WOMEN, METHOD ACTING, AND THE HOLLYWOOD FILM

Women, Method Acting, and the Hollywood Film is the first study dedicated to understanding the work of female Method actors on film.

While Method acting on film has typically been associated with the explosive machismo of actors like Marlon Brando and Robert De Niro, this book explores an alternate tradition within the Method—the work that women from the Actors Studio did in Hollywood. Covering the period from the end of the Second World War until the 1970s, this study shows how the women associated with the Actors Studio increasingly used Method acting in ways that were compatible with their burgeoning feminist political commitments and developed a style of feminist Method acting. The book examines the complex intersection of Method acting, sexuality, and gender by analyzing performances such as Kim Hunter's in *A Streetcar Named Desire*, Julie Harris's in *The Member of the Wedding*, Shelley Winters's in *The Big Knife*, Geraldine Page's in *Sweet Bird of Youth*, and Jane Fonda's in *Coming Home*. Challenging the longstanding assumption that Method acting's approaches were harmful to women and incompatible with feminism, this book argues that some of Hollywood's most interesting female actors, and leading feminists, emerged from the Actors Studio in the period between the 1950s and the 1970s.

Written for students and scholars of Film Studies, Cultural Studies, Theatre and Performance Studies, and Gender Studies, *Women, Method Acting, and the Hollywood Film* reshapes the way we think of a central strain in American screen acting, and in doing so, allows women a new stake in that tradition.

Keri Walsh is Associate Professor of English and Director of the Institute of Irish Studies at Fordham University in New York. She is the author of *Mickey Rourke* in the BFI Film Stars Series and editor of *The Letters of Sylvia Beach*. In 2018 she was named an Academy Film Scholar by the Academy of Motion Picture Arts and Sciences.

WOMEN, METHOD ACTING, AND THE HOLLYWOOD FILM

Keri Walsh

Taylor & Francis Group

NEW YORK AND LONDON

First published 2021
by Routledge
605 Third Avenue, New York, NY 10017

and by Routledge
2 Park Square, Milton Park, Abingdon, Oxon OX14 4RN

Routledge is an imprint of the Taylor & Francis Group, an informa business

© 2021 Keri Walsh

The right of Keri Walsh to be identified as author of this work has been asserted by her in accordance with sections 77 and 78 of the Copyright, Designs and Patents Act 1988.

All rights reserved. No part of this book may be reprinted or reproduced or utilised in any form or by any electronic, mechanical, or other means, now known or hereafter invented, including photocopying and recording, or in any information storage or retrieval system, without permission in writing from the publishers.

Trademark notice: Product or corporate names may be trademarks or registered trademarks, and are used only for identification and explanation without intent to infringe.

Library of Congress Cataloging-in-Publication Data
Names: Walsh, Keri, author.
Title: Women, method acting, and the Hollywood film / Keri Walsh.
Description: New York, NY : Routledge, 2021. |
Includes bibliographical references and index.
Identifiers: LCCN 2020049106 (print) | LCCN 2020049107 (ebook) |
ISBN 9780367463465 (hardback) | ISBN 9780367636067 (paperback) |
ISBN 9781003119944 (ebook)
Subjects: LCSH: Method acting. | Motion picture acting. | Actresses–United States. | Motion picture actors and actresses–United States. | Women in motion pictures.
Classification: LCC PN2062 .W35 2021 (print) |
LCC PN2062 (ebook) | DDC 792.02/8082–dc23
LC record available at https://lccn.loc.gov/2020049106
LC ebook record available at https://lccn.loc.gov/2020049107

ISBN: 978-0-367-46346-5 (hbk)
ISBN: 978-0-367-63606-7 (pbk)

Typeset in Bembo
by Newgen Publishing UK

CONTENTS

Acknowledgments   *vi*

    Introduction   1

1 Women and the Method   22

2 Kim Hunter's Feminist Method   49

3 Protest Performances: Actor Rebellion as Feminist Critique   80

4 Jane Fonda: Method Auteur   104

5 Epilogue: Barbara Loden's *Wanda* (1970)   127

Bibliography   *135*
Index   *143*

ACKNOWLEDGMENTS

I would like to thank the Academy of Motion Picture Arts and Sciences for an Academy Film Scholar fellowship in 2018, which allowed me to conduct research at the Margaret Herrick Motion Picture Arts and Sciences Library, and to participate in programming at the Pickford Center for Motion Picture Study. The research made possible by the Academy fellowship provided a restorative break from the usual pressures of academic life, and I also forged a long-distance friendship with my fellow Fellow, Glenn Frankel: we cheered each other on while completing our projects.

Along the way I benefited from the help of many skilled archivists, including those at the Herrick Library: Louise Hilton, Rachel Bernstein, Warren Sherk, Kevin Wilkerson, Clare Denk, Kristine Krueger, and Lea Whittington. Maya Montañez Smukler at UCLA's Film and Television Archive helped me to locate the few surviving episodes of the *Actors Studio* television show (and her book *Liberating Hollywood: Women Directors and the Reform of 1970s Cinema*, provided both inspiration and erudition). I would also like to thank the archivists at Yale's Beinecke Library for assistance with the Geraldine Page Papers, and those at the New York Public Library for the Performing Arts where I studied Kim Hunter's *Streetcar* script notes. I am also indebted to the librarians at my home institution, Fordham University: Tierney Gleason, Charlotte Labbé, and Jean Walsh helped to locate materials, garner interlibrary loans, reserve screening rooms, and scan much-needed documents as I completed this book during a pandemic. Thank you also to my research assistants Amal Zaman, Molly Henschke, and Daniel Heffernan, as well as to the deeply engaged students in my "Modernism, Cinema, and Literature" graduate seminar in spring 2020.

At Routledge I would like to thank Lucia Accorsi and Stacey Walker for giving my argument a forum. Routledge has been at the vanguard of publishing exciting work on feminism, film, and acting for decades, and a glimpse at my bibliography will reveal that this book could not have been written without the Routledge catalogue. And, thank you to Suba Ramya at Newgen Knowledge Works for preparation of the manuscript.

As is perhaps to be expected when the subject is popular culture, often it was journalists, cultural critics, and reviewers who helped to illuminate my path when there was little academic criticism on a subject. I am especially grateful for the work of Richard Brody, Cintra Wilson, Sheila O'Malley, and Angelica Jade Bastién.

Among my colleagues in film studies, I was happy to have before me the work, support, and example offered by David Greven, George Toles, Rochelle Sara Miller, Kristen Hatch, Emily Carman, Lilya Kaganovsky, Jacqueline Reich, and Catherine O'Rawe. I would also like to thank Amanda Konkle who served as technical editor for comments that helped me to introduce some "bold nuance" during the book's final stages. My thanks are also due to Pamela Robertson Wojcik, Joy Schaefer, and Beth Corzo-Duchardt for advising on image use and permissions. Thank you also to my fellow speakers in various conference sessions that have been essential to my thinking about Method acting: "Modernism and the Actress" at the Modernist Studies Association conference in Boston in 2015; "Auteurism and After: Film Authorship and Culture Industries" at the Modernist Studies Association conference in Pasadena in 2016; "New Directions in Feminist Media Studies" at the American Comparative Literature Association conference in Los Angeles in 2018; and "Stardom in Transitional Moments in Hollywood" at the "Stars and Screen: Film and Media History Conference" in Glassboro, New Jersey in 2018.

This project required me to expand my understanding of theatre as well, and I am indebted to the stellar friends and colleagues whom I was able to consult in the field, especially Paige McGinley, Allan Pero, and Brian E. Herrera. I would also like to thank the speakers in the 2014 Rethinking Realist Acting Colloquium that I convened at Fordham University with Shonni Enelow and Mary Luckhurst: Martin Shingler, Cynthia Baron, Jacqueline Reich, Sharon Marcus, Rosemary Malague, Joseph Roach, Stuart Sherman, Jacob Gallagher-Ross, Kenny Leon, and Sharon Marie Carnicke. Thank you also to Callie Gallo for her skill in organizing that conference. I am also grateful to Tom Oppenheim at the Stella Adler Studio of Acting in New York, a great public-facing institution, for meeting with me and sharing stories and family history.

Colleagues and mentors from my home discipline of literature have also been supportive at every stage. John Farrell, John Harrington, Missy Bradshaw, Patricia Juliana Smith, David Yaffe, James Morrison, Audrey Bilger; Scott Poulson-Bryant, Glenn Hendler, Mary Bly, Corey McEleney, Jordan Stein, Anne Fernald, Eva Badowska, Jean Walton, Mary Cappello, Phil Sicker, Moshe Gold, Julie Kim, Sarah Zimmerman, Susan Wolfson, Ron Levao, Diana Fuss, Maria DiBattista, Lucy McDiarmid, Michelle Coghlan, Vlasta Vranjes, and Saikat Majumdar deserve special mention. I am indebted in some way to every member of my department, and also to Fordham University for the Faculty Fellowship that allowed me to spend an uninterrupted semester working on this project. And it is with particular love that I thank Daniel Contreras and Ryan Carmichael for always knowing just a little bit more about Tennessee Williams and Broadway history than I ever will.

One of the greatest discoveries of middle age has been the joy and power of writing groups. Thank you to Briallen Hopper, Beth Boyle Machlan, Rebecca Rainof Mas, Lauren Arrington, and Emily Bloom for their support and insight delivered sometimes over Zoom and sometimes over cocktails at the Algonquin. Thank you also to my friends Amy Eli Trautwein and Heather Clark for offering both intellectual and practical sustenance. I would also like to thank my family: Deirdre, John, and Melanie Walsh; David, Julia, and Jane Huber; Geraldine O'Shea; and Margaret, Peter, Emily, and Daniel Larlham.

This book is dedicated to three friends whose writing I admire deeply and whose company and belief sustained me through its completion: James Morrison, Briallen Hopper, and Shonni Enelow.

Finally, as ever, I would like to thank John Bugg. He helped me translate my love of Method acting from personal obsession to professional contribution, and I couldn't have finished this monograph without him.

INTRODUCTION

In Otto Preminger's World War II epic *In Harm's Way* (1965), Patricia Neal appears as Naval Lieutenant Maggie Haines, a character whom Bosley Crowther described as a "weary" and "tough" nurse.[1] Lieutenant Haines delivers her life story matter-of-factly: first she divorced her husband, and after that went to nursing school and joined the navy. Throughout the film, she appears in uniform. Her affect is consistently practical and calm. She is as confident directing a large medical ward as she is expressing her sexual desires. As she moves to take John Wayne's Captain Torrey to bed, she maintains steady eye contact as she removes her cap, and the camera pans down to her feet where one by one, she pulls off her orthopedic white nursing shoes. Lieutenant Haines is not a nubile nurse fantasy. Instead, she is a hard-working middle-aged professional with sore feet and desires of her own. Such unflappable, disciplined, mature, and grounded women were Neal's trademark—she had played similar parts in Elia Kazan's *A Face in the Crowd* (1957) as the radio producer Marcia Jeffries who sabotages a populist demagogue with a hot mic, and in Blake Edwards's *Breakfast at Tiffany's* (1961) as Emily Eustace Failenson, who pays for the upkeep of her young lover. Given the niche Neal had carved for herself in Hollywood as the purveyor of midlife cool, it was not surprising that she was the first to be offered the part of Mrs. Robinson in Mike Nichols's *The Graduate* (1967). When she turned it down, her fellow Method actor Anne Bancroft stepped in, giving an iconic performance of her own, one that drew some of its energy and inspiration from Neal's screen persona. Critics have rarely traced such genealogies between women of the Method, but in this book I show that female Method actors were often in dialogue with each other. Just as Robert De Niro's performances speak back to Marlon Brando's, Anne Bancroft's speak to Patricia Neal's, and to those of other women in the tradition that I describe as feminist Method acting.

One can see what attracted Neal to the role of Lt. Haines in *In Harm's Way*: the chance to play a competent, professional, three-dimensional woman. But in this film, and others that I study in this book, we can also see some of the limitations that actors like Neal faced as they tried to bring the realist values of the Actors Studio to bear on expressing the complexities of women's lives. In a subplot of *In Harm's Way*, Lt. Haines's younger roommate and mentee, Ensign Annalee Dorne, is raped by a superior (played by Kirk Douglas). After learning that she is pregnant, Dorne commits suicide. Neal's Lt. Haines discovers her body and a note. She tries to bring the truth surrounding her roommate's death to light by passing along the note to her naval superiors, but Captain Torrey has a different sense of how the situation should be handled—he thinks that because the crime is shameful, it should be covered up. Dorne's rapist is never brought to justice: instead, he "redeems" himself at the film's end by dying in a sacrificial mission that saves other lives. Lt. Haines's concern to expose the truth is quickly passed over, swallowed up in the imperatives of battle. While Preminger's film could plausibly be read as a criticism of the navy's response to sexual violence (it does, after all, dramatize the cover-up), the fact remains that only Neal's character pushes to tell the truth, and suggests a more accountable way of responding. Only her presence in the film suggests to the audience that the way the navy responds to sexual violence is a problem. She is the feminist witness to Ensign Annalee Dorne's death.[2] This dynamic, in which a female Method actor inhabits and infuses feminist insight and potential into a film that is not necessarily fully hospitable to it, is one I encountered commonly in films made before 1968, when the Production Code (or Hays Code) was converted to a Ratings System that gave filmmakers, and audiences, more freedom to explore social issues in a forthright manner. After 1968, subjects of feminist concern like rape, abortion, and harassment could be addressed explicitly, and, thanks to the rising energy of second-wave feminism, they increasingly were. Before 1968, however, which is the period that is under consideration in the first three chapters of this book, these moments of feminist critique can be seen struggling to assert themselves in conditions either censored, hostile, or indifferent. But they are there. As it turns out, they are a recurring feature of women's performances in the Method tradition.

Neal's portrayal of Lt. Haines in *In Harm's Way*, like so many of her performances, exemplifies the body of work I bring to light in this book, that of feminist Method acting in Hollywood. For the purposes of this study, by feminism I mean second-wave feminism, the mid-twentieth century explosion of consciousness and activism that emerged alongside other liberation struggles of the time. Whereas feminism's first wave (which lasted from the mid-nineteenth century until the years following World War I) had focused on securing women's right to vote, second-wave feminism fought for a host of social issues related to women's lives, protesting against their status in the household, demanding equal compensation and opportunities in the workplace, and agitating to gain reproductive, sexual, and other rights.[3]

I have opened this study with Patricia Neal because her unflustered style is the last thing that would usually be conjured by the phrase "Method acting," and yet she was a dedicated Method actor. Whereas the male stars associated with the Method, like Marlon Brando and James Dean, expressed the anarchic energies of youth culture and the troubles of returning World War II veterans, Method women carved different paths. They did not trade in brooding misunderstoodness; they were not sex symbols (at least not of a stereotypical variety); they did not live fast or die young. Instead, they built sustained careers, often performing memorably into old age. While these Method actors inhabited characters of many ages and types, from Eva Marie Saint's troubled young wife Celia Pope in Fred Zinnemann's *A Hatful of Rain* to Jo Van Fleet's raging matriarch Ella Garth in Elia Kazan's *Wild River*, there was often something decidedly midlife about their collective ethos—an ethos that Crowther's assessment of Neal as "weary" and "tough"—captures well. But theirs was not the toughness of sweaty undershirts and explosive emotionality. It was instead an attempt realistically to portray women's domestic and professional lives at the mid-century. These Method actors have rarely been thought of, except by themselves, as participants in second-wave feminism. And yet to look back at their work and their statements about their work is to see that their performances consistently documented and protested against the limitations imposed on women's lives in the years following World War II. They were determined to change the conventions governing women's screen performance and the idealizations Hollywood so often applied to women's lives. To do so, they employed the realist values of the Actors Studio, the New York institution from which the Method emerged, as a counterweight to Hollywood's default setting of glamor. Method women consistently pushed to allow more of women's ordinary lives onto the screen, and to make their protests seen and heard.

Women, Method Acting, and the Hollywood Film is an inaugural study of the work of this often-overlooked group of Method actors in Hollywood, grounded in close analysis of significant performances by Kim Hunter, Julie Harris, Geraldine Page, Shelley Winters, and Jane Fonda. I hope it will be a step toward a larger revival of interest in their work. Kim Hunter as Stella Kowalski in *A Streetcar Named Desire* challenged audiences with the complex portrayal of a veteran's wife's attempts to survive an abusive marriage, Julie Harris as Frankie Addams in *The Member of the Wedding* played the queer child Frankie Addams who protests against the demands of gender conformity, and Geraldine Page as movie star Alexandra Del Lago in *Sweet Bird of Youth* offered a powerful rebellion against the industry limitations placed upon older female actors.[4] Why are their names so often missing from conversations about the history of Method acting on film? Though they worked alongside Brando, Dean, and Clift at the Actors Studio and in Hollywood, and turned in groundbreaking performances, they have often been elided in accounts of the Method acting canon. In this book I restore them, and their fellow female Method actors, to view. And I argue that it is not enough that we remember them individually: we need to consider them as a community of actors who admired each other's work, who often performed together, and whose professional values were shaped by a shared genealogy.[5]

There are four key arguments that I hope the reader of this book will take away: first, that there is a strong tradition of women's Method acting in Hollywood, one that expresses itself in a variety of recognizable ways; second, that the screen performances of female Method actors both challenged and expanded Hollywood's capacities for representing women's lives; third, that these actors used their Hollywood careers to become powerful exponents of second-wave feminism; and fourth, that contrary to a commonly held idea that Method women's work was marred by a subservience to mid-century Freudian ideas, in practice the version of the Method these women enacted was much more concerned with social criticism than with psychoanalysis, and was eminently capable of its own feminist engagements with Freud. In fact, Freudian elements in mid-century films often provide cultural openings and a new language for exploring and expressing women's burgeoning rebellion.

Consider Joanne Woodward's performance in Nunnally Johnson's *The Three Faces of Eve* (1957). Woodward plays a character with dissociative identity disorder, a role that effectively requires her to play three different parts: Eve White, a depressed housewife, Eve Black, her sexually confident and socially rebellious alter ego, and Jane, a moderate woman who emerges as the integration of the two. The film begins with a documentary-style narrator informing the audience that Eve's story is based on an actual case study. The plot follows Eve as she undergoes psychiatric treatment and is eventually able to heal, guided by her doctor (played by Woodward's fellow Method actor Lee J. Cobb). Standard readings of women and the Method might argue that the film's presentation of a male doctor/female patient power dynamic is troubling or worry that the film promotes a view of women as fundamentally unstable or hysterical. But looked at from a different angle, *The Three Faces of Eve* suggests that the limits and demands placed on women as housewives and mothers are literally driving them crazy, and that their own rebellious subconscious selves might save them.[6] *The Three Faces of Eve* suggests that inside each docile and downtrodden housewife lurks a force struggling to get free, and that women's identities are actually much bolder and more various than the roles of domesticity they have been shoehorned into. Providing an uninhibited display of what American housewives might say, if they felt free to speak their minds, Eve's alter ego says of her husband that she would never marry "a jerk like that" and "I ain't gonna go through the rest of my life with that creep." It is she who tells the doctor about Eve White's suicide attempt, and who encourages her to "leave Ralph, take Bonnie and run away." In one scene, Eve's bolder self gets dressed seductively and shows her husband a sexually forward side of her personality of which he disapproves, and then informs him "There's a lot of things you've never seen me do." By the end of the film, Eve has gotten divorced from her husband and found a new one, having gained more assertiveness, control, and happiness. The film provides a bravura, Oscar-winning role for Woodward: Bosley Crowther noted that she gives a performance of "superlative flexibility and emotional power."[7] When she shifts from one personality to another, Woodward's body language changes entirely: she leaves behind her tense, hunched posture and leans back relaxed, smiling, and taking up space.

Even though Woodward and her contemporaries often generated such compelling and memorable screen performances, the women of the Method have often been left behind in both popular and academic memory. Noticing this absence, Karen Hollinger has raised the question of why the title of "Method actor" has so seldom stuck to female performers, and why their tradition has become so submerged both in cultural memory and scholarly accounts of screen acting.[8] Hollinger points out that there were plenty of "notable female Method performers" during the period of Method acting's ascendance in Hollywood after World War II, yet somehow, she notes with perplexity, in the popular imagination all of the "exemplars of Method acting were men" (14). Hollinger points out that the unwritten history of female Method actors remained a missing chapter in screen acting that made her own study of later performers (even those not from the Method tradition) including Meryl Streep and Angela Bassett more difficult to undertake.

In offering some of this missing history, I seek to provide a greater understanding of what women have contributed to Hollywood cinema as Method actors. One reason we have not recognized their work is that it often looks so different from that of their male peers. To include them in our critical accounts, we need to learn to see the Method in broader ways, and not just in the images of Brando, Clift, Dean, De Niro, or successive waves of male actors who traffic in the angst-to-explosion arc. When I started writing this book, a Google search for the phrase "women Method actors" yielded a list of eight male actors. Now, thanks to feminist critics taking a new interest in this topic, it yields several articles querying why there has been a dearth of attention to female Method actors in Hollywood.[9]

Given their low profile now, it might come as something of a surprise to learn that in the golden age of Method acting (from the 1950s to the 1970s), the work of female Method actors was in fact recognized in Hollywood, even if it was not recognized as Method acting per se. While the images of Brando, Clift, Dean, Newman and others became synonymous with the idea of the "Method actor" as a new disruptive and exciting star type, women of the Method were equally celebrated for their work in awards season. Brando received an Academy Award nomination for his performance as Stanley Kowalski in *A Streetcar Named Desire* (1951), but he did not win; Kim Hunter, however, did win the Best Supporting Actress Oscar for her performance as Stella Kowalski. Other Best Actress and Best Supporting Actress winners who honed their craft at the Actors Studio in this period include Joanne Woodward for *The Three Faces of Eve* (1958), Anne Bancroft for *The Miracle Worker* (1963), Patricia Neal for *Hud* (1964), Eva Marie Saint for *On the Waterfront* (1955), Jo Van Fleet for *East of Eden* (1956), Shelley Winters for *The Diary of Anne Frank* (1960) and *A Patch of Blue* (1966), Jane Fonda for *Klute* (1971) and *Coming Home* (1978), Sandy Dennis for *Who's Afraid of Virginia Woolf?* (1967), Estelle Parsons for *Bonnie and Clyde* (1968), and Ellen Burstyn for *Alice Doesn't Live Here Anymore* (1975).[10] These performances have rarely been considered collectively or studied in relation to the influence of the institution where they originated.

The only comprehensive history of the Actors Studio, Forster Hirsch's *A Method to Their Madness* (1984), holds that Hollywood served Method women poorly. Beginning with an acknowledgment of the ways in which the path to stardom was more uphill for female actors who embraced the intensity and realism of Method acting, Hirsch's account ultimately lapses into the pejorative critical paradigm that he had initially seemed prepared to question:

> Unwilling (or perhaps unable) to play the sexy image that American movies often force on women, these actresses have either retuned to stage work whenever they could or else been cast in supporting roles as an assortment of oddballs and weirdos. Dressed in fright wigs and camouflaged with garish makeup, they have sometimes been cast unflatteringly, their individuality mocked rather than protected by the romantic aura that cradled Montgomery Clift and James Dean.[11]

Hirsch is right when he proposes that Method women were unwilling to conform to Hollywood's norms governing femininity. Their quest to depict female characters who were less compliant, less available to the gaze, and less normative in a variety of ways, was simply more challenging than male Method actors' presentation of masculinity in a more troubled, erotic, and counter-cultural image. Hirsch dismisses Method women's work on screen as "too batty," "too quirky," and "a sideshow," rather than reading their performances sympathetically to see what they might have been trying to say with such convention-breaking work.[12]

Despite Hirsch's account, not only did the Method did serve women well in Hollywood, but female Method actors' challenges in turn served Hollywood well. The award statistics suggest that their performances were both relevant and exciting to critics, audiences, and the industry. Drawing on the processes and values they developed at the Actors Studio helped them to develop careers as acclaimed actors operating successfully in the years marked by the dissolution of the Hollywood star system. In fact, Method women often worked to upend terms like those of Hirsch's critique that were used to describe women (batty, quirky, sideshows) along with adjacent pejorative terms used to dismiss non-conforming women: spinster, frigid, hysterical, offbeat, plain, frumpy, ugly. It was often through their conscious engagement with such pejoratives that women Method actors began to carve out new and resistant domains for female performance on screen, and to seek out strategies to flip, resist, and reframe such dismissals.

One of their best allies in this campaign was Tennessee Williams, the playwright deeply associated with the Method whose queering of American theatre provided many resources for thinking about gender and sexuality, resources that female Method actors drew on and adapted. Williams placed great emphasis on female characters who resisted normative identities. As Blanche Dubois asks in *A Streetcar Named Desire*: "Straight? What's 'straight'? A line can be straight, or a street. But the heart of a human being?" Williams's resistance to norms provided an inspiration to deviate for many Method women's performances. Like Williams as a playwright, female Method actors were realists in many regards, but were more than capable of irony, camp, comedy, and various forms of disidentification. Similar encouragement to express feminist and queer perspectives came from their appearances in adaptations of works by women writers such as Carson McCullers, Lillian Hellman, and Shirley Jackson.

Off-screen, the politics of Method women were typically liberal and/or left, and many became involved with political campaigns and causes, including the civil rights movement, the peace movement, the anti-nuclear movement, campaigns for reproductive freedom, activism against the death penalty, movements for economic justice, and feminist campaigns against harassment and inequality and in favor of more equitable media representation. This was not surprising, given that the Actors Studio descended from the group of directors and actors involved with the legendary leftist 1930s theatre collective, The Group. For many years the politics of the Actors Studio have been suspect because of the notorious actions of one of its founders, Elia Kazan, who named names of Communist Party members to the House Un-American Activities Committee (HUAC) in order to protect his burgeoning film career (an act that Arthur Miller, whose attitudes captured those of many of Kazan's fellow theatre workers, referred to as a "moral defection" and a decision that "disserved both himself and the cause of freedom.")[13] But Kazan's action was notorious precisely because it represented such a dramatic departure from the politics embraced by most members of the Actors Studio and the Group Theatre before them. For instance, Milly S. Barranger's *Unfriendly Witnesses: Gender, Theater and Film in the McCarthy Era* dedicates a chapter to Kim Hunter's principled stand against McCarthyism, one that barred her from working in Hollywood in the years following her Oscar win for *A Streetcar Named Desire* (by her own account, Hunter was never a member of the Communist party, but she contributed to various progressive causes, including peace and civil rights, and she raised funds for the defense of the Hollywood Ten, the group of writers and directors accused of having Communist sympathies). Hunter stood up to the HUAC-supporting blackmailers who offered her "clearance" from Communist suspicions, and in 1962 she testified before the New York Supreme Court to expose them. Geraldine Page, meanwhile, was blacklisted after her Oscar win for *Hondo* (1953)—she thought it was because she had studied with another Stanislavsky-based teacher based in New York, Uta Hagen, who was also a suspected Communist. Page did not work on film again until *Summer and Smoke* (1961).[14] But even though their appearances on screen were curtailed by this ugly interlude in American history, women from the Actors Studio persisted in both their political activism and their film work. For their artistry, their social engagement, their adept and creative navigations of both censorship and sexism, and their rich and challenging feminist realism, these actors' riveting performances deserve our fresh attention.

"Method acting" is a term that seems to have gotten away on us: it is a descriptor that carries great cultural weight and evokes some indelible images, but it is often used without much accuracy. It is therefore worth pausing here to say a few words about the basic definition of Method acting. Most simply and least contentiously, the term refers to Lee Strasberg's particular adaptation of Konstanin Stanislavsky's ideas about acting, and specifically, to Strasberg's fusion of Stanislavsky's techniques with Freudian psychoanalysis in workshop sessions at the Actors Studio. However, the term has sometimes been applied to a broader set of Stanislavsky-derived acting techniques and approaches (for instance, those associated with the teachings of Stella Adler, Uta Hagen, and Michael Chekhov), or used even more capaciously to describe any actor who goes to great lengths to prepare for a role, particularly those who undertake feats of immersion such as weight gain or loss, temporarily living in a particular subculture, or not breaking character while in rehearsal or on set. I have tried to avoid these more sprawling uses of the term. For the purposes of this book, I use "Method actor" with historical specificity to refer only to those who were members of the Actors Studio, the non-profit workshop for actors, directors, and playwrights.[15] Founded in New York in 1947, the Actors Studio charged no membership fees, and admission was by either audition or invitation. At its heart were weekly sessions at which feedback was given on scenes performed by various members. Though different facilitators inhabited the role of session leader, beginning in 1951 Lee Strasberg became most associated with the weekly sessions. Strasberg's style was personal, intense, and often polarizing. His philosophy included the need for both "work on the self" and work on the role, and in some cases he encouraged actors to begin psychoanalysis to deepen their artistry. In keeping with his interest in the connection between acting and therapy, he developed the "emotion memory" or "affective memory" exercise through which actors could access personal memories for use in their performances. These practices led Method acting to become associated with—and sometimes mocked for—what was seen as its tendency to promote self-indulgent introspection and hyperbolic moodiness. But a turn to psychoanalysis was hardly the sole characteristic of the Method (either at the Actors Studio, or in related Stanislavsky-based New York institutions, or in Hollywood).

Though Strasberg's linking of psychoanalysis and acting was a key theme of his actor preparation techniques, it was not the only element of Method acting, and it has sometimes been overemphasized in critical accounts. Looking at Method acting in mid-century Hollywood film suggests that the Method is better understood as a set of approaches that combined psychological insights with urgent sociological and political concerns, priorities in evidence in films starring Method actors directed by Elia Kazan, Fred Zinnemann, László Benedek, Martin Ritt, and others. Method acting's chief aim was realism, whether it construed this primarily in psychological or sociological terms (most often it combined them), and the scenes studied and rehearsed at the Actors Studio were usually (but not exclusively) drawn from the canon of dramatic realism. Most esteemed were those realist works that had been composed and performed during the late nineteenth century, some of which focused on the oppression of women and became rallying points for feminist activism (Ibsen's *A Doll's House* of 1879 was the most notable play in this regard). Chekhov, whose oeuvre had formed the cornerstone of Stanislavsky's Moscow Art Theatre repertoire, was the most highly valued playwright at the Actors Studio, and his works also provided nuanced, complex roles for women (in 1966 the Actors Studio released a film adaptation of Chekhov's *Three Sisters* starring Geraldine Page, Shelley Winters, Kim Stanley, and Sandy Dennis in the roles of Olga, Natalya, Masha, and Irina). Twentieth-century playwrights associated with the Method, beyond Williams, included William Inge, Horton Foote, and Arthur Miller, and when the Method came to Hollywood it was often in adaptations of their work.

In offering this relatively straightforward definition, I join a recent critical turn away from debates about the process of Method acting (and from the field-preoccupying questions of whether it is a valid interpretation of Stanislavsky's system, and even whether it is an advisable approach to the craft of acting) and toward a cultural studies approach that looks outward to study the Method's connections to the intellectual and political formations of the 1950s and beyond. Technical debates about the Method's value (or lack thereof) as an acting preparation process are certainly warranted in scholarship by acting teachers, but my purposes here do not require such judgments. I therefore join recent critics including Shonni Enelow and Jacob Gallagher-Ross in resisting what Gallagher-Ross has called "the factional squabbles and terminological disputes" that have tended to saturate critical work on the Method. Instead, I focus my attention on the film performances of women who were members of the Actors Studio, to see what new light can be shed by a close study of their work.[16]

It was in the early 1950s that "The Method" first caught the notice of a broad American public through press coverage of films like Elia Kazan's *A Streetcar Named Desire* (1951) and *On the Waterfront* (1954). But the ideas that shaped what became known as Method acting had in fact arrived in the United States over two decades earlier, with the Moscow Art Theatre's American tours of 1923 and 1924. Two members of the ensemble, Maria Ouspenskaya and Richard Boleslavsky, stayed in New York to found the Laboratory Theatre, and it was here that Stanislavsky's "System" for actor training was introduced to American students. Those who trained at the Laboratory Theatre included Lee Strasberg and Stella Adler, who would become Strasberg's chief peer and rival as a teacher of Stanislavsky-based acting. In the 1930s both Strasberg and Adler, as well as Elia Kazan (who would become Hollywood's highest-profile Actors Studio-affiliated director), had been members of the Group Theatre, the influential theatre collective that adapted Stanislavskian principles to the American stage in the works of playwrights such as Clifford Odets and Irwin Shaw.[17] After the dissolution of the Group Theatre, three of its members (Kazan, Robert Lewis, and Cheryl Crawford) founded the Actors Studio in 1947, with a view to developing actors to feature in their own productions. Adler, meanwhile, founded a teaching studio of her own, breaking with Strasberg's techniques after a meeting with Stanislavksy in Paris in the mid-1930s, and promoting approaches that deemphasized psychoanalysis in favor of script analysis, imagination, and dramatic circumstances. In Hollywood, the Group Theatre alumnus John Garfield is often considered the earliest ambassador of what would later come to be called Method acting, but that title might also be given to Ouspenskaya, who moved to Los Angeles in the mid-1930s and found success in a series of scene-stealing supporting roles.[18] By the 1940s, Stella Adler too was in Hollywood advocating for Stanislavskian realism. She appeared in several films and spent time as an acting coach at MGM where she worked under Arthur Freed on *For Me and My Gal* (1942) and *Du Barry Was a Lady* (1943).[19] Like Ouspenskaya, she used the cultural prestige of her theatre background to exert an influence in Hollywood. Later, Strasberg would also set up shop in Hollywood, traveling between the Los Angeles and New York locations of the Actors Studio.

Method acting came to the fore during a crucial decade of change in Hollywood, and it even came to represent the crossover between the classical studio system and the New Hollywood which was characterized by burgeoning independent production companies, the decline of the star system, increasing challenges to the Production Code, and the rise of a variety of new technologies and strategies to compete for television's audiences. The post-war period, when the major studios were forced to sell off their theatres by anti-trust lawsuits that gave them much more limited control over distribution, led to the biggest transformation in Hollywood since the move to sound two decades before.[20] Perhaps it was no accident that Method acting came to the attention of the public at this moment, nor was it surprising that Method actors became symbols of Old Hollywood's demise, exposing through their discontent with studio norms the need for change. In the post-war period, just as smaller production companies rose to challenge the studio system's hegemony, Method actors challenged what had been the studio era's corporatization and control of the actor's work. This resistance to the status quo was also deeply related to the Method's theatrical origins: early films featuring Method actors moved from Broadway to the screen with casts nearly intact. Resisting the star system, these films introduced actors who were unknown to screen audiences and foregrounded ensemble casts. Elia Kazan insisted on casting Julie Harris in *East of Eden* even though studio executives deemed her not pretty enough, while Kim Hunter mocked Warner Brothers' demand that she dye her hair blonde to play Stella Kowalski. Because of their challenges, Method actors were branded disruptors of the Hollywood status quo, and while they were officially derided for it, their fascination also depended on this idea of disruption. If much more attention has been given to male Method actors' industry rebellions, it is worth noting that 20 years before Marlon Brando skipped the Academy Awards in protest in 1973, Kim Hunter refused to collect her Oscar for *A Streetcar Named Desire*, fearing that such ceremonies diminished the ensemble values of the craft. The idea of Method rebellion has gathered firmly around figures such as Brando and Dean, but it is important to remember that the Method's women were rebellious too. While Method men famously refused to perform traditional masculinity—suit-wearing and job-holding, law-abiding and barbecue-owning—female Method actors too refused expectations that they would vacate the jobs they had taken during the war and content themselves with domestic lives of child-rearing in kitchens graced with new appliances.

To identify a tradition of feminist Method acting is not, however, to claim that the Actors Studio was free from sexism, any more than other cultural institutions of the 1950s (or our own time) are. The point of reclaiming the work of women Method actors is not to idealize the Actors Studio or its key personalities, but to wrest from this tradition – which has been almost completely discredited from a feminist perspective—the socially aware women's acting that it produced. Female Method actors often had to correct and guide their directors' impulses and educate them about their own biases, a process I trace most thoroughly in my chapter on Hunter's performance in Kazan's *A Streetcar Named Desire* (1951). But Method acting's ways of working privileged the input of actors and valued these kinds of negotiations. The women who came out of the Actors Studio made conscious choices about how to translate to the screen the approaches and techniques practiced there. They engaged critically with Hollywood's constrictions, creating work that pushed at the boundaries of convention and censorship and challenged audiences to see women's lives in new ways.[21] We have yet to recognize the extent to which female Method actors urged—and persuaded—directors like Elia Kazan, Fred Zinnemann, and Martin Ritt to amend and nuance their representations, in order to show that women's lives were less contented and more complex than Hollywood had previously allowed. I show how they negotiated with directors to make room for feminist interpretations of characters, scenes, and situations.

In arguing that feminist Method actors influenced the films they were in, I participate in an ongoing effort within film studies to challenge received ideas about women's work in Hollywood. Recent scholarship has sought to restore to view the agency that women exerted over their careers (in an industry where they were not usually treated as equals), and to deepen our understanding of the artistic range of their work. Much of this research has focused on the silent and studio eras. Jane Gaines's *Pink-Slipped: What Happened to Women in the Silent Film Industries?* charts first the influential presence then the mass eviction of women from Hollywood leadership positions at the end of the silent era, and Shelley Stamp's *Lois Weber in Early Hollywood* argues for Weber's status alongside Cecil B. DeMille and D.W.

Griffith as a foundational filmmaker.[22] Challenging the premise that the end of the silent era spelled massive disempowerment for women, Emily Carman, meanwhile, has shown that studio-contracted stars of the 1930s and 1940s, such as Irene Dunne, Janet Gaynor, and Carole Lombard, used their box office power to gain a greater measure of professional control than previously imagined, negotiating such elements as script approval and choice of director.[23] And J.E. Smyth's *Nobody's Girl Friday: The Women Who Ran Hollywood* also questions the hypothesis that the studio era was repressive to women, arguing instead that it was "the most important and empowering chapter in women's employment in the film industry."[24] More work is needed that reassesses axioms about women's presence and achievements in film history, both in front of and behind the camera, work that is as attuned to resistance as it is to repression. This is especially the case for Hollywood's other great transitional moment, the one following World War II that I am concerned with in this book. On the surface, the 1950s, when the story of Method women begins, may seem a step back for women in Hollywood. Certainly female screen actors of the 1950s worked in the formidable shadow of the great female stars of the 1940s, stars like Joan Crawford and Bette Davis.[25] But the massive changes of the decade also allowed women to reformulate norms and participate in building Hollywood along new lines. One recent welcome development in the feminist historiography of this period has been the renewed attention to the works of Ida Lupino, a successful screen actor who became one of Hollywood's few working female directors of the post-war period. Like the Method performances I study here, Lupino's films presented women's lives in new ways: *Never Fear* (1949) told the story of a dancer's rehabilitation from polio, and *Outrage* (1950) was one of the few films of the period to deal with rape.[26] In the chapters that follow I show how female Method actors, by entering Hollywood from a performance environment that held an alternative set of priorities and values, also helped to enlarge the possibilities for women in terms of casting, subject matter, performance styles, and creative control.

My focus on women's contributions as actors, rather than as directors, writers, or other film workers, presents its own set of challenges. In film studies there are certainly classic works on screen acting, such as James Naremore's *Acting in the Cinema* (1988) and Charles Affron's *Star Acting: Gish, Garbo, Davis* (1977), but there is also a tradition of subordinating the creative contributions that go into a film to the authorship of the director. There is sometimes even an animosity toward acting in film studies. Suggesting that attention to acting is often associated with fanship rather than scholarship, Paul McDonald argues that the field has "developed an intellectual agenda with lines of inquiry that have firmly encouraged a disregard for acting."[27] The more recently emergent field of Star Studies moves the focus back to screen performers, but attends to many elements of a star's image and influence in addition to their acting, and as the name suggests, it focuses on the phenomenon of stardom, which leaves numerous screen performers outside its purview. The mid-century was a moment of struggle between actor and director, with the Actors Studio strongly championing the role of the actor in shaping the meaning of films, while certain of the critics associated with the journal *Cahiers du Cinema* elevated the importance of the director. Certainly it is important to remember that actors' performances emerge complexly through direction, writing, and technical mediations such as editing and lighting. Critical analyses of screen acting must remain alert to the complex questions of film authorship, but it is worth considering what is eclipsed by the lingering influence of the auteur model that privileges the director. The study of screen acting invites a corrective that advocates for actors as meaningful film artists. Sometimes there is simply not enough information to say with certainty who contributed what to a film, but in a surprising number of cases research can shed light on these processes and reveal the negotiations among directors, writers, editors, and actors that gave rise to the performances that appear on screen. In *Theorizing Film Acting* (2012), Aaron Taylor argues for the value of actor-centric approaches to the study of film,[28] and while he acknowledges that the methodological and theoretical issues of screen acting are far from simple, he suggests that these issues may nonetheless be illuminated by close and careful study of particular screen performances (Taylor positions his book as part of "the emergent tradition of film acting studies").[29] In the case of women and the Method, examining materials such as script annotations, personal correspondence, biographies, memoirs, interviews, and other published and unpublished material uncovers many ways in which female actors exerted influence and claimed authorship.

Examinations of Method acting may have a particularly valuable contribution to make to this relatively recent turn to the actor in film studies. The Method's emphasis on such values as improvisation, workshopping, research, script analysis, and "work on the self" all developed from the conviction that actors should do much more than simply learn their lines and not bump into the furniture, and that they belonged to the same creative sphere as directors, playwrights, and screenwriters. Directors who cast Method actors tended to want to share creative control, and Method actors were prepared to collaborate with them in this way. And yet, despite the Method's potential to broaden our understanding of how actors contribute to film authorship, Method acting has rarely been the subject of sustained academic inquiry.[30] As their titles suggest, recent works on screen acting, such as Baron, Carson, and Tomasulo's *More than a Method: Trends and Traditions in Contemporary Film Performance* (2004) and Scott Balcerzak's *Beyond Method: Stella Adler and the Male Actor* (2018), tend to begin from the premise that the Method has monopolized critical attention and that new studies need to displace its influence. This perception has led to a curious critical situation in which Method acting is considered too hegemonic for further study, despite the serious gaps in its history, particularly of women's contributions. Ironically, a distaste for the Method's assumed sexism has prevented scholars from recognizing the feminist work the tradition contains.

To expand our view of Method acting on film and the kinds of performances it gave rise to, we must become better historians, documenting more accurately who Method actors were and what they did on screen in the foundational decades at mid-century. We are perhaps most accustomed to narratives of the Method's empowerment of actors as it pertains to the highest-profile male stars and their collaborations with directors, such as De Niro's with Scorsese in *Mean Streets* (1973), *Taxi Driver* (1976), and *Raging Bull* (1980). Adam Baker claims Robert De Niro as an auteur based on his choice of roles, his changes in physical appearance to play them, and above all, the way his improvisations significantly shaped the scripts of his films.[31] De Niro's capacity to collaborate in this way, Baker argues, is grounded in the Method's consistent encouragement of actors to take active roles in script analysis and scene development. It is less often noted that the Method also offered these possibilities to female actors, resulting in collaborations no less fruitful, such as Fred Zinnemann's work with Julie Harris in *The Member of the Wedding* (1952), Kazan's with Jo Van Fleet in *Wild River* (1957), Scorsese's with Ellen Burstyn in *Alice Doesn't Live Here Anymore* (1973), and Martin Ritt's with Sally Field in *Norma Rae* (1979). Furthermore, the Actors Studio generated not only performers but also producers including Cheryl Crawford, Marilyn Monroe, and Jane Fonda.

Various factors have converged to obscure women's work in the Method, from Hollywood casting practices and media coverage in their own day to the insufficiently inclusive work of historians and preservationists in our own. This imbalance needs to be approached with the restorative effort brought to any case of exclusionary cultural canonization. There is little danger of losing sight of men's accomplishments in the Method. In 2016 Martin Scorsese released a newly restored version of Brando's only directorial effort, *One-Eyed Jacks* (1961), and books like Susan L. Mizruchi's *Brando's Smile: His Life, Thought, and Work* (Norton, 2015) and William J. Mann's *The Contender* (Harper, 2019) continue to reassess Brando's legacy in light of evolving critical perspectives. Meanwhile, *The Member of the Wedding* (1952), which includes an Oscar-nominated performance by Julie Harris (and has other significant claims on our attention: it was directed by Fred Zinnemann, features an extraordinary performance by Ethel Waters, and is based on a novel by Carson McCullers) has yet to become available in an accessible streamed version: it can only be found on VHS, DVD, Blu-Ray, and sporadically on YouTube. In the process of completing this book, it was disheartening to find how many films featuring notable women's Method performances were inaccessible in high-quality digital versions, from Kim Stanley's in *The Goddess* (1958) to Jane Fonda's in *Coming Home* (1979). And while the stream of male Method biographies shows no sign of abating, we still lack biographies of Kim Hunter, Julie Harris, and Geraldine Page (to name some of the most notable oversights). How might the work of recovering these actors and their performances begin? Jon Krampner provides a good example by including several appendices in his book on Kim Stanley that document her performances, including one simply entitled

"Where You Can See the Work of Kim Stanley," which provides a list of archives containing footage of her work that is not otherwise available.[32] Krampner's appendices perform a dual function, making visible the fact that Stanley's work has not been given the curating it merits, and beginning the work of doing just that. Finally, we need to do close studies of these women's performances, reading them for their distinctive qualities but also for shared themes and styles. While the phrase "the Method" has tended to call to mind a particular type of masculine performance—working-class characters, mumbled lines, explosive intensity—until now there has been little consideration of what recurring themes and features characterize the work done by female Method actors and how existing ideas about Method acting need to be re-thought in light of their work.

Thanks to the critical consciousness they brought to their performances, the women of the Actors Studio were at the forefront of challenging Hollywood's accepted templates for femininity after World War II. They resisted conventional expectations for their conduct and appearance. They wore less makeup. They cut their hair short. If we view their performances as a body of work, we notice a few significant features: from Kim Hunter in *Streetcar* to Geraldine Page in *Sweet Bird of Youth* to Anne Bancroft in *The Graduate*, female Method actors tend to be purveyors rather than objects of the gaze. Their performances often refuse, resist, complicate, depart from, or critically appropriate the familiar norms of male Method actors, such as the privileging of emotionality or mumbling style. From Kim Hunter's maternity clothes in *A Streetcar Named Desire* to Jane Fonda's curlers in *Stanley and Iris*, they rupture glamor with ordinariness. They also provide critiques of marriage, family, and heterosexuality that participate in second-wave feminism. These characteristics of Method acting by women recur across the range of their work.

Introducing the issues shaping women's Method performances, my first chapter, "Women and the Method," traces how the Actors Studio in its early years became a rare and appealing space for female actors, a community where they held leadership roles, where plays by women were studied and staged, where artistic craft was valued above profit and physical beauty, and where the material studied, developed, and performed tackled pressing social problems. The women who emerged from this environment had a greater sense of their entitlement to shape their careers and a greater expectation that they would play roles of gravity and import. As they worked on films amidst the complicated and shifting gender roles of the post-World War II era, I show how the techniques and processes valued at the Actors Studio— ensemble work, improvisation, script analysis—helped to empower them as co-authors.

No film is more strongly associated with Method acting than Elia Kazan's *A Streetcar Named Desire*, and so any effort to redirect our understanding seems to demand revisiting and rereading this film. My second chapter, "Kim Hunter's Feminist Method," considers *A Streetcar Named Desire* beyond Brando's epochal turn by attending to Kim Hunter's performance. Specifically, I argue that Hunter's performance challenges Kazan's view of the character of Stella Kowalski. Studying Hunter's performance alongside her notes on her acting script, I show how she uses Method values to develop an interpretation that critiques traditional versions of femininity and wifehood, and also draws upon contemporary sociological discourses of veterans' reintegration. To develop this interpretation of Stella, Hunter plays the role in two ways simultaneously: as a "perfectly normal" post-war wife, and as a potentially queer bohemian. Her double performance, I suggest, is characteristic of the Method's nuanced understanding of the relationship between normativity and deviance, its complex treatment of sexuality, and a less essentialist approach to identity that we have generally acknowledged.

In my third chapter, "Protest Performances: Actor Rebellion as Feminist Critique," I focus on three Method women who played discontented actors drawing attention to the difficult conditions of their work: Shelley Winters in Robert Aldrich's *The Big Knife* (1955), Julie Harris in Henry Cornelius's *I am a Camera* (1955), and Geraldine Page in Richard Brooks's *Sweet Bird of Youth* (1962). I argue that the figure of the dissenting actress becomes an allegory for women's feminist demands more broadly. While I am considering these depictions of rebellious female actors, I also look at several other significant performances by Winters, Harris, and Page to show how they moved from protest to carving out more satisfying cinematic careers for themselves than those of the actor characters they played.

In my closing chapter, I turn to the career of Jane Fonda. The feminist interpretations that I uncover in women's Method work of the 1950s and 1960s were often located in supporting roles, and were undertaken in films that were not focused centrally on feminist themes. This changed with the career of Fonda, who, at the height of her career, produced her own feminist films. Tracing Fonda's work beginning in the 1960s allows us to see the extent to which she made explicit connections between Method acting and feminism. Through considerations of Fonda's oeuvre, I show her influential presence as a feminist Method auteur.

Finally, in a brief epilogue, I consider Barbara Loden's film *Wanda* (1970). Loden, a longtime Actors Studio member, wrote, directed, and starred in *Wanda*, a film that has become a recognized milestone of feminist independent cinema. Loden's masterpiece shows her operating simultaneously as feminist Method actor and director, and simultaneously inhabiting, extending, and interrogating the Method tradition.

Women, Method Acting, and the Hollywood Film seeks to understand a contentious but enduringly influential screen acting tradition in more capacious, sympathetic, and dynamic ways than we have so far done. Given this remit, I necessarily challenge a series of received ideas about the Method: that it left no room for the female actor; that its processes were a self-indulgent disruption to the business of filmmaking and the command of the studio or auteur; that it could only express masculinity; that its realism was incompatible with feminist approaches to performance; and that it mystified oppressive social structures and reinforced the status quo. Through their persistent tailoring and deepening of roles, and by seeking to tell new kinds of stories about their disaffection with the repressive gender regimes of the post-war years, female Method practitioners developed a performance tradition that remains among the most resonant, arresting, and provocative modes for voicing feminist dissent. The film performances of the women of the Method deserve more critical attention than they have been given, and both the Method and the history of post-war Hollywood look different from their point of view.

Sometimes recent feminist thought and activism can provide helpful tools for understanding the work of female Method actors. The "Me Too" movement has drawn our attention to the long history of double standards and sexual violence in Hollywood, phenomena that the women I study here also noted and resisted. The feminist philosopher Sarah Ahmed's concept of "the feminist killjoy" is also useful here. That is the name Ahmed gives to women who contest assumptions of contentment because what they knew from experience requires them to disrupt the supposedly good time being had by all: "That's not fun, Stanley," says Kim Hunter as Stella Kowalski, rebuking her husband when he slaps her in front of his poker night friends.[33] The insights of Deborah Nelson regarding Cold War era literature might usefully inform our thinking about women and the Method as well. In *Pursuing Privacy in Cold War America*, she argues that the Cold War brought with it a contested definition of privacy, one worked out both in legal battles, in psychoanalysis, and in Confessional poetry. This fraught status of the "private" is one we would do well to think about in relation to Strasberg's "private moment exercise," undertaken in an era when feminists declared that the personal was political. Continuing her investigation of post-war culture in her second book, *Tough Enough*, Nelson argues that certain influential public intellectuals and artists of the post-war period, such as Susan Sontag and Joan Didion, resisted "demands for female warmth and sympathy" and cultivated an anti-sentimental affect of "toughness"—an affect similar to the one I note in a number of the performances I study.[34] Finally, Emma Copley Eisenberg has given new attention to the feminist uses of the aesthetic sometimes called "frump," a style which she calls "a whole sensibility in and of itself," and one that "denies the male sexual gaze" by its embrace of clothes and style that contravene the dictates of fashion and instead embrace comfort.[35] I thought of "Notes on Frump" many times while writing this book, and especially when Joanne Woodward, in a scene in *The Fugitive Kind*, flaunts a pair of "granny panties."

The feminist Method tradition is various: it looks not just like Patricia Neal's insouciant cool, but also like Jo Van Fleet's incendiary maternal ambivalence in *East of Eden* and *Cool Hand Luke*, or Carroll Baker's startling study of PTSD following rape in *Something Wild*, or Ellen Burstyn's attempts as a widow and single mother to make a new life in *Alice Doesn't Live Here Anymore*. I hope that in

18 Introduction

our own moment of renewed feminist energy there may be an audience for their work, and that their re-entry into the Method canon will be lasting.

Notes

1 "John Wayne Starred in Preminger Film," *New York Times*, April 7, 1965.
2 Two years before she played Maggie Haines, Neal had exposed sexual violence in her Oscar-winning performance in Martin Ritt's *Hud* (1963), a film in which she plays the housekeeper of the anti-social Hud (played by Paul Newman). One night, he attempts to rape her. A family member intervenes. Neal's Alma quits her job as his housekeeper and leaves the house. Neal won the Best Actress Oscar for her work in *Hud*.
3 For surveys of second-wave feminism, see Alice Echols and Ellen Willis's *Daring to be Bad: Radical Feminism in America, 1967–1975* (Minneapolis: University of Minnesota Press, 2019); Lynn S. Chancer's *After the Rise and Stall of American Feminism: Taking Back a Revolution* (Stanford, CA: Stanford University Press, 2019); Kirsten Swinth's *Feminism's Forgotten Fight: The Unfinished Struggle for Work and Family* (Cambridge, MA; Harvard University Press, 2018); Rory S. Dicker's *A History of U.S. Feminisms* (Berkeley, CA: Seal Press, 2008, updated 2016); Victoria Heresford's *Feeling Women's Liberation* (Durham, NC: Duke University Press, 2013); Benita Roth's *Separate Roads to Feminism: Black, Chicana, and White Feminist Movements in America's Second Wave* (Cambridge University Press, 2010); and Gail Collins' *When Everything Changed: The Amazing Journey of American Women from 1960 to the Present* (London: Little, Brown, and Company, 2009).
4 Bosley Crowther, "Screen: Sweet Bird of Youth opens: Adaptation of Williams Play at 2 Theatres," *New York Times*, March 29, 1962.
5 Examples of Method women working together or in conversation with each other include the following: in John Cromwell's *The Goddess* (1958), Kim Stanley plays a character partly based on her fellow Method actor Marilyn Monroe; in Fred Zinnemann's *A Hatful of Rain* (1957), Eva Marie Saint plays the part Shelley Winters had originated on Broadway; in Ralph Nelson's *Requiem for a Heavyweight* (1962), Julie Harris plays the social worker originated by Kim Hunter in the television version; in Woody Allen's *Interiors* (1978), Geraldine Page and Maureen Stapleton plays opposite each other as the mother and step-mother of the same family, and in Lee Strasberg's film of Chekhov's *Three Sisters* (1964), four Actors Studio members appear together: Kim Stanley, Shelley Winters, Geraldine Page, and Sandy Dennis.
6 Justine Lloyd and Lesley Johnson have presented one feminist reading, suggesting that the film explores "a tension between discourses of modernity and femininity. We suggest that the housewife in such popular cultural forms of the period must work through the problem of the modern individual's relationship to home." Justine Lloyd and Lesley Johnson, "Three Faces of Eve: The Post-war Housewife, Melodrama, and Home," *Feminist Media Studies*, 3.1, 7–25.
7 Bosley Crowther, "Screen: '3 Faces of Eve, Personalities Study Opens at Victoria,' *New York Times*, September 27, 1957.
8 Karen Hollinger, *The Actress: Hollywood Acting and the Female Star* (New York: Routledge, 2006).
9 Angelica Jade Bastién, "Hollywood Has Ruined Method Acting," *The Atlantic*, August 11, 2016; Chris Bodenner, "Does Method Acting Disadvantage Actresses?" *The Atlantic*, August 13, 2016.

10 Other Method women's work recognized by Oscar nominations included Julie Harris for *The Member of the Wedding* (1953), Carroll Baker for *Baby Doll* (1957), Maureen Stapleton for *Lonelyhearts* (1959), Shirley Knight for *The Dark at the Top of the Stairs* (1961), Lee Remick for *Days of Wine and Roses* (1963), Kim Stanley for *Séance on a Wet Afternoon* (1965), Anne Bancroft for *The Graduate* (1968), Joanne Woodward for *Rachel, Rachel* (1969), Patricia Neal for *The Subject Was Roses* (1969), Estelle Parsons for *Bonnie and Clyde* (1968) and *Rachel, Rachel* (1969), Jane Fonda for *They Shoot Horses, Don't They?* (1970), *Julia* (1978), *The China Syndrome* (1980), *On Golden Pond* (1982), and *The Morning After* (1987). Geraldine Page was nominated seven times—for *Hondo* (1954), *Summer and Smoke* (1962), *Sweet Bird of Youth* (1963), *You're a Big Boy Now* (1967), *Pete 'n' Tillie* (1973), *Interiors* (1979), and *The Pope of Greenwich Village* (1985)—before eventually winning the Best Actress Oscar in 1986 for *The Trip to Bountiful*.

11 Foster Hirsch, *A Method to their Madness: The History of the Actors Studio* (New York: Da Capo Press, 2001), 319.

12 Ibid., 320–321.

13 Arthur Miller, *Timebends: A Life* (New York: Grove Press, 2013), 529.

14 "Geraldine Page," *Dictionary of Missouri Biography* (Columbia, MN: University of Missouri Press, Lawrence O. Christensen, et al., eds.), 590. Page comments: "Even though I was nominated for an Academy Award for *Hondo*, I wasn't offered any kind of film role for seven years."

15 See Forster Hirsch, *A Method to their Madness: The History of the Actors Studio* for an introduction to the institution. See Sharon Carnicke's *Stanislavsky in Focus* (London: Routledge, 1998) for an introduction to the Stanislavskian roots of Method acting. The term "Method" has been used to refer both to members of the Actors Studio and to those affiliated with other Stanislavsky-based groups in New York, such as those surrounding Stella Adler, Sanford Meisner, and Uta Hagen. While all of the actors I study were members of the Actors Studio, some had affiliations with these other teachers as well (for instance, Shelley Winters was coached by Stella Adler for her performance in *A Hatful of Rain*; Sandy Dennis and Geraldine Page studied with Uta Hagen). Others may identify as Method actors, or be identified with Method acting, but for the purposes of creating a specific historical genealogy I have limited this study to those who were members of the Actors Studio.

16 Jacob Gallagher-Ross, *Theatres of the Everyday: Aesthetic Democracy on the American Stage* (Evanston, IL: Northwestern University Press, 2018). On Stanislavsky's varying receptions in American and Russia, see Carnicke's *Stanislavsky in Focus* (Routledge, 1998). On the American side of this reception, see Enelow's *Method Acting and its Discontents* (Evanston, IL: Northwestern University Press, 2015). For a history of the institution of the Actors Studio, see Forster Hirsch's *A Method to Their Madness: The History of the Actors Studio* (Da Capo Press, 1984; repub. 2011) and David Garfield's *The Actor's Studio: A Player's Place* (New York: Macmillan, 1980).

17 The Group Theatre was founded by Harold Clurman, Lee Strasberg, and Cheryl Crawford in 1931. Its goal was to adapt Stanislavsky's ideas to American actors and to generate a canon of new American plays.

18 On stage, John Garfield (1913–1952) originated the role of Ralph in Odets's *Awake and Sing* (1935), and in the 1940s and 1950s he brought a naturalistic style to his roles in films like Robert Rossen's *Body and Soul* (1948) and Robert Aldrich's adaptation of Odets's *The Big Knife* (1955). Ouspenskaya forged a successful Hollywood career in the roles of Russians and matriarchs, including in James Whale's *Waterloo Bridge* (1940) as the sadistic ballet teacher of Vivien Leigh's character.

19 In addition to her substantive theatre resume, Adler had acted on film in Elliot Nugent's *My Girl Tisa* (1948), a New York immigrant drama set in 1905, as well as in *Shadow of the Thin Man* (1941) and *Love on Toast* (1937).
20 Cynthia Baron, *Modern Acting: The Lost Chapter of American Film and Theatre* (London; Palgrave Macmillan, 2016).
21 Women of the Actors Studio often worked in television. From 1948 to 1950, many Method actors appeared on the Actors Studio's television series *Actors Studio* (renamed *The Play's the Thing* as it neared its end), which was broadcast on ABC. On television Method performances, see Molly Schneider, "Television's Tortured Misfits: Authenticity, Method Acting, and Americanness in the Midcentury 'Slice of Life' Anthology Drama," *Journal of Film & Video* 68.3-4 (2016), 30–50. Friedan's *The Feminine Mystique* cites a 1959 television broadcast of Ibsen's *A Doll's House*, starring Julie Harris as Nora, as a key moment of feminist awakening for American women (140).
22 Shelley Stamp, *Lois Weber in Early Hollywood* (Berkeley: University of California Press, 2015).
23 Emily Carman, *Independent Stardom: Freelance Women in the Hollywood Studio System* (Austin: University of Texas Press, 2015).
24 J.E. Smyth's *Nobody's Girl Friday: The Women Who Ran Hollywood* (Oxford: Oxford University Press, 2018).
25 Christina Crawford notes that Joan Crawford even tried her hand at Stanislavsky-based acting for a brief moment. When describing Crawford's marriage to former Group Theatre member Franchot Tone, Crawford's daughter reports: "Mother said she was fascinated by his stories of the Group Theatre and acting lessons patterned after those of the great Russian director Stanislavsky.... As she listened attentively to the instructions, her heart sunk.... What Franchot wanted was for her to be a carrot. She was to stand like a carrot, and feel like a carrot. For several minutes she stared at him in total silence while the full impact of what was expected of her crept through her consciousness. ... She rose to her feet and took her position as a carrot. No one will ever know the extent of her performance as the ill-fated carrot because at this point in the story she burst into laughter. She said that she told Franchot she thought this was ridiculous. She was never going to be cast as a carrot and she couldn't imagine how in the world this could possibly help her career or get her better parts." *Mommie Dearest*, p. 20.
26 Therese Grisham and Julie Grossman's *Ida Lupino, Director: Her Art and Resilience in Times of Transition* (2017) is a valuable new contribution to the history of women's post-war work in Hollywood, as is Maya Montañez Smukler's *Liberating Hollywood: Women Directors and the Feminist Reform of 1970s American Cinema* (2018).
27 Paul McDonald, "Why Study Film Acting? Some Opening Reflections," in *More Than a Method: Trends and Traditions in Contemporary Film Performance*, Cynthia Baron, Diane Carson, Frank P. Tomasulo, eds. (Detroit: Wayne State University Press, 2004), 23.
28 Aaron Taylor, "Introduction: Acting, Casually and Theoretically Speaking," *Theorizing Film Acting*, Aaron Taylor, ed. (London: Routledge, 2012), 1–18.
29 Taylor, 12.
30 The closest we have to a sustained critical study is Richard Blum's *American Film Acting: Stanislavski Heritage*, but as the title indicates, Blum focuses on the broader influence of Stanislavksy in Hollywood, and not on the Method particularly (Champaign, IL: UMI Research Press, 1984).
31 Adam Baker," "Robert De Niro: Star as Actor-Auteur," *Acting for America: Movie Stars of the 1980s,* Robert Eberwein, ed. (Rutgers University Press, 2010), 19–35.

32 Krampner, *Female Brando: The Legend of Kim Stanley* (New York: Back Stage Books, 2006).
33 Sara Ahmed, "Feminist Killjoys (and other Willful Subjects)," *The Scholar and Feminist Online* 8.3 (Summer 2010), Polyphonic Feminisms: Acting in Concert. Accessed June 8, 2020, http://sfonline.barnard.edu/polyphonic/print_ahmed.htm
   See also Sarah Ahmed, "Feminist Killjoys," in *The Promise of Happiness* (Durham: Duke University Press), 2010.
34 Deborah Nelson, *Pursuing Privacy in Cold War America* (New York: Columbia University Press), 2001 and *Tough Enough: Arbus, Arendt, Didion, McCarthy, Sontag, Weil* (Chicago: University of Chicago Press, 2017), 3.
35 Emma Copley Eisenberg, "Notes on Frump: A Style for the Rest of Us," *Alma* 10 (August 2017). Accessed June 8, 2020, www.heyalma.com/notes-on-frump-a-style-for-the-rest-of-us/

1
WOMEN AND THE METHOD

In 1962 the *Saturday Evening Post* announced the rise of a new kind of film actor, one who "prefers a little apartment in New York's Greenwich Village to the magnificence of a 10-room California pad" and is "aware that a world of crises exists beyond what is reported in Hedda Hopper's column."[1] The intellectual, bohemian figure being described was Geraldine Page, by then a multiple Academy-Award nominated actor for her roles in *Hondo* (1953) and *Summer and Smoke* (1961), and soon to be recognized again for *Sweet Bird of Youth* (1962). Given Page's stature, the *Post* is surprised at how firmly she has rejected the trappings of Hollywood glamor to pursue a career grounded in an alternative set of values: the craft of acting, hard work, intellectual development, and social engagement. The photograph that illustrates the article emphasizes that Page rebuffs familiar ideas of an actress's glamor: no filter hides the wrinkles under her 38-year-old eyes or the weathered skin on her cheeks, and no dye covers her greying hair. Both text and image emphasize Page's actorly versatility over Hollywood's preferred qualities of beauty and star quality: she wears a "plain brown dress and sports tousled hair," her is face "unremarkable" but "expressive," and she has "an ability" to "play almost any heroine between the ages of twenty-five and fifty-five."

Where would such an actor come from? From the world of New York theatre, perhaps unsurprisingly, but from a very specific corner of it that was still an object of public fascination in 1962: the Actors Studio, home of "the Method" that had emerged ten years earlier as a galvanizing force in American screen acting with the compelling performances of *A Streetcar Named Desire*, and which, by the time of Page's interview, was associated in the public mind (erroneously, according to her) with working-class masculinity, mumbled delivery, and youth cultural angst. It was decidedly not associated with actors like Page whose rebellion was of a different variety—that of asserting the right to a new range of roles in the decades following World War II. Page is determined in the *Post* interview to overturn and expand the public perception of what Method acting is, and perhaps more importantly, *who* a Method actor is. She insists that Method acting is not the sole province of intense male actors like Brando, James Dean, and Steve McQueen, and that the Actors Studio, rather than being a site of misbehavior or cultish, Freud-obsessed neurotics, was a serious crucible for the development of actorly craft, including her own. While the *Post*'s interviewer may have expected to be compiling an ordinary celebrity profile, Page has other plans in mind: to offer a tutorial about the Method as a broad and empowering approach to acting for both men and women.

Page's account attempts to provide a corrective to common understandings of the Actors Studio—the place where Marlon Brando pretended to be a chicken and an ape, or where actors substituted Freudian therapy for art—and draw attention to the Studio as she saw it: as a much-needed working environment for maintaining and expanding the skills of actors, and a welcoming home where members were encouraged to challenge stereotypes and break out of ruts, both their own and those imposed by the commercial theatre and film worlds. It is worth pausing over this 1962 interview because the stereotypes that Page says had already started to accrue around the conception of Method acting ended up ossifying into axioms. The masculinist view of Method acting today is not far removed from the one she was seeking to overturn in 1962, and Page's invitation to look at the Studio's work from other points of view—specifically her point of view as a female actor—has never been taken up. This is even more remarkable given that, beginning in the late 1940s, a dynamic group of women—artistically ambitious, feminist, and identified with the burgeoning counter-culture—shared experiences like Page's at the Actors Studio, finding there a place where they could generate a new relationship to acting, including new kinds of roles and positions of artistic leadership.

Given the strong association of Method acting with masculinity, one might assume that the Actors Studio did not focus on developing the talents of women, yet this is far from the truth. Women have been foundational to Method acting since its inception in the New York theatre world of the 1940s. One of the Studio's three co-founders (alongside Elia Kazan and Robert Lewis), was Cheryl Crawford, drama alumna of Smith College, a queer woman who had co-founded the Group Theatre with Harold Clurman and Lee Strasberg (she was also the co-founder of the American Repertory Theatre with Eva Le Gallienne). The Actors Studio's first Broadway production was the work of a female playwright—Bessie Breuer's *Sundown Beach* (it opened at the Belasco Theatre on September 7, 1948), a drama that grappled with the challenges facing women in their relationships with men returning home from World War II (Julie Harris played a character who gets pregnant while her husband is at war). The first cohort of the Actors Studio, the one that boasted Marlon Brando, Montgomery Clift, and Karl Malden, also included Julie Harris, Patricia Neal, Maureen Stapleton, and Anne Jackson. Women played powerful roles at the Actors Studio, in New York's broader Stanislavsky-based acting circles, and subsequently in Hollywood, where several generations of female Method actors carved rich careers. For over half a century, women have been working as Method actors, contributing high-quality, challenging, and often feminist performances, and leaving statements about the mutually enriching relationship between feminism and Method acting, yet there has been almost no sustained attention to their work, or to how it helped to reshape the possibilities of film acting for women.

The Method and Masculinity After the War

Before we can restore women's work in the Method, it is necessary to pause over the many overdetermined meanings that became associated with male Method actors at mid-century. In László Benedek's *The Wild One* (1953), Marlon Brando plays the brash motorcycle gang leader Johnny Strabler. When he is asked by a young woman in a soda shop "Hey Johnny, what are you rebelling against?" he answers ""Whaddaya got?" Johnny's anarchic, open-ended rebellion sent shock waves through popular culture. When Brando came to prominence in Hollywood, he not only became synonymous with Method acting—he also became perhaps the most globally resonant icon of his cultural moment. The Method rebel, particularly Brando, but also James Dean and Montgomery Clift in their performances of social alienation and youthful angst in films like George Stevens' *A Place in the Sun* (1951), Elia Kazan's *On the Waterfront* (1954), Nicholas Ray's *Rebel Without a Cause* (1955), and Kazan's *East of Eden* (1955), came to embody energies of opposition to the imperative of social conformity that accompanied Cold War America's programs of containment and consensus. The figure of the male Method actor, in his poetic and leather-clad resistance to authority, gained a cultural status that no female Method actor was granted—the privilege of being considered the representative type of society. Looking back from 1966, Pauline Kael called Brando "the major protagonist of contemporary American themes in the fifties" and "the hero who really strikes a nerve."[2] Kael sees in Brando "a reaction against the postwar mania for security" and "a contemporary version of the free American," and suggests that when a delinquent is elevated into a hero, it is because his stance "expresses something in many people that they don't dare express" and that, in this case, it was "the courage to act out a *no* to a whole system of authority, morality, and prosperity."[3]

For Kael, as for others of her generation, films starring Method actors, no less than Beckett's *Waiting for Godot* (1953), Camus's *The Stranger* (1942) or Kurosawa's *Rashomon* (1950), represented a significant artistic response to the crises of moral and political authority unleashed by the war. The Method actor's disgust at the world he had inherited, and his struggle to find a place within it on new terms, made him a compelling archetype for the era of existentialism.[4] His appeal transcended US borders—he was received with enthusiasm by the French intellectual coterie of *Cahiers du Cinéma* who, in the process of elevating Nicholas Ray to high stature in the pantheon of auteurs, also found themselves enthralled by James Dean's "youth," "stubborn intensity," and "futile heroism" (112) in *Rebel Without a Cause*, as well as his emergence "from inauthenticity" (114) at the film's end in which they saw resonances with French absurdism and existentialism.[5]

Not only did male Method performances transfix critics and the film-going public. In what became one of the more curious culture wars of the period, the techniques of Method acting, its theories and preparation processes, also became an object of fascination, concern, adulation, skepticism, mockery, and suspicion. Debates, diatribes, and defenses of the merits and perils of Method acting as well as parodies of Method actors as neurotics peppered popular culture. In 1957, Robert Lewis, one of the co-founders of the Actors Studio, even felt the need to give a series of public lectures in New York in an attempt to demystify Stanislavsky's System and describe the work done at the Actors Studio with hopes of quelling some of these stereotypes (it was published by Samuel French in 1958 as "*Method— or Madness?*"). Also in 1958, Bette Davis filmed a pilot for a television series called *The Starmaker* in which she plays a theatrical agent comically trying to manage a male Method actor client who bursts into her office with the words "Paula, I'm suffering!" and who runs the gamut of supposed Method tics and antics: impulsive, quasi-suicidal, histrionic, mumbling, and alternating between outbursts of anger and quaking on the couch in the fetal position.

Why did the Method have such power to amuse, enthrall, and fluster midcentury Americans? Perhaps its roots in techniques developed by the Russian theatre director Konstantin Stanislavksy brought a provocative Cold War era charisma to Method acting by making it seem proximate to America's great geopolitical foe. Scholars of the Method have accounted for its highly fraught status at mid-century in a variety of ways. Nathan D. Allison posits that Stanislavsky's theories provided an ingenious way of managing post-war crises of subjectivity, agency, and authority. For Allison, though the war had shaken confidence in liberal humanist concepts of the self and the capacity of western aesthetics to address such moral horror, Stanislavsky's "as if" (a speculative orientation toward the real through concepts like "the given circumstances" of a play) provided a way of simultaneously affirming traditional concepts of subjectivity while also disavowing them. Via Method acting, Allison's argument goes, one could continue to pretend that humans were three-dimensional beings possessed of interiority and depth— one could proceed largely as before, even while knowing on some level that this was merely a convention, an "as if." For Allison, it is this quality that gives Method acting its appeal to early Cold War culture:[6]

> The rise of the Method can be understood as symptomatic of the sense of perceived loss (of agency, personal identity, and human uniqueness) occasioned by consensus culture. By this account, the Method becomes more than an approach to acting; it functions as a mode of being and

understanding the world, creating a space for the postwar subject to cultivate the perception of autonomy and a coherent personal identity, while acknowledging its limits.[7]

In short, Allison argues that Method actors came up with tricks to reassure a shaken world that humans were still human after all, of recuperating lost realness effects, and in so doing, tending to wounds that needed salving.

But it is also important to remember that Method performances provoked as much as they healed, and were not so much at odds with the newly emergent sociological worldview as they were a part of it. And the social meaning of these performances was not just existential. Male Method actors, with their brash attitudes, social contempt, psychological probing, and naturalistic style, were received as a bold generational challenge not just to society at large but also to film industry norms. The new male Method stars, as Steve Cohan and others have noted, played roles that were much more "neurotic" than those of any male stars before them, and were uninterested in taking up the mantle of manhood as it had been left at the beginning of the war. The gap they embodied between pre- and post-World War II generations was often played out in conflicts over acting styles, with Orson Welles, Katherine Cornell, Laurence Olivier, and others speaking for the old guard's confusion or hostility in the face of the Method's challenges to the star system and norms of acting decorum (Welles even dedicated himself to making a documentary film about his dislike of the Method).

The Method's disruptive power was partly a function of its reconfiguration of pre-war aesthetic hierarchies in ways characteristic of late modernism: Marianne Conroy locates its provocation in a "middlebrow disposition" that "[i]n the view of many intellectuals of the period...threatened the orthodox cultural distinctions between popular and prestigious forms on which the entire notion of a national style depended, in that the style combined high cultural purpose with a popular commercial ethos."[8] Jacob Gallagher-Ross sees the Method on film's challenge in its foregrounding of its own technological mediation. Richard Maltby suggests that the erotic, suffering presence of the male Method actor was a spectacle that allowed black-and-white social dramas to compete with other "cinemas of attractions" of the 1950s, from 3D to Biblical and Roman epics.[9] For Maltby, such displays of emotion had not been seen in Hollywood since the silent era. Shonni Enelow, meanwhile, suggests that the Method's rocky entrance into American popular consciousness had to do with the way in which it facilitated the mainstreaming of psychoanalysis and raised important questions of race and class integration in post-war American society. Both Enelow and Michael Trask have also suggested that the Method actor's aversion to "scriptedness" in general stood for a larger impulse to rewrite cultural scripts that foreshadowed the breaking with oppressive structures evident in the civil rights, feminist, and other social movements. Both Trask and Enelow also note that America's preoccupation with the Method was consistent with a broader turn to performance as a site of inquiry and relevance, one that was also evident in sociological works like Goffman's *The Performance of Self in Everyday Life* (1956).

The two directors who most clearly mediated the Method's entry into Hollywood were Elia Kazan and Fred Zinnemann.[10] Kazan was a co-founder of the Actors Studio, whereas Zinnemann was not officially affiliated with the Studio, but often cast Method actors in his films.[11] Both made films that spoke directly to the concerns of the post-war moment. The Method actors who came to prominence after the war were mostly too young to be veterans themselves (Karl Malden was an exception—he had been in the Air Force), but they often played veterans on screen in Kazan's, Zinnemann's, and other films that investigated the challenges of soldiers' reintegration and America's continuing commitments in Europe. Films like Zinnemann's *The Search* (1948) and *The Men* (1950) featured American soldiers abroad or trying to readjust to life at home after the war. Zinnemann presided over both Brando's and Clift's screen debuts. In 1948's *The Search*, he cast Clift as an American G.I. stationed in Germany who befriends a child survivor of a concentration camp and helps him find his mother. The film was shot on location in the US-occupied zone of Germany, and Clift helped to shape the screenplay through improvisation during filming. Two years later, Zinnemann's *The Men* took up the struggles of wounded soldiers on the home front, with Brando in the role of a veteran with paraplegia. It was filmed on location at the Birmingham Veteran's Hospital in Van Nuys, California, and, like William Wyler's post-war classic *The Best Years of our Lives* (1946), featured non-professional actors (hospital patients) in supporting roles. Both *The Search* and *The Men* eschewed simplistic returning-hero narratives in favor of more complex stories that acknowledged the difficulties of the post-war transition and the feelings of vulnerability, guilt, anger, and frustration that veterans and their families felt, as well as the ongoing obligations that both support for returning soldiers and the process of European reconstruction required (Figure 1.1).

FIGURE 1.1 Marlon Brando with Teresa Wright in Fred Zinnemann's *The Men* (1950). Credit: ©iStock.

In the decade following *The Search*, Zinnemann often cast Actors Studio members in projects designed to help Americans come to terms with their wartime experiences and expand their social consciences. A defining quality of his films is that they often encouraged audiences to question and relax rigid gender roles. In *The Member of the Wedding* (1952), Zinnemann directed Julie Harris in Carson McCullers's story of a gender non-conforming child growing up during the war, longing to be part of its adventures as a way of escaping from a loneliness. Zinnemann's *From Here to Eternity* (1953) also captured the post-war mood and its social and sexual dynamics. Based on the novel by James Jones, it became a blockbuster that swept the Oscars in 1954.[12] Among its ensemble cast, Zinnemann cast Clift in the role of Robert Prewitt, a soldier who expresses his love for his fallen comrade Maggio (who died in his arms) by playing a trumpet solo with tears rolling down his cheeks. Clift's performance acknowledged the deep bonds that had developed between men in the war and validated their need to mourn such losses.[13] Three years later, Zinnemann directed Eva Marie Saint, Don Murray, and Anthony Franciosa in *A Hatful of Rain* (1957), an adaptation of Michael Gazzo's Actors Studio-developed play that focused on a Korean War veteran's struggle with the morphine addiction he acquired in a military hospital.

In general, Zinnemann took a gentle, humanistic approach to characters and situations, and one undercurrent of his films was their consistent suggestion that relaxing strict gender roles would lead to greater happiness for all. And while Kazan's aesthetic was seemingly more invested in violent and toxic forms of masculinity, certainly his dystopian representations of authoritarian men in films like *A Streetcar Named Desire* (1951) and *East of Eden* (1955) could be seen as suggesting the need for the reform of gender roles as well. But Kazan's feminist consciousness was more limited than Zinnemann's (see Chapter 2 on Kim Hunter and the Epilogue on Barbara Loden for a more detailed consideration of Kazan's relationship to female actors). In addition to Kazan and Zinnemann, directors including Edward Dymtryk, George Seaton, László Benedek, and Martin Ritt also worked with Method actors to develop realistic portraits of the war and its aftermath. Their films too explored the uncertain cultural terrain of the post-war. Dymtryk's *The Young Lions* (1958, based on Irwin Shaw's 1948 novel) cast Brando as a Nazi officer and Clift as an American Jewish soldier facing prejudice in his own army. Seaton's *The Big Lift* (1950), filmed in Germany, portrayed the American Air Force's lift of supplies into Berlin. Clift plays an Air Force sergeant who finds himself bewildered as he negotiates the uncertain political terrain of East Berlin. In a key scene, his character's masculine pride is challenged when he must sit by and watch as the German woman he loves works a hard labor job from which he cannot relieve her. Early films featuring Method actors often showed the influence of the high-profile documentaries of the war years, and of Italian neorealism, in their preference for on-location filming, incorporating non-professional actors, and addressing social themes. They also reflected the expansion and popularization of the discipline of sociology and tracked the post-war dysphoria that was experienced by both women and men as they were expected to transition from the gender fluidities and reversals of their wartime experiences back to traditional roles. Because of the cultural crisis of gender assumptions from which they originate, early films featuring Method actors tend to treat disorientation surrounding gender expression as a kind of norm in itself: these films emerge out of a moment in which traditional roles had been exposed as arbitrary by the independence and professional competence women had shown during the war, and by the physical vulnerability and dependency of so many returning wounded men. These films and the performances they contained emphasized the fragility and exploitation of male bodies by war, capitalism, and the ideological imperatives of strength and violence.

The Method's interest in masculinity at its breaking points may have come to cultural prominence as a result of wartime experience, but it was also informed by leftist theatre and film, including works such as Clifford Odets's *Golden Boy* (1937) and Robert Rossen's *Body and Soul* (1947) which dramatized the narrow options, ethical compromises, and sacrifices required from those trying to achieve class mobility or ethnic assimilation. Explorations of male melancholia are prominent in the early screen appearances of male Method actors, and masculinity often appears as troubled construct, either something desired but unreachable, or as hideous and hostile.

An obsession with interrogating masculinity was certainly a defining trait of early films featuring Method acting. But this destabilization of masculinity brought with it new film roles for female actors informed by their own wartime experiences—performances of marginalized masculinity like Julie Harris's in *The Member of the Wedding,* or portrayals of the struggles of managing men's trauma, such as Kim Hunter's in *A Streetcar Named Desire.* The Method's concern with masculinity, in other words, is tied both to frequent depictions of male characters' complex identifications with femininity and queerness (particularly in the work of Clift) and to female characters' often tortured negotiations of masculinity. Given this dynamic, the female actors who work in such films have great revelations to offer. While feminist criticism has noticed that women often played domestic roles in these films, not enough credit has been given to the ways in which these performances were targeted critiques of the dissatisfactions and dangers of women's experiences in the late 1940s and 1950s.

The concern to represent the social changes wrought by the war was an important driving force of these early projects featuring Method actors. In one case, this impulse gave rise to a performance so arresting and influential that it transcended its specific historical context with results that have left a long and difficult shadow on the Method ever since. I refer here to Brando's performance as veteran Stanley Kowalski in Kazan's *A Streetcar Named Desire* (1951), which resulted in a phenomenon that might be called the reification of "Method PTSD." The result of Brando's generation-defining performance was the popularization of a performance style that followed the explosive patterns of post-traumatic stress disorder, which included among its symptoms irritability, outbursts, and aggressive behavior. The style Brando forged for his performance as Stanley Kowalski, in keeping with the imperative of Williams's play to depict the mood swings of a veteran, was one of alternation between periods of calm and explosive outbursts. Brando's performance was an effort realistically to portray symptoms of what was then called "combat fatigue," not a general Method stylistic, but so influential and charismatic was Brando's performance that it ended up being enshrined and imitated as the Method's signature style (not necessarily at the Actors Studio, where such imitation was discouraged, but certainly beyond it in many film performances of the "Angry Young Man" generation and beyond). And so, at the moment of its Hollywood inception, rather than being understood as a set of processes or approaches that could lead to widely divergent performance styles, the Method became conflated with performances of explosive masculinity. This particular performance, including the details of its costume and speech patterns, came to be seen as representative of, and even synonymous with, the Method. As Angelica Jade Bastién's recent article "Hollywood Has Ruined Method Acting" suggests by proposing that the Method is organized around and legitimates "destructive ideas of masculinity," we are still living in the shadow of Brando's Stanley Kowalski and its endless imitations.[14]

The Method and Feminism

Geraldine Page's forthright and anti-glamorous self-presentation in the *Saturday Evening Post* profile, as well as her claim that Method acting had been misunderstood as a male tradition, were in keeping with the broader growth of feminist consciousness in the 1960s and 1970s, when Eleanor Roosevelt chaired President Kennedy's newly created Commission on the Status of Women, a body designed to reintroduce legislation on women's rights. The rise of feminist energy would be a defining force of the: not only in acting but across the professions a generation of women sought equality of access and compensation in male-dominated industries. Scholars have been more inclined to historicize the Method in relation to the Cold War and McCarthyism, but it is worth locating it in relationship to the burgeoning feminist movements of the post-war as well.

The years between 1945 and 1960 have sometimes been mistaken as being practically devoid of feminist activity, but there were important changes afoot. The release of the second Kinsey report in 1953, the bestselling *Sexual Behavior in the Human Female*, was based on interviews with more than 6,000 women and disrupted sentimental discourses and tackled sexual taboos. The FDA approved the first oral contraceptive in 1960, and in 1965 the Supreme Court's *Griswold v. Connecticut* decision allowed married women to use birth control (the 1972 decision *Baird v. Eisenstadt* would make birth control legal for all). Even earlier than this, the 1950s in fact harbored a fair amount of feminist energy, although this has sometimes been forgotten because the pressures of McCarthyism led the relationship between feminism and the Left to be suppressed. As Kathlene McDonald argues: "the issue of women's oppression received unprecedented attention within the [American Communist] Party and wider left and Labor circles just after the war," and an emphasis on recruitment of women activists, "unionization of domestic workers, equal pay and job training for women, workplace discrimination, daycare, and national health insurance' meant that a "Left feminist community" began to emerge. McDonald advises that it is important to insist on these connections between feminism and the Left in the period, because of how badly warped our understanding of them has been by anti-Communist ideologies: "because of cultural repression of…activism during McCarthyism, the cultural history of Left feminist thought from this era is almost lost." McDonald cites Daniel Horowitz's research on Betty Friedan's intellectual roots in labor activism and reflects on the ways in which, when she came to publish *The Feminine Mystique* (1963), she "completely disavows her Left past and reinvents herself as a middle-class housewife" and yet, "many of the ideas in *The Feminine Mystique* are deeply rooted in the Left's critique of domestic ideology in the 1940s and 1950s." Horowitz argues that rescuing works like Friedan's "from their Cold War exile and analyzing them in the context of postwar Left feminism helps to rewrite US feminist history in a way that acknowledges a continuous tradition of resistance, a tradition that has been largely erased by the red-baiting of the McCarthy era."[15]

Together, Friedan's *The Feminine Mystique* and Simone de Beauvoir's *The Second Sex* (1949) were among the feminist texts that helped to reshape views of women in the post-war. And significantly, both Beauvoir and Friedan considered actors important figures in the history of feminism. For Beauvoir, they belonged to that rarest class of women who had "escaped feminine servitude": by making their own livings "for three centuries," she wrote, they "have been almost the only ones to possess concrete independence in society."[16] Beauvoir reserved her greatest admiration for those who went beyond gaining financial freedom from men and became "authentic artists."[17] Her idol was the same as Lee Strasberg's, Eleonora Duse, whom she lauds as follows: "she will really be an artist, a creator who gives meaning to her life by lending meaning to the world."[18] Beauvoir's sense of acting as a route to both economic and spiritual liberation for women was one that the first generation of Method women shared. Stanislavsky-based practitioners of the mid-century borrowed from feminist thought to note that while acting had been often been pejoratively associated with prostitution, vanity, narcissism, and hysteria, becoming an actor involved learning how to move beyond such stigmas, reclaiming the dignity of the profession and insisting upon its status alongside the other arts as a means of humanistic inquiry. Nowhere was this impulse clearer than in the title of Uta Hagen's 1973 book *Respect for Acting*, which distilled Hagen's many years of Stanislavsky-based teaching and performing into a guide for those who would take themselves seriously as actors. Hagen wrote that: "The profession of acting has been maligned throughout the ages" and has "been accused of prostitution and other vices of immorality," but the goal of the actor should be to resist this denigration and to make acting an intellectual, critically engaged, and rigorous pursuit: to "have a point of view about the world which surrounds you" and to "rebel or revolt against the status quo."[19] In these ways, according to Hagen, actors could "merit respect for our profession (221)." One aspect of this defense was particularly compatible with feminism. For Hagen, as for Strasberg and most Stanislavsky-based teachers, "Physical beauty is not a prerequisite to becoming an actor," and she wrote that the best actors, "men and women, can create beauty for an audience" (14). Hagen's ideal actor was also Duse, who in her view transcended stereotypical expressions of femininity and conventional modes of theatricality to become above all "a human being on the stage" (11).

If Beauvoir's *The Second Sex* (1949) was the feminist title that defined the immediate post-war years (it had appeared in H.M. Parshley's English translation in 1953), it was Friedan's *The Feminine Mystique* that would become most identified with middle-class American women. Friedan's book introduced two influential concepts: first was the "problem that has no name," her phrase for the generalized ennui which she claimed was broadly felt by suburban women and which culminated in the question "Is this all?"[20] Second was the book's title itself, which Friedan defined as follows: "the feminine mystique says that the highest value and only commitment for women is the fulfillment of their own femininity."[21] For Friedan, a demand for feminine performance extended beyond professional actors to include all woman in the pressure to cultivate a star-like charisma through make-up, clothing, grooming, and social behavior. The refusal to enact this "mystique," Friedan insisted, was an important step towards emancipation. Female Method actors, grounded in a naturalistic tradition that similarly sought to draw performance away from artifice, were well-positioned to model what it might look like to repudiate "mystique."

The Status of Female Actors in Strasberg's Method

While the culture at large focused on the rebellious images of male Method actors, at the Actors Studio in New York it could be argued that Lee Strasberg (who took over leadership in 1951 once Kazan's Hollywood commitments made it impractical to oversee the studio) was equally, and perhaps even primarily, concerned with the development of female actors. It would be an understatement to say that Strasberg's Studio sessions have been the subject of fierce controversy, and the most contentious issue of all has been the question of his work with female actors. The words "Strasberg" and "feminism" are often considered anathema. For instance, in her criticism of Method acting preparation techniques in *Feminism and Theatre*, Sue-Ellen Case writes that inevitably in the Method, "From Antigone to Blanche Dubois, the female actor works on the passive, broken sexual development of her character. ... From a feminist perspective, the Method techniques for building these characters lead the female actor into inaccurate analyses of female sexuality" (123). Further, Case argues that the Method's most influential playwrights

(Williams, Miller, etc.) develop their characters beginning with "Freudian biases" and "portray women's sexuality as subordinate and derivative in relation to that of the leading male characters" (124). In addition to its Freudian orientation, Case also faults the Method's investment in realism as one that "reifies the male as sexual subject and the female as sexual 'Other' and promulgates an "often defeatist, determinist view of the opportunities for change."[22] A more recent feminist challenge to Strasberg comes from Rosemary Malague's "Emotional Control: Lee Strasberg as 'Big Daddy' of the Method" in *An Actress Prepares*.[23] Malague rejects any compatibility between feminism and Method at the Actors Studio during Strasberg's long tenure, describing his approach to female actors as domineering, paternalistic, exploitative, and destructive. Drawing on transcripts of Strasberg's work with women and memoirs by those affiliated with the Actors Studio, Malague sketches a portrait of a thoroughly demoralized and victimized cadre of female actors, and suggests that Strasberg was particularly drawn to vulnerable women over whom he could exert emotional control and sometimes profit from financially (this, for instance, is Malague's reading of the relationship between Marilyn Monroe and Strasberg).

On the other hand, Shonni Enelow, another leading feminist scholar of the Method, expresses reservations about Malague's account, noting that its characterization of the women who worked with Strasberg as victims perpetuates anti-Semitic discourses of "Jewish parasitism" and also that it denies female actors like Monroe any artistic or personal agency in their decision to join the Actors Studio. In light of these concerns, Enelow suggests that "it's time for a new feminist reading…of Method acting" (35) and asks "what if there really was something that some women found both intellectually stimulating and gender nonconformist about their work at the Actors Studio?" (27). I approach this question by arguing for the presence of feminist currents—or at least, currents that were compatible with feminism—in Strasberg's comments and session-leading practices. While it is certainly true that there were actors (of all genders) who found Strasberg's personality and processes estranging, these narratives have received far more attention than the accounts of female actors who found their experiences at the Actors Studio positive, and so here I revisit Strasberg's work with a view to identifying the aspects of his approach that may have been constructive, in order to begin to answer the question of why certain female actors found the Actors Studio to be a welcoming and congenial environment. Using the same source that Malague uses to critique Strasberg's work with women (transcripts from Actors Studio sessions published under the title *Strasberg at the Actors Studio*, edited by Robert H. Hethmon), I will lay out what I see as the potentially enabling currents in Strasberg's work with female actors. Certainly, both positive and troubling strains exist in Strasberg's practice. Different actors responded to different elements of Strasberg's pedagogy, and took different things from it. Until now, however, feminist critiques have almost exclusively explored what they consider to be the problematic dimensions of Strasberg's session-leading practices. For the sake of a fuller picture that might help to explain why female Method actors in Hollywood so consistently intervened in their scripts in feminist ways, let me enumerate a few of the ways in which Strasberg's remarks and perspectives might be viewed as compatible with feminism.

Feminist critiques have often singled out Strasberg's "Affective Memory" exercise as a pernicious practice, one supposedly geared at breaking through the inhibitions of actors—particularly female actors—by bringing them to the point of emotional breakdown in sessions.[24] This practice has been viewed as excessive and invasive, and scholars have suggested that Strasberg was more interested in pushing female than male actors toward these shows of emotion. There is a longstanding stereotype of the female Method actor as a teary-eyed mess, emotionally assaulted by Strasberg or other powerful male teachers created in his image. Gallagher-Ross has suggested that we might even distinguish between the male and female Method traditions according to what is believed to be Strasberg's emphasis on female emotional breakdown, proposing that: "If the characteristic unit of noisemaking for the male Method actor was the mumble, we could even say that for female members of the studio, the corresponding quantum of authenticity was the sob."[25] But in fact, while Strasberg did emphasize the need for all actors to be able access personal emotions, and while actors did sometimes cry during Affective memory exercises, in work on scenes at the Actors Studio, Strasberg often actively discourages displays of sobbing and "hysteria" from female actors. Most often, what Strasberg advises female actors to do is to refuse the association between femininity and hysteria. Instead, he encourages them to find logic in their parts. "One of the most serious misunderstandings of actors is to assume that to act truly and believably means to forget what you are doing," Strasberg tells one of his studio sessions, "But," he warns, "that's hysteria" (166). Working with "Actress O" (all of the actors in the book are anonymized) on the character of Lady Anne in Shakespeare's *Richard III*, he tells her that the most effective moment of the performance was the one in which "You turned your face away. You seemed to say, 'Please, I don't want to, but I have to cry,' which was 'a logical and human response.'" (220). In another scene, when Strasberg works with "Actress RR" on Juliet, he steers her away from her inclination to weep and toward the delivery of the words. "Don't worry about the crying. Let's hear the words" (238) Strasberg tells her, and also encourages her to follow her impulse to express anger, to yell and kick instead of crying, to see what would happen if she allowed herself to transform tears into rage. Here, Strasberg suggests that a female actor is entitled to perform the same kind of explosive rage that her male counterparts made famous, and that Juliet could be interpreted as an Angry Young Woman.

When working with "Actress N" on the final scene from Tennessee Williams's *Summer and Smoke*, Strasberg counsels her to resist emotion in order to think logically about why Alma confronts her suitor at the end of the play. He asks her:

You were ill. Is this scene a continuation of the illness? Or have you come out of the illness? It seemed to me that you did not ask these questions. The girl actually had had a breakdown. For months she sat and did not speak to anyone. She was mentally disturbed, but now she has come out of it. What did she come out of and with what attitude?

(123)

Strasberg next proposes an interpretation that emphasizes Alma's attainment of clarity and a kind of self-realization at the end of the play, but he does not prescribe the details of the interpretation:

…she was looking herself straight in the eye for the first time. This is why she said to herself before this scene begins, "This is what I want, and this is what I must have."

…there must also be the other thing that makes her face herself and makes her face him in this scene. I don't know what it is. I don't know whether it's strength or something else. You find out. Your way of doing it, your imagination, your awareness, may be different from anybody else's idea."

(123)

Here, Strasberg's comments might be read as compatible with feminism in two ways—first, he interprets Williams's character as more than a pathological specter of female madness and instead sees her as one who is "looking herself straight in the eye for the first time" (123)—as a woman waking to herself, attaining self-consciousness. In addition to this potentially feminist reading of Alma, Strasberg reminds Actress N that the freedom to interpret the role is her own. Belying his domineering image, Strasberg encourages her to find "Your way of doing it" (123). Similarly, with another actor working on Juliet, he remarks "You tell me what a girl who fantasizes at a moment like that [falling in love] is *really* concerned with" (308–9). And to another, he remarks: "nobody makes your instrument on the stage except you" (260).

Another frequent feminist critique of the Method (one that has been articulated by Elizabeth Stroppel and Sue-Ellen Case) is that it encourages women to identify themselves with harmful gender stereotypes perpetuated in the works of male playwrights. When helping female actors to explore their characters, however, Strasberg often counsels them to interpret these roles in ways that challenge conventional expectations for femininity. For instance, when working on the role of Irina from Chekhov's *Three Sisters* with "Actress O," Strasberg suggests that she try to present Irina as *less* resigned to the sacrifices she is going to make: "Only the things Irina is going to accept are here, not this other thing which she still desires and thinks she is going to give up" (125). Strasberg encourages "Actress O" not to romanticize what Irina is giving up but to make the cost of her sacrifice more legible to the audience. Strasberg shows a similar feminist awareness when "Actress

DD" brings in a scene from Stringberg's *The Stronger*, one between two characters who are actors in which one has lines and the other has none. First, Strasberg mocks Strindberg for including the silent female character, and then he suggests that the actor might bring a similar insouciance to her performance and fill in the scene herself by thinking, 'Well, the damn author doesn't give me the words. He made a stunt out of this, so I guess I won't, but I could if I wanted to,' so that you constantly feel the need and the desire and the willingness to speak" (183). And he counsels her to find ways to assert herself physically in the scene and to project that: "You're sure, strong. You know your power" (183). Working with "Actress U," he advises her not to worry about making her character likeable by the inclusion of endearing physical gestures: "We like these things. They show you're human. They call out our sympathy. I do not want you to put us in a position where we should sympathize with you. You do not need our sympathy" (217). Finally, in his work with an actor playing Lady Macbeth, Strasberg manifests a kind of androgynous sensibility. In workshopping the sleepwalking scene, he enters into her problem imaginatively by remarking, "I have thought about it. I think I know what work I would do emotionally and dramatically" (333). And then he uses this scene as an example of how an actor can solve problems of interpretation and staging that may be beyond the director's understanding. He explains that he could never figure out how to stage the scene until seeing a performance by a Lady Macbeth who put down her candle and sat on the floor. "From the actress we got not only expression but staging" (333).

Strasberg's conviction that performers had the right to contribute to the interpretation and development of scripts was never limited to male actors. And yet, one of the most significant differences between the scholarly conversations about male and female Method actors has been the way in which the actor-director relationship has been understood. Typically, male Method actors are viewed as having more power and freedom than other actors because they are involved in creative collaborations with their teachers and directors (i.e., the relationships between Kazan and Brando or Scorsese and De Niro). By contrast, female Method actors have often been portrayed as unusually disempowered parties in these same relationships. But in the Lady Macbeth example above, Strasberg insists on female actors' equal rights to contribute artistically from their point of view.

Perhaps Strasberg's particular commitment to working with female actors came from his admiration for Duse, whose portrait hung in the Actors Studio alongside Stanislavky's. He had seen Duse perform in her farewell tour of 1923 and often invoked memories of her work in sessions at the Actors Studio. He lauded her efforts to play against gender stereotypes, and to resist the pressure on female actors to show unrestrained emotion, and he appreciated her insight into dramatic characterology. Reminiscing about her performance in Ibsen's *The Lady from the Sea*, he told an Actors Studio session:

> One of the most memorable evenings in my theatergoing life was when Duse stood on the stage and smiled. She did literally nothing but smile.... When I walked home after that performance of *The Lady from the Sea*, I was a little bit let down. I had gone expecting to be bowled over, and I had watched her perform very simply and easily. But as I started to think of what she had done, I said, "My God—it's funny, I never quite understood that play, but when she smiled, for the first time I knew what this woman is about. She doesn't really want to leave when she asks her husband to let her go. She only wants the freedom to make her own decision. When the husband finally said, 'go, go,' at that moment the most beatific smile came over her face. It started in the face, but it actually took in the whole body. She doesn't want to go. She only wants the freedom to make the choice." I think I finally understand the play.[26]

Strasberg was particularly struck by Duse's eschewal of emotionality. When he recalls having seen Duse's performance in Ibsen's *Ghosts*, he again mentions her emotional calm and subtlety at the play's end when "She did not become hysterical. She saw something, and it had an effect on her, and that was all."[27] According to Strasberg, Duse's excellence lay in her understanding of "the way in which the actor must learn to lose the conventional, imitative parts" of the self (368). And he speaks about the distinction between physical beauty and the artistic beauty that arises from her "expressivity" (369). He admires Duse's theatrical intellect ("Duse could act whatever problem was set for her"), her ability to play what was "between the lines" (which, he says, Duse called "the third dimension" in acting), as well as her capacity to do much more than simply inhabit her role: "She played the significance, the meaning, and the reality of each play through herself" (370–371). Finally, for Strasberg, she achieves better than any other actor the fusion of the personal and the artistic that Method acting seeks—"she had the ability to be most herself and yet highly theatrical" (371). To summarize, for Strasberg a great actor—to him Duse was universalizable as a great actor—does not require physical beauty, restrains her emotion, interprets the play, and brings her whole life to the role but does not forget that she is acting.

Under Strasberg's influence, Duse became the Method's model of the actor, and Studio members aspired to be her heirs. Such an aspiration—to be analytical rather than emotional, expressive rather than beautiful—may have seemed the antithesis of Hollywood's blonde bombshells (Marilyn Monroe) and happy housewives (Debbie Reynolds)—in other words, the normative female images of the 1950s, but by 1954, the Method's artistic ideals had captivated even Monroe: she moved to New York, joined the Actors Studio, allied herself with one of its leading playwrights, and ended her career in a film role (*The Misfits*) that critically investigated the kind of Hollywood glamor she had previously represented. Film scholar Amanda Konkle, in a chapter on Monroe's relationship to the Method, challenges Rosemary Malague's reading of Monroe as Strasberg's passive victim, arguing instead that Monroe's time at the Actors Studio was productive and empowering, and that her experiences in Strasberg's workshop sessions helped her to bring depth and complexity to the kinds of roles in which she tended to be cast in Hollywood.[28]

This interpretation seems confirmed—albeit in a strangely roundabout way—by Arthur Miller's report on Monroe's work with Strasberg. Speaking of Monroe's preparations for *The Prince and the Showgirl* with the assistance of both Paula and Lee Strasberg, Miller opines that Monroe should have realized how superficial her role was and not tried to infuse it with Method complexity: "her want of training, as she saw it, in high comedy, ... pressed her to try to delve too deeply into a character that was essentially a series of lines crafted to address a situation, an outside with no inside" (422). However, when he saw the final version, Miller was impressed by how Monroe's performance lent "the film a depth of pathos it did not really have" (422), a comment that suggests that her acting preparations in fact may have contributed something valuable that was lacking in the script.

Another defining element of feminist wariness of the Method has been its association with Freud and psychoanalysis both through the Affective memory exercise and more broadly (as Enelow notes, "Both the techniques and the aesthetics of Method acting were linked to the look and feel of hysteria, neurosis, and psychic excess" (33).) Feminist scholarship in many disciplines has undertaken a critique of Freud, in some cases rejecting his work wholesale and in others repurposing it to feminist ends. In light of feminism's critique of Freud, the pedagogical structure of work at the Actors Studio—an actor processing personal traumas in the presence of Strasberg in studio scenes that replicated the logic of psychoanalysis—has often seemed suspect, paternalistic, and off-putting. But such skepticism should not distract attention from the occasions on which the Method's feminist practitioners showed that they were capable of a critically engaged Freudianism similar to the kind feminists forged in other disciplines.[29]

Nor should psychoanalysis be the only context in which we view the Method. As I mentioned in this book's Introduction, scholarship has often tended to overemphasize the Method's psychoanalytic concerns at the expense of its sociological ones: Method actors of the 1950s and 1960s spent as much time engaged in research geared at understanding social problems as they did gazing inward. In fact, both Kim Hunter and Julie Harris played social worker characters in the television and then film versions of *Requiem for a Heavyweight*, with Kim Hunter presenting a burned-out but heroic character improving the lives of people in her community, while Julie Harris turned the same figure into a more skeptical study of social work's bureaucracy and hypocrisy. The Method is often associated with narcissistic self-indulgence, but it was equally invested in tackling pressing social questions, even at the height of anti-Communist persecution and substantial film censorship from both the Production Code, the Catholic Legion of Decency, and other local and national bodies. Method practitioners often craftily and courageously worked around such censorship in order to present unsanitized treatments of such phenomena as post-traumatic stress disorder, disability, drug addiction, racism, and homophobia. Kazan is usually more associated with what we might call the Method's sociological wing than Strasberg is, but even Strasberg's approaches were more timely and politically engaged than they have been given credit for. For instance, the Method's supposed fetish for "authenticity" has long been pilloried, but it might be understood more contingently than is usually done. Rather than representing a kind of vacuous humanism, it could be connected to the values of existentialism that became ethically pressing in the 1940s, and that ultimately offered important intellectual resources to American leftist politics and civil rights struggles. In keeping with Sartre's and other existentialists' understanding of "authenticity," this was not necessarily the belief in an essentialist, transcendent self but rather, a performative notion of identity grounded in action and choices. Strasberg's understanding of characters and actors as making interpretive choices (such as the one he describes Duse making at the end of *The Lady from the Sea*) is compatible with existentialism's notion of authenticity, and was one that could be—and would be—activated for feminist ends by Method actors.

Women and the Question of Method Style

> James Dean was credited, if it could be called credit, with representing what was thought of as the Actors Studio style. It involved slouching, mumbling and wearing dirty, torn jeans. In truth, there was no such style. If a lot of Studio people wore T-shirts and jeans, it was usually out of economic necessity; they were, after all, struggling young actors. The notion of a Studio actor as a self-absorbed, inarticulate proletarian derived mainly, I think, from the much-publicized tough, sensitive loners that Brando and Dean played in films.
>
> —*Cheryl Crawford*[30]

Cheryl Crawford was not alone in refusing the premise that there is such thing as a Method style—most teachers and practitioners emphasize that it is a process or technique, not an end result. However, scholars have nonetheless tried to codify recurring stylistic features of Method performances. All of these efforts have taken male actors as their yardstick, but many of the qualities associated with male Method actors are not applicable, not prominent, or are actually reversed or otherwise transformed in performances by female Method actors. The very notion of a women's Method style has seldom come up.[31] Because of this oversight, codifications of Method acting style require re-examination. For instance, James Naremore cites "heightened emotionality" as typical of Method acting, while Forster Hirsch calls it "defiantly emotional," and both assume that displaying emotion is itself a kind of protest. This may well be true for male actors, but because emotionality is a traditional expectation for women, for female actors the more defiant choice was often its refusal. A flatter affect is the strategy that Kim Hunter pursues in *A Streetcar Named Desire* and that Patricia Neal employs in *A Face in the Crowd* and *Hud*. Rather than being "defiantly emotional," female Method actors often defied gendered expectations by refusing to conform to expectations of hysteria, tears, loss of control, or other manifestations of emotional excess. Instead, they were often defiantly unemotional.

Patricia Neal's work in *Hud* provides a useful example. To watch Neal as the housekeeper Alma calmly offering Paul Newman's Hud (Figure 1.2) a section of an orange is to witness her putting a well-practiced stopper on his escalating toxicity: she treats his bad behavior as no more than a blood sugar crash. As her performance unfolds, it becomes apparent that this scene sets the tone for her practical refusals to be drawn into his emotional games, and for her wary management of his advances. In this opening scene, Alma, stranded with a broken-down truck and two bags of groceries, flags down the anti-social Hud, who is cruising by in his convertible on his way back from a rendezvous with a married woman. He scarcely slows down to let her into the car, does not offer to help with the groceries, and starts speeding away even before she closes the door. This scene might easily have been played according to stereotypes on Neal's part. But instead of interpreting Alma's lines as needy, desperately unrequited, pathetic, or accepting of Hud's abuse, Neal uses her lines to develop Alma as a character who can not be ruffled. She starts teasing Hud about the gossip she has heard about his afternoon romp, and asks how women have enough time on their hands to have escapades with him. When he tries to threaten her with the words "our maid's gonna get canned because she talks too much," she responds with deflating laughter. As the film progresses, she plays Alma as a skeptical figure who sometimes performs attraction to Hud but just as often recognizes his behavior as harassment. It is a controlled, ambivalent performance that brilliantly explores the uncertainties and discomforts of Alma's simultaneous position as a member of the family

FIGURE 1.2 Patricia Neal and Paul Newman in Martin Ritt's *Hud* (1963).

and its employee. The key to this performance is Neal's purposeful resistance to "heightened emotionality," as she develops a feminist performance that subtly lingers at the borders of livelihood, desire, and abuse.

Tied to the assumption of emotionality is another common characterization of the Method, one that has to do with its physical style—what Colin Counsell calls its "disinhibition" or its "new 'ease' or naturalness."[32] This quality has generally been exaggerated in treatments of the Method, even for men. A naturalistic ease characterizes some Method performances (such as Brando's in *A Streetcar Named Desire*), but it does not account for the range of even male Method performances that purposefully dwell in unease (such as Montgomery Clift's in *Terminal Station* and *A Place in the Sun* or James Dean's in *Rebel Without a Cause*). More often, the Method explores the difficulty of attaining the "natural," and in doing so suggests that such "naturalness" is a performance given at considerable cost. There is much anxiety in Method embodiment, in other words, and much effort put forth to create the effect of ease (even preparation practices such as the "Mirror Exercise" suggest the great effort involved in making the most everyday tasks, such as combing one's hair, look "natural"). It is particularly problematic to suggest that women's Method performances are characterized by "disinhibition" or "ease," for female Method actors often expose the labor required to generate "feminine mystique." Harris, Hunter, Neal and others draw attention to femininity *as* performance, and a tiring one at that. For instance, Ellen Burstyn as the newly widowed Alice Hyatt in Martin Scorsese's *Alice Doesn't Live Here Anymore* (1974) wonders if she can perform the kind of attractiveness that will allow her to support herself and her young son, and fears that sexual allure is a requisite of female breadwinners. When Alice dons her "sexy" attire, Burstyn might easily have played a successful transformation from dowdy mom to diva, but she resists the performance of seamless glamor. Rather, she shows how difficult this transformation is for a shocked woman in financial crisis, emphasizing Alice's sweat, her discomfort at finding herself in an unfamiliar town, her strained resources, and her awkwardness in trying to perform the kind of femininity that men in the bars and nightclubs where she seeks work might consider "sexy." Her performance neither feeds a fantasy of transformation nor makes Alice a laughingstock in her efforts to look like a nightclub singer. Burstyn's strategies of identification and empathy-building are geared toward helping audiences identify with the dilemmas of its female protagonist whose situation demands that she grow beyond conventional roles but who continues to be held to conventional standards of female beauty. This is the bind that Burstyn's subtle performance captures so well (Figure 1.3).

Beyond reassessing the tendency to associate the Method with emotionality and ease, several other qualities often tied to the Method must also be reexamined to account for women's work in the tradition. In an interview, Kim Stanley directly rebuffed the stereotypical image of the Method actor in both inarticulacy and costume: "Wearing a leather jacket does not make you a Method actor, and

FIGURE 1.3 Ellen Burstyn in Martin Scorsese's *Alice Doesn't Live Here Anymore* (1974).

Method actors do NOT mumble."[33] Geraldine Page made a similar point about speech to the interviewer who visited her at the Actors Studio: "maybe now you'll believe that we teach the classics and speech here—and that we don't all scratch and mumble and belch"[34] (rebutting claims of mumbling seemed to be a particularly strong concern for Method women).

Histories of screen acting have often overlooked female Method performers. When James Naremore offered a few sentences on Method women in *Acting in the Cinema* (1988), he wrote that they did not emerge until the 1970s, completely overlooking the groundbreaking work of women in the tradition in the previous two decades. Nor did he suspect that the performance styles women developed in the Method differed from those of men due to the different parts they were assigned and the different pressures they faced. It is necessary to re-open academic discussions of the Method with an awareness of the ways in which these conversations, even when they have aimed to be explicitly feminist ones, may have unwittingly participated in effacing the work of female Method actors.

By the time the rediscovery of female artists became a priority in the 1970s, the Method was already out of fashion in academia, its canon of male angst seemingly closed to further contestation. The strongly pejorative academic characterization of the Method has been difficult to reconsider or complicate. For several decades now, feminist approaches to the Method have tended to characterize it as a reactionary style, one that reinforces conservative notions of gender and limits women to the roles of hysterics and housewives. But such dismissals are often at variance with accounts by Method actors like Shelley Winters, Jane Fonda, and Ellen Burstyn who identified feminist potential in the Method. Instead of beginning with the assumption that the Method and its approaches are uniquely hostile to women, it would make more sense to analyze women's Method film performances and historicize their accomplishments within the context of post-war Hollywood.

To do so is to find that they were often present at the scene when gender norms were stretched and broken. This is no accident: in the 1950s, 1960s, and 1970s Method practitioners were interested in investigating and challenging social roles, for both women and men. To date, however, attention has been paid only to how male Method actors mounted these challenges. In the 1990s, film scholars like Virginia Wright Wexman and Steve Cohan documented the ways in which male Method actors transformed existing templates of Hollywood masculinity to forge more tentative, neurotic, fluid, and feminine star images. While popular stereotypes of our own time equate the Method with machismo, these scholars suggested that Method "masculinity" was actually always less stable and dominant than we might imagine.[35]

It is now worth listening to the women who worked at the Actors Studio in its early days and who described it as a welcome refuge in a period of reactionary gender norms. While most of the cultural dictates of the 1950s counseled women to stay home and raise families, Patricia Neal recalled playing scenes at the Actors Studio while pregnant, and Shelley Winters noted how belonging to the Studio restored her artistic confidence and sense of vocation when she was a single parent.[36] Because of its professed aim of developing artistry without regard to the marketplace, the Actors Studio often served as a useful counterbalance for female actors who were judged in Hollywood by their age, weight, or looks. And because it was tuition-free and non-profit, it was a plausible starting place for actors from working-class backgrounds: membership in the Method community could supply a body of knowledge and cultural capital comparable to a college degree. Carroll Baker was effusive in her praise on this point: "The Actors Studio was free of charge! They required no qualifications whatsoever! It wasn't necessary to have acting credits, or experience, or looks, or even money! The only criterion was talent; the only admission was by audition" (76).

Ellen Burstyn (who currently serves as co-President of the Actors Studio) commented in a 2017 interview on what the Studio represented for her: she remarks that she had survived a number of difficult experiences—an illegal abortion in 1950, a sexual assault—and that it was not until she became a member of the Actors Studio that she became politicized and self-conscious about the meaning of these experiences and capable of addressing them in her art. "Thank God I got to Lee Strasberg. Because when I got to him, he approved of me for me, and I never had that. You know, without wanting sex from me." She continues: "It was just a revolution in my psyche. … What he [Strasberg] really asked for was for people to be honest about who they were" and that it was "the beginning of my real life." She explains how she brought these revelations to her performance in *Alice Doesn't Live Here Anymore*. She recalled how she used one of her actual experiences—being denied the right to buy car insurance in her own name because she was married, even though her husband was abusive, and how she used memories of such experiences to build her character using the Method's emphasis on personal connection to the role. Burstyn explains how "Out of that came *Alice*

Doesn't Live Here Anymore. The realization of a woman as a human being, not an appendage of a man. You know, that line I put in, 'It's my life, it's not some man's life I'm helping him out with.' That's what I learned in this period."[37] Sally Field recalls similar experiences when she was in her early twenties and had just had her first child:

> For sure, my restless generation was pushing me to rethink everything I had always accepted as "the way things are." Betty Friedan's book *The Feminine Mystique* had begun to trickle into my awareness. And I eventually heard the challenge from Germaine Greer in *The Female Eunuch*, inviting women to own their bodies, to examine that mysterious part of themselves by holding a mirror between their legs, to taste their menstrual blood and, most important, to be outraged…
>
> …Much of the change in me had to do with my constant participation at the Actors Studio and the secure place it gave me to experiment with myself. No longer an observer, I had been accepted as a member after doing a scene…from *A Taste of Honey* by Shelagh Delaney. Unfortunately, Mr. Strasberg had returned to New York for the winter and wasn't sitting in his familiar front-row chair for my audition. Instead I performed for a group of longstanding alumni, which included Bruce Dern—who was frequently the moderator in Lee's absence and for whose focus and support of me I will always be grateful. Ultimately, I was given a lifetime membership.[38]

Revisiting assumptions about the gender politics of the Method by listening to the narratives of women who found their time there artistically generative as well as feminist can help to create a new context for the reception of their performances. Working with other Method actors, and with directors like Kazan, Zinnemann, and Martin Ritt, often gave female performers greater control over their work than was typical in Hollywood. The Actors Studio should be understood not as a lab of Freudian repression geared at training women to believe they were hysterics, but as an interesting and accomplished corner of post-war bohemia that opened up new possibilities for women. Male Method actors have been associated with the bohemian rejection of mainstream values—Steven Cohan writes of Brando, Clift, and Dean that "With its key note of social disengagement, the new star's rebel persona paralleled the nonconformist beat movements in Greenwich Village and San Francisco, making a deliberate contrast to the era's hegemonic masculinity."[39] Female Method actors, however, have never been given the credit of their own rebellions. They too were nonconformists, seeking disengagement from normative social expectations, and from the late 1940s onward, they found at the Actors Studio a receptive environment for artistic growth, community, and experimentation.

Notes

1 Bill Davidson, "Geraldine Page: Diamond Who Likes it Rough." (*Saturday Evening Post* November 17, 1962), 30–31.
2 Pauline Kael, "Marlon Brando: An American Hero," *I Lost it at the Movies*, p. 190.
3 The first quotation in the sentence is from Kael, "Marlon Brando: An American Hero" (190); the second is from Kael, "The Glamour of Delinquency" (46). Bruce McConachie unearths an interesting contradiction in the male Method actor's presence. For him, the male Method actor is a paradoxical figure who simultaneously embodies resistance to Cold War conformism and complicity with those same norms, in so far as his presence and freedom to rebel supposedly index a kind of belief or investment in the liberal humanist subject, and that the Method male became the icon of "the free world" as American popular culture's takeover of global entertainment began. The Method man may have felt constrained by American society, but he also represented that society's freedom to rebel (*American Theater in the Culture of the Cold War: Producing and Contesting Containment, 1947–1962*).
4 The rebel Method actor was not the only newly prominent star type to signify larger social trends on the 1950s screen. Steve Cohan has codified the dominant male stars of the era as follows: "the man in the grey flannel suit" (symbol of conformism), the criminal psychopath, descended from the tough guys and noir heroes of the Forties, the "beefcake" (making the 1950s "the age of the chest"), the western and epic heroes like John Wayne and Charlton Heston. In male Method actors, Cohan locates a generational challenge to predecessors like Grant and Gable—the new Method stars—"boys who are not men"—dared to be more neurotic than any male stars before them.
5 Eric Rohmer: "Ajax ou le Cid?," *Cahiers du Cinéma* 59 (May 1956), in *Cahiers du Cinema The 1950s: Neo-Realism, Hollywood, New Wave*, Jim Hillier, ed. Translated by Liz Heron (Cambridge, MA: Harvard University Press, 1985), 112, 114, 111–115.
6 Nathan D. Allison, "Method Acting, Autonomy, and the Curious 'as if' of the Postwar Subject in Nicholas Ray's *Rebel Without a Cause*," *Arizona Quarterly: A Journal of American Literature, Culture, and Theory*, 73.2 (2017), 103–124.
7 Ibid., 105.
8 Marianne Conroy, "Acting Out: Method Acting, the National Culture, and the Middlebrow Disposition in Cold War America." *Criticism* 35.2 (1993).
9 Richard Maltby, *Hollywood Cinema* (Oxford: Wiley-Blackwell, 2003), 98.
10 Kazan (1909–2003) was born in Istanbul to Greek parents. An alumni of Williams College and the Yale School of Drama, he was strongly influenced by Harold Clurman and Lee Strasberg as a member of the Group Theatre and, in addition to co-founding the Actors Studio in 1947, would have an acclaimed career in both theatre and film directing, with his best-known film works including *A Streetcar Named Desire* (1951), *On the Waterfront* (1954), and *East of Eden* (1955). The Austrian-born Zinnemann (1907–1997) directed some 50 films across his career, including *High Noon* (1952), *From Here to Eternity* (1953), *A Man For All Seasons* (1966), and *Julia* (1976). Zinnemann came to the United States in 1929, and his training as a filmmaker had included an apprenticeship with documentary pioneer Robert Flaherty (director of *Man of Aran*). Zinnemann's parents were murdered in the Holocaust, and his works maintained a commitment to promoting awareness about human rights and the legacies of war. Zinnemann worked with a number of prominent Method actors, including Brando, Clift, Harris, Eva Marie Saint, and Anthony Franciosa. Of his practice of working

with actors, Zinnemann remarked that "whether the part is large or small, I spend much time discussing it with each of the actors separately, and in depth—the way their character develops and their relationships with other people in the film" (*Fred Zinnemann: An Autobiography*, Bloomsbury), 223.

11 Kael contrasted their approaches in 1955, finding Zinnemann to be the more nuanced, and contrasting the triumphalist ending of *On the Waterfront* unfavorably with Zinnemann's *From Here to Eternity*, remarking that Zinnemann's "did not reduce issues to black and white" nor "convert its hero into a socially acceptable leader" and still managed to be "was a huge popular success" ("The Glamour of Delinquency," *I Lost it At the Movies*, 49).

12 *From Here to Eternity* won Academy Awards in 1954 for Best Picture, Best Director, Best Screenplay, Best Supporting Actor and Actress, Best Cinematography, Best Film Editing, and Best Sound.

13 In his autobiography, Zinnemann recalled the difficulties he had in persuading the President of Columbia Pictures, Harry Cohn, that Clift was right for the role of Prewitt, a talented boxer who refuses to fight matches for the army. Zinnemann reports that he came close to resigning as the film's director over the matter of Clift's casting, though he eventually won the day (*Fred Zinnemann: An Autobiography* (London: Bloomsbury, 1992), 121)).

14 In a 2016 *Atlantic Monthly* article ("Hollywood Has Ruined Method Acting") Angelica Jade Bastién diagnoses a problem with Method acting's status in contemporary Hollywood. She began by distinguishing between two ways of understanding the Method. First there is the technical definition: "the Method" refers to a set of actor preparation techniques descended from the teachings of Konstantin Stanislavksy as interpreted by Lee Strasberg and others at the Actors Studio, an approach to acting that, according to Bastién, has "fuelled many of cinema's greatest performances and can be a useful way of approaching difficult roles." In the second definition, which she deems a looser—but still powerful—assemblage of pop cultural ideas and industry practices, "the Method" has come to stand in for a pernicious culture of machismo and marketing that has little to do with the acting approach itself. In this toxic formulation, which Bastién dates to Robert De Niro's Oscar win for Martin Scorsese's *Raging Bull* (1980), the performances of male Method actors—she cites Daniel Day-Lewis, Philip Seymour Hoffman, Christian Bale, and Leonardo DiCaprio as examples—command undue acclaim for their assertion of "destructive ideas of masculinity." According to Bastién, these toxic performances of gender are then licensed and authenticated by appeals to the artistic authority of the Method. Bastién cites Jared Leto's performance as the Joker in David Ayer's *Suicide Squad*, and the behaviors attributed to Leto during the making of the film, as typical of the kind of conduct for which "the Method" serves as an alibi. Allegedly, as part of his "Method" preparations for his role, Leto surprised his colleagues with a used condom, live rat, and dead pig, gestures that were not only tolerated but even promoted by the film's marketing team as signs of Leto's Method performance's "legitimacy, verisimilitude, and importance." Bastién faults this re-branding of harassment as "Method acting" not only for its inherent violence, but also for unduly influencing conceptions of what "good acting" looks like and thereby limiting the kinds of performances that receive acclaim. Bastién suggests that disproportionate attention goes to Method performances involving masculine aggression, extremes of experience, or intense immersion in "masculine" feats of endurance—DiCaprio's wilderness survivalism in *The Revenant* (2015), for instance, or Shia LaBeouf's pulling of his own tooth in preparation for his performance in *Fury* (2014).

15 McDonald, Kathlene. *Feminism, the Left, and Postwar Literary Culture* (Jackson: University of Mississippi, 2012), 5,7, 108.
16 De Beauvoir, Simone. *The Second Sex*. Trans. Constance Borde and Sheila Malovany-Chevallier. (New York: Vintage, 2009), 356, 835.
17 Ibid., 765.
18 Ibid., 834.
19 Uta Hagen, *Respect for Acting* (New York: Macmillan, 1973), 221.
20 Friedan, Betty. *The Feminine Mystique*. Introduction by Gail Collins. New York: Norton, 2013 [1963], 15.
21 Ibid., 43.
22 Sue-Ellen Case, *Feminism and Theatre* (New York: Routledge, 1988), 124.
23 Rosemary Malague, *An Actress Prepares: Women and "the Method"* (New York: Routledge, 2012), 30–71.
24 In the Affective memory exercise, actors are asked to evoke and dwell with a memory from their own past in front of the group. Strasberg describes the exercise as follows: "Affective memory is not mere memory. It is memory that involves the actor personally, so that deeply rooted emotional experiences begin to respond. His instrument awakens and he becomes capable of the kind of living onstage which is essentially reliving. The original emotional experience can be happy or frightening or fearsome" (109). He also notes that "The important thing in using affective memory is to maintain one's concentration, not on the emotion, but on the sensory objects or elements that form part of the memory of the original experience.…You try to remember through your senses what your mouth tasted and what you wore and the feeling of that garment against your body. The emotion you try not to remember at all" (110). Finally, he explains that "after the actor has discovered an affective memory that is really serviceable, he still faces the problem of bringing it into the scene he is playing. He must fuse his personal emotion with the character and event he is portraying" (111).
25 Jacob Gallagher-Ross, *Theatres of the Everyday*, 93.
26 Lee Strasberg, *Strasberg at the Actors Studio: Tape-recorded Sessions*. Robert H. Hethmon, ed. (New York: Theatre Communications Group, 1993), 191.
27 Ibid., 371.
28 Amanda Konkle, *Some Kind of Mirror: Creating Marilyn Monroe*. (New Brunswick: Rutgers University Press, 2019). See Chapter 5: "The Actress and Her Method: Resisting Playing 'Marilyn Monroe.'"
29 When Kim Stanley appeared on Broadway as a patient of Freud's in Henry Denker's *A Far Country* in 1961, she describes how, to prepare, she "read Freud's 'Studies in Hysteria,'…and also Freud's letters—I had read his biography some time ago—and I talked to several doctors about the clinical nature of the patient" (Stanley qtd. in "First Into the Depths:" *A Far Country, Newsweek*, 17 April 1961, 69). Stanley also based her interpretation of Freud's patient on other research: she studied Viennese prints because they showed "the physical constriction of women of the time" (Stanley qtd. in "Kim Stanley Plays with a Full Deck," *Los Angeles Times*, 10 January, 1982, Paul Rosenfield, 22). Of her performance in the Freudian drama, for which she was nominated for a Tony, Stanley commented in the *Newsweek* article cited above: "I put the pieces of the character together like a mosaic. The rest of it? Let's just say that's my secret," a remark that suggests that her approach was not entirely intellectually dependent on Freud's perspectives (69). (For another example of how female Method actors engaged with Freud, see Chapter 4 in which I explore Jane Fonda's performances as both a therapy patient and a psychoanalyst in *Klute* and *Agnes of God*).

30 Cheryl Crawford, *One Naked Individual: My Fifty Years in the Theatre* (Bobbs Merrill, 1977), 222.
31 Steve Vineberg's work is an exception. In *Method Actors: Three Generations of an American Acting Style*: there, he divides female Method actors into two groups—the "neurosis kids" and "Method sanity."
32 Colin Counsell, *Signs of Performance: An Introduction to Twentieth-Century Theatre* (London: Routledge, 1996), 54.
33 Stanley quoted in Jon Krampner, *Female Brando: The Legend of Kim Stanley* (New York: Back Stage Books, 2006), 59.
34 Page quoted in Bill Davidson. "Geraldine Page: Diamond Who Likes it Rough," *Saturday Evening Post*, October 27, 1962, 30.
35 See Virginia Wright Wexman's description of Brando in *On the Waterfront* as "a figure of ambiguous gender possibilities" (171) in *Creating the Couple: Love, Marriage, and Hollywood Performance* (Princeton: Princeton University Press, 1993), 160–179. See also Cohan's *Masked Men*, particularly Chapter 6: "Why Boys are Not Men" (201–263), for a thoughtful challenge to the idea of Method claims to "authenticity" and machismo in performances by Dean, Clift, and Brando. Steven Cohan. *Masked Men: Masculinity and the Movies in the Fifties* (Bloomington: Indiana University Press, 1997).
36 Patricia Neal, *As I Am* (New York: Simon and Schuster, 1988), 173; Shelley Winters, *Shelley II: The Middle of My Century* (New York: Simon and Schuster, 1989), 17.
37 "Ellen Burstyn's Lessons on Survival," *Sex, Death, and Money*, October 4, 2017. Interview with Anna Sale.
38 Sally Field, *In Pieces* (New York: Grand Central Publishing, 2018), 229–230.
39 Cohan, *Masked Men*, 202.

2
KIM HUNTER'S FEMINIST METHOD

The most iconic moment of *A Streetcar Named Desire*—so familiar that the tone in which it is cited is almost always parody—is Marlon Brando as Stanley Kowalski's late-night wail for his wife's forgiveness and care: "Stellaaaaaaaaaa!" The single most famous utterance in the Method canon, in other words, is the name of a female protagonist. It is astonishing how attention to this utterance has been so exclusively dedicated to the affect of its utterer, rather than to his referent, his wife who has taken refuge upstairs from his violence just moments before. Kim Hunter's performance as Stella Kowalski has long been overshadowed, and her achievement in what we might call "Feminist Method" has never been adequately apprehended.[1] Drawing on Hunter's own script notes and comments, I show how director Elia Kazan's approach to the Method, especially his emphasis on the value of ensemble work, enabled Hunter to develop her performance in a way that made possible a feminist interpretation of the role of Stella. Thanks to the modes of working established by Kazan, as well as the flexibility of Tennessee Williams as a screenwriter, Kazan's cast was able to respond welcomingly to Hunter's innovations and to produce a film that featured one of the most serious and nuanced studies of intimate partner violence yet to be presented on the Hollywood screen.

In what follows, I argue that *A Streetcar Named Desire* (Warner Bros., 1951) was a landmark feminist production, both in what its actors were able to express, and in the story of its promotion by a team of committed, powerful women. At every stage in *Streetcar*'s journey it was women who responded to its themes and worked to ensure that it reached the public. Tennessee Williams's agent Audrey Wood wooed Irene Selznick to produce the play on Broadway; Molly Thacher Kazan persuaded her husband to take on the task of directing it; Irene Selznick urged the casting of Hunter as Stella Kowalski; and Hunter herself brought to the part of Stella its materiality, three-dimensionality, and feminist critique.[2] With her performance, Hunter influenced first the play's and then the film's presentation of marriage, in particular the toll exacted by the post-war emphasis on the nuclear family. Hunter drew out feminist elements that Kazan had missed in Williams's play and contextualized them in the light of contemporary social developments, especially the pressures surrounding veterans' wives.

A Streetcar Named Desire had been one of the biggest Broadway hits of the 1940s. The New York production ran for two years beginning on December 3, 1947, and the original cast was preserved nearly intact in the move to the screen.[3] This continuity was also preserved in the film's writing and direction, with Tennessee Williams taking the role of screenwriter and Kazan at the helm of both the stage and film productions.[4] This history meant that the *Streetcar* film performances had benefited from long workshopping and development, including substantive changes to the characters and their relationships over time. Such development was Kazan's common practice and a keynote of his style. For *Streetcar*, this long collaboration among performers, director, and playwright accommodated growing revelations about each of the characters and their relationships to one another. The performance most transformed through this process was Kim Hunter's. In the role of Stella, Hunter was assigned a part with many fluencies, ambiguities, and mysteries, but when Broadway rehearsals began, Kazan presented her with his own reading of Stella—a trite, flat stereotype of a passive housewife. Hunter suffered the setbacks inherent in such limiting advice, including mixed reviews of her performance when the play opened on Broadway, but she persisted in her work on the character, bringing new values to the role until she had shaped it into a compelling milestone of mid-century feminist realism on screen. This chapter is primarily a study of Hunter's performance in the 1951 film, but it also draws on the longer story of her development of the part on Broadway, making use of theatre archives that show how much changed from Kazan's initial notes on Stella to Hunter's eventual interpretation of the character on film. Hunter's feminist performance worked vigilantly to challenge and overturn Kazan's sexist reading of Stella point by point. Hunter and Kazan's agonistic collaboration suggests an alternative model to the account usually given of the disempowering relationship between the Method director and female actor.

Kazan's original view of the character of Stella was not the nuanced portrait of a woman contending with abuse that Hunter would create. Instead, Kazan's initial reading blamed Stella for failing to hold her family together. Kazan advised Hunter to present Stella as a character who takes the path of least resistance, and who walks around "as if in a daze." His director's notes insist: "Give her all kinds of narcotized business."[5] This interpretation suggested a character who was both lazy and hypnotized by sexual addiction to Stanley. For Kazan, seeing Stella as "narcotized" was a way of reconciling her "refined" class background with her current domestic disarray.[6] But Kazan's director's notes also reveal that he tended to focalize his remarks on Stella through Stanley, as though he could only think of her from Stanley's point of view. Some of his characterizations even contradict each other (for instance, Stella "can't really cook" but all she does in a day is make Stanley's dinner):

> Stanley thinks Stella is very badly brought up. She can't do any of the ordinary things—he had a girl before her who could really cook, but she drank an awful lot. ...Stanley has made her a woman. ... She walks around as if in a daze. She's waiting for the dark where Stanley makes her feel only him, and she has no reminder of what she has given up. She does not want the other world to intrude. She's in a sensual stupor. She shuts out all challenge all day long. She loafs, does her hair, her nails, fixes a dress, doesn't eat much, only prepares Stanley's dinner and waits for Stanley. She searches for no other meaning from life. Her pregnancy just makes it more so. She is buried alive in her flesh. She doesn't seem to see much. She laughs incessantly like a child tickled and stops abruptly as the stimuli, the tickling, stops, and returns to the condition of pleasantly drugged child. Give her all kinds of narcotized business. ... She has sold herself for a temporary solution. She's given up all hope, everything, just to live for Stanley's pleasures. So she is dependent on Stanley's least whim. ... Stella is plain out of her head about Stanley. She has to keep herself from constantly touching him. She can hardly keep her hands off him. She is setting little traps all the time to conquer his pretended indifference (he talks differently at night, in bed). She embarrasses him (though he is secretly proud) by following him places. They have a game where he tries to shake her all the time and she pursues him, etc. He makes her a panther in bed. He fulfilled her more than she knew possible, and she has to stop herself from crawling after him. She's utterly blind as to what's wrong with Stanley, and she doesn't care, until Blanche arrives.[7]

Kazan's approach to Stella overlooks certain elements of the text, its historical context, and Stella's given circumstances. It was this overlooked matter that interested Hunter as she wrested the part from Kazan's vision and developed her own version of the role.

Before Hunter pursued her own interpretation, however, she first tried it Kazan's way. Hunter's handwritten notes in her original acting script reveal that in rehearsals and then early in the play's long Broadway run she was trying to carry out Kazan's interpretation of the character. Her playscript notes emphasize her efforts to communicate sexual satisfaction and a "drugged" state. When Stella wakes up the morning after Stanley's poker party outburst and their late-night stairwell reunion, for instance, Hunter's script notes read: "Leisurely start—a new day," "Dippy—lazy—drunk with happiness," and "Shuffle around." She notes her movements in the scene as follows: "Stretches out on chair—bedroom—feet on stool—finish putting polish on nail—wave it to dry (whole hand) other hand on tummy." Her stage action of nail-painting comes from Kazan's notes, and the gesture of putting her hand on her stomach immediately after reminds viewers of her pregnancy and associates it with femininity and sexual fulfillment rather than anxiety and domestic entrapment. Hunter's Kazan-inflected script notes continue as though in defensive response to Blanche's criticisms of Stella's state: "Drunk with happiness. Leave me alone—I'm happy."[8]

But Kazan's circumscribed view of Stella rendered her character perplexing to reviewers. Presenting Stella as lazy, passive, and happy undermined the play's presentation of the cyclical patterns of intimate partner violence. *A Streetcar Named Desire* contains more feminist insight than its first Broadway production revealed. In 1947, intimate partner violence had not been codified—it was not until the 1970s that the concept of the "battered wife," followed by the codification of domestic violence, would enter public awareness through the work of feminist activism. Thirty years earlier, however, Williams's play provided a textbook presentation of its dynamics. *Streetcar* shows an abuser controlling through money ("Stanley doesn't give me a regular allowance, he likes to pay bills himself, but—this morning he gave me ten dollars to smooth things over." (78)); escalating violence in times of pregnancy, childbirth, and new parenthood (Stanley's rape of Blanche on the night when Stella is at the hospital giving birth); justifying control by appeals to male privilege ("Remember what Huey Long said—'Every Man is a King!' And I am the King around here, so don't forget it" (131)). Stanley also isolates Stella (for instance, by destroying Blanche's chance of marrying Mitch and sending Blanche away); he minimizes, denies, and blames ("it's going to be all right after she goes and after you've had the baby" (133)); and his behavior falls into typical abusive cycles of escalating tension that culminate in acts of violence, followed by reconciliations and periods of calm (for instance, he smashes a radio and beats Stella behind a door and then calls her downstairs and cries in her arms).[9]

However, largely because of the first Broadway production's characterization of Stella as enjoying her abuse, early reviewers did not heed the urgency of the play's critique of the Kowalskis's marriage. Howard Barnes of the *New York Herald Tribune* wrote that Stella "has welcomed marriage to a tough factory worker of Polish descent and does not care if he beats the daylights out of her."[10] Similarly, Irwin Shaw noticed the conflicts in Stella's character, but for him they did not add up to a persuasive whole: "The idea of the character is interesting—the upper-class girl who for the overbearing pleasures of the flesh has willfully and delightedly allowed herself to become the slattern her husband can desire and understand. But in its development the character is skimped; neither the slattern nor the belle is convincing."[11] What is missing in these reviews, and what Hunter introduced to the part in its transition to film, were not only the complex, ambiguous, and discordant notes that could be located in her character, but also a plausible and contemporary explanation for the performance of submission, conformity, and happiness that Stella seemed to be carrying out so diligently, especially as it pertained to her status as the wife of a war veteran. Crucial to Hunter's revised interpretation was her suggestion that Stella's contented behavior *was* a performance. Between Broadway and Hollywood, Hunter would take possession of the role, remodeling it to elaborate a feminist analysis and bringing out the play's critical consciousness about post-war gender roles, marriage, and the nuclear family.

In the 1951 film, Hunter simultaneously amplifies two different interpretations of the role which are grounded in Williams's play but were undeveloped on Broadway: the post-war veteran's wife and the bohemian. Both of these interpretations help to account for Stella's behavior in more contemporary, empathetic, and materially grounded ways. Ultimately, Hunter's performance in the film reveals a feminist actor working within the tradition of the Method to insist upon a multifaceted, sophisticated, and politically engaged realism.

The Post-War Veteran's Wife

Just as Brando's career was launched by a series of troubled veteran roles, Hunter carved out a niche playing wartime women.[12] Her breakout role came in a supporting part in the 1943 RKO film *Tender Comrade*, a morale-boosting tale of women who work in a factory and room together while their husbands are at war.[13] She followed this with a portrayal of a Women's Army Corps (WAC) member in Powell and Pressburger's *A Matter of Life and Death* (1946).[14] And while scholarship on *Streetcar* has recognized the importance of Stanley's veteran status, no less important is Stella's status as a veteran's wife.[15] The end of war was certainly difficult for soldiers, but it was also a challenge for many women on the home front, especially those who had headed their households or enjoyed careers and possibilities for advancement in them during the war. Films of the 1940s like *Tender Comrade* (1943), *The Best Years of Our Lives* (1946), and *The Men* (1950) gave careful attention to women's roles during wartime, as well as their transitions from war to peace.

Tennessee Williams had an ongoing interest in the problem of soldiers' reintegration and the effects of war experience on relationships and behavior in civilian life. To study *Streetcar* in its immediate historical context is to realize that Williams's play closely responds to the national obsession with "reintegration" and documents its sometimes great cost to wives and families. "Reintegration literature" was a body of advice produced by sociologists and other military and academic researchers (and disseminated more broadly via journalism and popular culture). It described common problems surrounding the return of veterans and gave instructions for how to address them. These works used the keyword "adjust" as a euphemism for this often tumultuous transition, a term that would become so ubiquitous that Williams would mock it in his later comedy *Period of Adjustment* (whenever the veterans and their wives in that play encounter marital difficulties, they reassure each other with the words, "You're just in a Period of Adjustment").[16]

In *Streetcar*'s more serious register, Williams treats the issue of reintegration comprehensively, allowing it to shape the beliefs and behaviors of the characters. One of the more disturbing and coercive aspects of this advice was its normalization of intimate partner violence as a symptom of "combat fatigue" (the name then in use for PTSD), a normalization that encouraged victims of violence to stay with their partners and discouraged witnesses from intervening. In *Streetcar*, Mitch participates in this process when he brushes off Blanche's distress at having seen Stanley beating Stella behind a door: "Ho-ho! There's nothing to be scared of. They're crazy about each other" (68). Though Mitch's anxious chortles might betray some anxiety of his own, his excuses for Stanley's violence seek to normalize it. Similarly, Stanley's keen sense of entitlement to have his needs met evokes reintegration discourse's strong privileging of men's needs over those of women and children. Stella's circumstances, meanwhile, replicate those of many women who struggled to be primary—and sometimes, sole—caregivers to husbands who needed professional therapeutic help, even while suddenly renouncing the independence they may have gained during the war.

Post-war sociologists were concerned with the arrangement of the family and with documenting the social habits of veterans, both of which are addressed in Williams's play.[17] In fact, the dynamics of reintegration in *Streetcar* closely resemble the case studies from Robert V. Havighurst's *The American Veteran Back Home* (1951), an influential sociological text on soldiers' reintegration. Havighurst's book paints a picture of bowling alleys, movie theatres, and nightclubs emerging as hangouts for returning soldiers who were restless, bored, and sometimes unemployed, and whose nocturnal habits indicated not merely a post-war party spirit but also the sleep disruption, irritability, morose moods, and anti-sociality that were symptoms of "combat fatigue." Havighurst's subjects consistently reported a sense of letdown, of a limited future, and a feeling that after long anticipation of the joys of returning home, they had outgrown their former lives. This feeling was often exacerbated by the fact that they were returning to less than a hero's welcome in terms of jobs, housing, and opportunities for social mobility. All of these strains are present in Williams's play and are given even greater emphasis in Kazan's film. The film, for instance, relocates Stanley's first appearance to inside a bowling alley, where Stella points him out to Blanche as the one roughhousing more violently than anyone else. The play's setting in the French Quarter of New Orleans invites us to see the family home as an extension of a nightclub, and in the film, a neon saxophone advertising a jazz club is attached to the outside window of Stella and Stanley's bedroom, suggesting that they live upstairs from a club. The discontents of reintegration can also be felt in the crowding of the Kowalski's apartment (they have no spare room to offer to Blanche), in Stanley's fight with Mitch on the floor of the plant where they work, and in Blanche's history with the soldiers of Laurel.

If an elaborate propaganda campaign had lain behind the mobilization of women into factories and fields during the war, so too did the push for reintegration give rise to an equally elaborate campaign geared at reversing the trajectory of women once the jobs they held were considered again the rightful property of men. The result could be a strong sense of dissonance as women were sent from the public, corporate, and industrial roles they had inhabited to the more traditional ones that were now demanded by the return of soldiers. Ultimately, reintegration research was driven by fears of what might become of the men recently returned from service. Experts worried that if veterans could not be treated for their physical and psychological wounds, placed in well-paying occupations, and tended to by wives in homes of their own, they would grow restive. A range of legislation was aimed at directing veterans toward constructive paths and creating opportunities for them. But given the immense scale of the task, those advising on post-war social problems suggested that such official channels were not enough: psychologists and military doctors also sought to recruit an unpaid workforce by casting wives and girlfriends in therapeutic roles. Women were counseled to recognize the extent of men's sacrifices and to understand that their husbands had a claim on their caregiving energies. They were advised to cede the autonomy they had gained during the war and return home to supply the stability their husbands required. This they should do, experts advised, even if their husbands had not yet managed to return to work. As described in the reintegration literature, their therapeutic role entailed a range of challenging duties, such as allowing their husbands' service friends to come before family obligations (Stella allows Stanley's poker night with his war buddies to take precedence over Blanche's visit), and learning to tolerate mood swings and even violent outbursts (Stella returns to Stanley moments after he has beaten her). There were also contradictions in what was demanded of women: they were to baby their husbands but not allow them to become babies, and to seem submissive and feminine in ways that would encourage the return of their husbands' masculinity, all while assuming the duty of maintaining the household and meeting all of their own physical and emotional needs while their husbands were recuperating.

This official advice spread to women's magazines, which took up the business of supplying wives with stories, resources, guidance and moral support. One such article appeared in *Ladies Home Journal* in February of 1945, and the many relays between this article and *A Streetcar Named Desire* not only illuminate the dynamics of Williams's play but also suggest it as a likely source.

"Meet Ed Savickas: A Victim of Combat Fatigue" was a profile by J.C. Furnas of a Polish-American veteran and his wife Stella.[18] Many details of the piece recur in Williams's play. Like Stanley Kowalski, Ed Savickas was a veteran of the Sicilian Campaign from the Engineer's corps. "Right now, Ed needs pampering and loving," his wife Stella remarks. *The Ladies' Home Journal* copyeditor adds: "But Stella must see that her husband becomes master and not baby of the household" (143). It was a month after the article's appearance, on March 23, 1945, that Williams wrote to Audrey Wood with his idea for a new play, one featuring a veteran's wife named Stella.[19] The Furnas article included a number of incidents and images that would turn up in Williams's play, including a nocturnal, watermelon-eating, card-game playing husband, a portrait of the stresses of cohabiting with extended family and the pressures introduced by a new baby, and a description of the street where the post-war couple lives as "rattle-trap" (Blanche uses the word when she describes "that rattle-trap street-car that bangs through the Quarter" (81)).

The article tackled one of the most challenging problems facing ex-combatants and their families: mental health. "After many weeks under fire, Ed was temporarily paralyzed from combat fatigue," the article reports, "He is still moody and restless, hates crowds and noise, suffers from insomnia and nervous indigestion." The article includes an image of Ed at the dinner table in a crowded kitchen, with a caption that reads:

> 'The boys overseas prey on Ed's mind,' says his wife, Stella, 'Some nights he can't eat a mouthful. I try to keep cheerful and never mention the war. Then some stupid friend has to ask him how many Germans he killed!' The Savickas' tried living with Stella's mother (left) when Ed was discharged a year ago, but he was too edgy. He got strange yens for food like watermelon in midwinter. Nights he'd prowl, sleepless, about, waking the others up.

The article toggles between Stella's situation and the official recommendations, making her a case study of their ideal execution. It ends by suggesting that a wife like Stella is the cure every soldier needs: "The best thing any employer could do for a returned case of combat fatigue, of course, would be to supply each with a wife like Stella…a companion intelligently dedicated to his needs and wishes."[20] And as though to show one wife's willingness to accept this charge, Stella instructs the magazine's readers, "You've got to go a lot farther than halfway with him." She uses the second-person pronoun in a way that makes it sound as though she's quoting from a handbook when she advises: "Time enough after he's adjusted to worry about how you like things done yourself. Right now everything is all his."[21]

Williams explores the dynamic in Furnas's article between a PTSD-suffering veteran and his caretaker spouse, but emphasizes the strains and sacrifices that are downplayed or repressed by the *Ladies Home Journal* portrait. In fact, *Streetcar* might be read as a critique of the article and especially of the ways in which it fosters the conditions for abuse. What Williams suggests as he imagines a dystopian version of Stella and Ed in the characters of Stella and Stanley is that the demand for such self-abnegating behavior on a wife's part was not necessarily a prescription for recovery from PTSD, but it was certainly one for male tyranny. These pressures imposed on post-war women can be useful in illuminating what might otherwise seem Stella Kowalski's undue preoccupation with observing norms. In the context of reintegration discourse, Stella's tendency not to share potentially upsetting information with Stanley, and her tolerance of her husband's violence, take on a new and culturally mandated cast. Williams's play considers and critiques the ideological regime surrounding post-war marriage specifically. Building on contemporary fears of disruptive men and the demand for submissive and accommodating wives, it is possible that Stella, rather than being a naturally submissive or passive person, is actually struggling quite actively to make herself adopt a pose of submission. For instance, Williams hints that Stella does not seem like the same person she used to be, and that she is artificially shaping her actions in an effort to perform the role demanded of her. Soon after their reunion, Blanche remarks to her sister, "I'd forgotten how quiet you were" (13). Later, Blanche tells Mitch that she is visiting because "Stella hasn't been so well lately, and I came down to help her for a while. She's very run down" (60). Although this was not the original reason for her visit, as a rationale it may contain a truth of its own, and it is a line that draws attention to the question of Stella's well-being. When Stella says to Blanche about Stanley, "of course there were things to adjust myself to later on" (18), Blanche guesses, "Such as his civilian background!" but Williams's stage direction instructs that "Stella laughs uncertainly" at this comment—perhaps because it is actually Stanley's wartime background that Stella having difficulty adjusting to. It is significant that here the word "adjust" migrates from the veteran's process to that of his wife, emphasizing her difficult period of adjustment to him.

One of the most challenging aspects of this adjustment was that women already bore the brunt of domestic labor in serving as the primary caregivers for children and ill and elderly relatives. Stella is attempting to care for Stanley while she is both pregnant and caring for Blanche. Also worn out from caregiving, Blanche tells her sister: "I, I, I took the blows in my face and my body!...You just came home in time for the funerals Stella. And funerals are pretty compared to deaths" (21). Blanche's monologue about how she cracked under the strain of the deaths at Belle Reve, and her accusation that Stella was not there to help, underlie her expectation that Stella will care for her as she faces her own mental health crisis. Blanche's words emphasize the high stakes and chronic strains of this usually invisible women's labor. And yet, despite these clues in the script and the way in which they were picked up by both Hunter and Leigh in their performances, *Streetcar* has never been adequately addressed as a drama about caregiving. Demanding that women prioritize the needs of veteran husbands placed them in very difficult dilemmas. How could they protect themselves along with their children and extended families from violence? Should they neglect their other responsibilities? The official advice to try to live apart from parents to re-establish male independence only exacerbated these difficult choices. Williams's play suggests how isolating this new emphasis on the nuclear family could be, and makes it clear that a wife who is not allowed to speak up for herself also cannot speak up for more vulnerable members of her family. The self-abnegating conduct advised for wives inflicted a great burden on women while nonetheless making their efforts invisible to their husbands. As Susan Hartmann points out, the expectation that wives adopt a therapeutic role did not bring with it any of the protections of a professional environment, such as time limits, payment, colleagues, or a safe physical space.[22] To be on the job constantly was a recipe for burnout. Williams's play is compatible with a feminist analysis of the role of women in the post-war family and Hunter's performance seizes upon this potential: the most important shift between Broadway and Hollywood is that Hunter's performance moves *Streetcar* in the direction of feminist realism, and Kazan follows her lead. To examine her acting choices is to realize how her interpretation of the role pulls *Streetcar* towards the outcome of Stella leaving Stanley, making Williams and Kazan's decision to end the film in this way in response to censorship pressures seem a motivated and intuitive choice.

Hunter's Performance: Acting Like a Feminist

Comparing Hunter's film performance to Kazan's original instructions reveals the pains she took to address and challenge almost every point in his sketch of Stella. What seems to have offended her most was Kazan's dismissal of Stella's agency and effort. In response, Hunter makes Stella the character who works harder than anyone else: she rarely appears in the film without a kitchen or laundry task in hand. We can begin to see Hunter's interpretation of the part maturing and diverging from Kazan's even in her Broadway script notes. In key moments, Hunter's notes suggest that Stella is making a conscious effort to stage an illusion of domestic contentment that she does not feel. When trying to appear non-threatening to Stanley, she notes: "Light and gay—giggly—get tickled at slightest thing 'Girls will be girls'"—the quotation marks revealing that she knows this to be a performance, and one that she must make to allow for Blanche's continued residency in their apartment.[23] At Blanche's birthday party, when household tensions have escalated significantly, Hunter's notes once more indicate Stella's attempt to perform a festive mood she does not feel: "See the party through—despite opposition." She writes in the margin of the scene, "Perfectly normal."[24] It is this awareness of Stella's strained performance that Hunter returns to and amplifies in the film. Using a variety of facial and bodily gestures, Hunter finds in Stella a character very different from the alternating "slattern" and "belle" that perplexed Broadway reviewers. Instead, she presents a caring but increasingly exhausted woman constantly trying to ameliorate her husband's behavior by strategies of the kind recommended to veteran's wives.

One of the most important changes Hunter brings to the role is her decision to play a range of responses which sketch a persuasive psychological portrait of abuse. In her efforts to survive and protect those around her, Stella modulates between attempts to placate her husband, attempts to resist him, and attempts to work around him. She also shifts between scenes in which she performs affection for Stanley and capitulates to his demands, and scenes in which she reveals disgust, anger, hurt and fear. In light of this interpretation, Stella's catering to Stanley, her efforts to accommodate his poker and bowling nights, his outbursts of violence and his cruelty look less like the consequence of pure desire, and more like a concerted campaign to protect herself and her sister. Hunter's performance carefully documents Stella's efforts to apply the recommended techniques—and also the limits of these techniques in ensuring her safety or her husband's recovery. The various and sometimes conflicting strategies that Hunter shows Stella adopting include hiding her tears, biting her tongue, speaking her mind, laughing at her situation, physically protecting Blanche, physically consoling Stanley, taking time-outs, confronting Stanley directly with words and with physical violence, listening to her husband's lectures, not listening to her husband's lectures, patching up everything Stanley breaks, ripping his shirt as she tries to stop him from going out to bowl, having sex with her husband, refusing to have sex with her husband, and vigilantly monitoring Blanche and Stanley's movements with a view to de-escalating conflicts between them. In Hunter's interpretation, Stella is fighting to survive her situation, grappling with the normalization of abuse mandated by "reintegration," her economic dependency on her husband, and the pressure of her pregnancy. This portrait is simultaneously much more sympathetic, psychologically and sociologically realistic, and feminist than the characterization of Stella first advised by Kazan for the Broadway production.

Near the beginning of the film, Hunter provides the first clue that Stella's emotions are not synonymous with her actions. She gives Stella a time delay between her first, unguarded reaction to a comment, which passes across her face, and the next, her prepared and disciplined response. In her first scene with Blanche, Stella's gut response to an insensitive remark about her weight flickers across her face for a moment—irritation—and then we see her compose a second face, one that smooths things over. With this moment Hunter teaches audiences to recognize that Stella is acting, and she makes the audience privy to the effort that goes into this attempt to maintain the peace—a style we might call "eggshells acting." When it is later revealed that Stella is pregnant, we realize that in choosing not to show her anger to Blanche in that early scene, Stella did more than not rise to the bait of a comment about her weight: she also chose not to reveal her pregnancy to her sister. Hunter picks up on ambiguities in Williams's script to suggest Stella's complex emotions surrounding her pregnancy. Throughout the film Hunter plants clues that Stella is ambivalent about becoming a mother, and that she would like to hide her pregnancy not only from Blanche but also from Stanley and even from herself.[25] In the scene in which she goes into labor, she escalates Williams's stage direction for this moment and actually has Stella walk to a door and hide her head behind it, removing herself from the view of Stanley and the audience (Figure 2.1).[26]

Stella's only line acknowledging that she has gone into labor is "Take me to the hospital," and this Hunter has Stella whisper into Stanley's ear. And even as she moves closer to her delivery date, her physical exertions do not abate: she continues with all of her household responsibilities and even becomes more physically engaged with resisting Stanley. After she gives birth, it is not until the last scene of the film, when Stella is leaving Stanley, that we see her holding the baby: until then it is the Kowalskis's upstairs neighbor Eunice who takes on this job. With such choices, Hunter makes it seem as if Stella is ignoring impending motherhood and

FIGURE 2.1 Stella hides behind a door as she goes into labor.

that it is an unwelcome further burden.[27] Her affect in this regard contrasts sharply with Stanley's, who on several occasions expresses his pride and excitement about having a child. Hunter's decision to suggest Stella's reluctance about her pregnancy contributes to the sense that she does not feel secure in her marriage or in her ability to care for a child in her current circumstances.

Instead of being related to her pregnancy, in Hunter's performance all of Stella's maternal gestures are directed at other adults—Blanche, Stanley, and even Mitch.[28] Through her mothering gestures toward them, Hunter insists that Stella is more than the "pleasantly drugged child" of Kazan's view. Hunter performs Stella's maternal approach to Blanche through a range of physically protective physical gestures which over the course of the film make it clear that Stella usually takes Blanche's side and is thus far from solely concerned with Stanley's well-being or her own sexual pleasure. When Blanche is being bullied by Stanley, Stella often stands behind her and places her hand over Blanche's shoulder, as though she is backing her up and putting the strength of two bodies against him. Hunter's performance, increasingly supported by Kazan's directorial decisions in the move from stage to screen, emphasizes various ways in which Stella cares for Blanche. For instance, in the first scene set in the Kowalskis's apartment, the opening shot is of Stella's arm sweeping a rag around the bath she is running for Blanche. Stella holds Blanche's hand as they walk through the streets, embraces her, and cradles her when she is agitated. She takes a similarly protective role toward Blanche's possessions, defending and wrestling them away from Stanley. Through these gestures, Hunter presents a Stella deeply concerned with caring for her sister. In addition to this protective behavior, the other pattern in Hunter's performance of Stella's treatment of Blanche is what we might call gestures of twinning. In these moments she performs in physical synchronization with Blanche in a way that suggests that they are mutual victims of Stanley. For instance, at Blanche's birthday

FIGURE 2.2 Stella and Blanche cower before Stanley's rage.

FIGURE 2.3 Stella holds her arm, marking the place where Stanley grabbed her.

party, we see Stella cowering in an identical posture to her sister, revealing that they both live in fear of Stanley's rages (Figure 2.2).

Hunter's performance also demonstrates a refusal to ignore or eroticize Stanley's abuse. Hunter finds numerous ways in which to draw attention to Stanley's violent treatment of Stella, using strategic gestures to mark it for the audience. As though directly challenging the Broadway reviewer who claimed that Stella "does not care if he beats the daylights out of her," Hunter's performance insists that Stanley's abuse is painful and real. When Stanley rummages through Blanche's trunk, Stella holds her arm (Figure 2.3) where Stanley has just grabbed her as though to draw attention to the place of an injury. The gesture insists that this moment should not just be passed over. Then, while still rubbing this spot, she makes a fist and raises it up to him, indicating Stella's anger and will to fight back (Figure 2.4).

62 Kim Hunter's Feminist Method

FIGURE 2.4 Stella raises a fist to Stanley.

FIGURE 2.5 Stella's alarm at the sound of Stanley returning.

When Stella wakes up the morning after her late-night reconciliation with Stanley, Hunter lifts her arm to reveal a bruise to the audience. Even though her lines suggest that Stella would like Blanche to forget what happened ("he was as good as a lamb when I came back and he's really very, very ashamed of himself"), the film's audience is not allowed to forget the bruise Stanley gave her the night before. Hunter again draws attention to the toll of Stanley's violence and her fear of his explosions in a scene that follows the monologue in which Blanche compares Stanley to an ape. Here Stella responds in anxiety and alarm to the sound of Stanley at the door as she realizes that he may have heard Blanche's words (Figure 2.5).

Even as Stella comforts Blanche, and before she flies to Stanley's side to embrace him, she looks up in alarm and fear, waiting for his reaction to Blanche's words. As the sisters embrace, Kazan films the back of Blanche's head and shows Stella's face

FIGURE 2.6 The pregnant Stella fights Stanley to save the radio.

FIGURE 2.7 Stella is dragged across the room as Stanley lurches toward the window.

in order to prioritize her anxiety and distress. This moment makes clear that she placates Stanley more out of fear than love.

There are also several moments in which Hunter depicts Stella fighting back physically against Stanley's violence. The most significant of these comes during the poker night scene in which Stanley beats her in front of his friends, precipitating her flight upstairs. The episode begins when Stanley becomes enraged by a German song on the radio.[29] He hurls the radio out the window, and Stella, while pregnant, jumps on Stanley's back (Figure 2.6) and is dragged across the room by him (Figure 2.7).

Williams's play gives no stage directions to Stella for this moment.[30] Here Hunter's physical action brings a visceral force to Stella's resistance. Similarly, right after this scene Stella goes back into the living room and pulls back a chair that one of Stanley's poker friends is sitting on, sending him flying to the floor and setting the light fixture careening (here, the stage direction is simply, "She rushes through to the poker table" 62).

These gestures of Hunter's are stronger and more dynamic than anything called for in the play's stage directions. In her characterization, Hunter insists that Stella is no passive victim but even goes so far as physically to confront her husband and his friends while she is pregnant. In her effort to save the radio in the moments before Stanley starts beating her, Hunter shows audiences what a PTSD outburst might look like from a wife's point of view, something that the article about Stella and Ed Savickas had not dared to broach. Later, when Stanley prepares to go bowling after giving Blanche a one-way bus ticket home at her birthday dinner, Hunter's Stella grabs and shakes him hard, using both of her hands. She rips his shirt as she confronts him: "You're not going bowling…Why did you do this? I want to know why! Tell me why!" This action is followed immediately by him shoving Stella violently toward the mantelpiece and then her going into labor. Hunter's performance escalates Stella's defiance of Stanley, and unlike the Broadway production, the film suggests that Stella's labor is induced by Stanley's violence.

Through an array of recurring gestures, Hunter builds up a portrait of Stella's frustration and exhaustion as well as her range of strategies for getting through the day. She very often wears a blank expression or looks down, absenting herself while Stanley lectures her (as in the scene in which he is talking about the Napoleonic Code). She fiddles with objects while he rants, as though she is just trying to wait it out. In response to one of Stanley's lectures, Hunter adds a gesture to Williams's line for Stella, "My head is swimming": she touches her hand to her head as though to suggest a headache, a gesture she repeats several times throughout her performance, most notably after Stanley tells her that he has informed Mitch of Blanche's sexual past. During Stanley's dinner tantrum, meanwhile, she bites her nails at the table.

Given these decisions in Hunter's interpretation, it is not surprising that in the film Stella turns more firmly and permanently against her husband than the Broadway production had suggested. In fact, Hunter prepares viewers for the film's new ending (one adopted to satisfy the demands of the Production Code)—Stella's statement that she is leaving Stanley for good, followed by her exit up the stairs to Eunice's apartment. One way Hunter communicates this rupture is by performing with her back turned to Stanley (Figure 2.8), as though to ostracize him and foreshadow the film's new ending for their relationship.

Hunter begins to assume this posture only after Stanley starts telling her what he has learned about Blanche's past—that is to say, Stella does not turn definitively against Stanley until she becomes aware of his ruthless campaign against her sister. After turning her back to Stanley at the window for a few moments, Stella walks across the room to the door to get away from him (Figure 2.9). He follows and she keeps her back turned as he continues to lecture her. When she walks away from the door, again trying to get away from him, she turns away so as not to have to make eye contact. With these tableaus, Stella progresses from staring

FIGURE 2.8 Stella turns her back on Stanley at the window as she learns of his plans to destroy Blanche's relationship with Mitch.

FIGURE 2.9 Stella walks to the door and turns her back on Stanley again as he continues to talk about his discoveries about Blanche.

out the window to staring out the door, and, in the final and most revealing of these scenes, she and Stanley stand near the staircase while Hunter casts her gaze upward to Eunice's apartment, the place to which she will eventually flee for refuge. Stella's repeated turning of her back on Stanley suggests her escalating will to escape, from gazing out the window, to facing out the door, to leaving the apartment and looking up to her only known sanctuary (Figure 2.10). As she grips the stair's railing, Stanley attempts to ingratiate himself, but her silent sobs and anxious glance convey her loneliness, anxiety, and despair. She doesn't share any of her feelings with him and he cannot see her tears. Even as Stanley touches Stella as though he is trying to appease her, he continues to tell her of his plans to expose and terrorize Blanche, and Kazan's camerawork makes use of dramatic irony to allow Stella's face to communicate to the audience the truth of her emotional state

FIGURE 2.10 At the stairs to Eunice's apartment, Stella gazes upstairs.

that Stanley does not see. At the end of this scene, she follows Stanley back into the house where he seems to improve his behavior for a moment—he picks up something from the floor—but only moments later he is smashing items again.

As Hunter's gestures and modes of interaction with Blanche, Stanley, and even the set suggest, in all of her choices Hunter insists upon a sociological view of Stella's situation as a wife subject to physical and emotional abuse. Her performance is a concerted refusal of the premise of Kazan's interpretation that Stella is under Stanley's sexual spell, and her attempt to wrest Stella away from this interpretation gives the film feminist significance.

"What Other Can I Be?"

The *Streetcar* film opens with a subtle but important difference from the play: it diverts attention from the relationship of Stanley and Stella to the lives of the women of the French Quarter. In the play, Stanley bellows "Hey there! Stella, Baby!"[31] as he hurls a package of meat towards her. The film, on the other hand, begins with women gossiping in the yard of the apartment, and includes this remark from Eunice: "When he got home, she was waiting for him. But he never heard nothing about that!" Though it is never revealed who Eunice is talking about in this scene, her comment suggests that women's wartime lives were considerably more complicated than propagandistic myths of fidelity insisted, and that the women who seemed to have been patiently waiting on the home front may not have been living in suspended animation.

Hunter's second, simultaneous interpretation of the role of Stella, both bohemian and homosocial, is less the opposite of the conforming post-war wife than one of its possible consequences. When Blanche accuses Stella of being too placid about Stanley's violence, Stella asks her, "What other can I be?" On the surface, this response shows Stella's pragmatism that offsets Blanche's poetic personality.

But as I argued in the first half of this chapter, it can also be interpreted as her sense that she must conform to official, widespread, and coercive advice. What if we read her question differently—as though she is asking sincerely: who else might I be? What else is there? What other way could I live? Perhaps her question (after all, it is a question) may not be a fatalistic statement of acceptance, but rather, a quest for alternatives of the kind that would also be asked by a range of post-war social movements, including feminism. The critical history on Stella has sometimes been too quick to assign her a normative role. In Williams's play, Stella is an open-ended character, and one full of interpretive possibilities—Stella Adler's notes on the play call her "rather indefinite" (249). Ambiguity permeates Stella's language: almost all of her statements are interrogative, qualified, conditional, vague, or phrased in the negative (to mention just a few: "I was—sort of—thrilled by it," "What other can I be?" "I wasn't blinded by all the brass," "It isn't on his forehead and it isn't genius," "I'm not sure it would have made any difference where I saw him"). This heavily qualified, uncertain language renders Stella *Streetcar*'s most mysterious character.

In her film performance, Hunter uses this language as an opening to challenge Kazan's reading of Stella as the passive, conformist, hopelessly straight wife and sister. When we go back to the play, we see Williams hinting that there are chapters of Stella's past we do not know about. Blanche's line "I haven't asked you the things you probably thought I was going to ask" draws attention to an aporia in the plot.[32] In *Streetcar*, we learn quite a lot about both Blanche and Stanley's pasts, but almost nothing about Stella's. This blank spot raises important questions, including: what exactly drove Stella to leave home at the age of 15, and what was she doing from that time until she met and married Stanley? Many women of Stella's generation found meaningful employment and gained financial independence during the war. One of these was Stella Savickas, the heroine of the *Ladies Home Journal* article: Furnas mentions that she worked as a factory inspector at her husband's plant during the war and saved $375. Looking at the historical picture of wartime suggests that Stella Kowalski too might have been engaged in war or factory work.[33] "The best I could do was to make my own living," Stella tells Blanche in response to the accusation that she abandoned her sister and the rest of her family at Belle Reve. Whatever path she has taken since leaving Belle Reve, Hunter's performance suggests that there is little of the Southern belle left in Stella. She walks around the house in her underwear. She pickpockets Stanley to fund her dinner out with Blanche. She does not wear makeup. She tosses a cigarette butt out her window carelessly from bed, and does the same with the core of an apple. Furthermore, she defines herself by her decision to live in a city and in a neighborhood that are not governed (she claims) by the same Southern divisions of race, class, and gender under which she was raised. "New Orleans isn't like other cities" she tells Blanche when her sister's sensibilities rankle at their surroundings. What Blanche perceives as downward mobility, Stella understands as a concerted refusal of middle-class standards of femininity and respectability.

In this attitude, she resembles another post-war figure—the Beat who resisted the conformity of suburbia to move into city neighborhoods such as Greenwich Village in New York or the French Quarter of New Orleans. Rather than failing to live up to genteel standards, Stella consciously refuses them. She embraces her neighborhood's diversity and anti-puritanism, joining Stanley in bowling, going to the movies, and staying up late, and she resents it when he tries to put her in her place in front of his friends. Williams's film script even adds a line for Stella which she delivers with a certain amount of pride to Blanche: "Some of your sister's friends have stayed in the city" (seemingly a reference to either Eunice or Steve having spent time in jail). And in her combination of domestic frustration and rejection of conventions of middle-class feminine behavior, we might even begin to see Stella as a nascent second-wave feminist. In her specific rebellions against the expectations of what constituted a "normal" life for a woman of her class, she bears similarities to the women whose lives Friedan considers in *The Feminine Mystique*.[34]

Hunter also challenges Kazan's idea that Stella is sexually or emotionally satisfied by her husband by going back to Williams's play in search of moments that allow her to complicate and resist his reading. In the scene in which Stella and Blanche discuss Stella's marriage, Hunter embraces a framed photo of Stanley as a kind of *memento mori*: even though Stanley survived the war, she plays the scene mournfully as though he had died. This staging recalls the *Ladies Home Journal* article in which Stella Savickas's young daughter reaches for the portrait of her fallen uncle; so too does it resemble a curious scene at the end of *Tender Comrade*, the Dalton Trumbo/Edward Dymtryck film that Hunter had appeared in alongside Ginger Rogers in 1943, in which Rogers plays an entire scene opposite a similar framed portrait of her husband who died in the war. In her handling of the scene with Stanley's photograph in the *Streetcar* film, Hunter conflates the two destinies—that of the war widow and that of the war bride—and re-purposes the photograph as a prop with which to mourn her still-living husband. But what, exactly, is she mourning (Figure 2.11)?

The sexual problems of returning veterans were often addressed in post-war reintegration films like *The Men* and *The Best Years of Our Lives*, and Williams provides a number of signals that the Kowalskis's marriage may have run into such difficulties. In the scene of Stella and Blanche's departure for dinner at Galatoire's, Stanley is ornery when Stella tells him: "I put you a cold plate on ice." The cold plate may be a metaphor for Stella's emotional temperature towards Stanley, or perhaps for the current state of their sex life—Hunter's playscript notes show her decision to have Stella lean on an ice box off and on throughout her Broadway performance. In the film, when Stanley returns from the station with Blanche's trunk, Hunter plays the scene without touching or kissing him in greeting upon his return. In fact, it is only when Stella starts describing the cold plate and asking Stanley for money that she touches him. To study the movements of Hunter and Brando in this scene is to realize that it is characterized most by her gestures of

FIGURE 2.11 Mourning for Stanley.

refusal. When Stanley rummages through Blanche's possessions, Stella blocks him item by item. This scene foreshadows Stanley's rape of Blanche, but it also signals Stella's own refusals.

Further clues suggest that Stella has lost her sexual relationship with or desire for Stanley. For instance, it is only to Blanche, and only defensively, that Stella makes claims about Stanley's sexual appeal. She never remarks on it to Stanley or to anyone else. In fact, she gets angry when he tries to call on her publicly as his submissive wife by slapping her in front of his friends. "That's not fun, Stanley" she tells him. When Blanche is lecturing Stella about Stanley's ape-like behavior, Stella is putting a pillow in a pillowcase, but she suddenly tosses the pillow away, a gesture that may indicate that Blanche is getting through to her. In fact, despite Stella's characteristically vague comments to Blanche about her nights with Stanley ("there are things that happen between a man and a woman in the dark— that sort of make everything else seem—unimportant"), it is actually Stanley who tries to persuade Stella that their sex life is good—or was once good. He blames Stella's pregnancy and Blanche's presence as the reasons for their fading fireworks, but he concedes that they have faded:

> Stell, it's gonna be all right after she goes and after you've had the baby. It's gonna be all right again between you and me the way that it was. You remember that way that it was? Them nights we had together? God, honey, it's gonna be sweet when we can make noise in the night the way that we used to and get the colored lights going with nobody's sister behind the curtains to hear us!

Even one of *Streetcar*'s most iconic scenes—Stella's late-night descent down the stairs to be reunited with Stanley moments after he has beaten her—demands a reexamination that pays closer attention to Hunter's performance.

Although the staircase scene is usually read as one of mutual erotic catharsis, the notion that Stella desires Stanley irresistibly is largely created by Alex North's sensual soundtrack. But focusing on just Hunter's performance, it becomes apparent that this scene is as much a demonstration of Stella's hurt and her internal fight to refuse Stanley's summons as it is an erotic return to him. Hunter shows Stella passing through a range of painful emotions before she reunites with Stanley at the bottom of the stairs. In keeping with her performance throughout the film, Hunter plays this scene as a series of conflicting moods and impulses. Even in the moments before she leaves Eunice's apartment, she alternates between two ways of playing the scene. The first is "narcotized tranquility" (the mood Kazan had assigned her on Broadway) and the second shows her breaking out of this trance and attempting to resist Stanley's calls. The first shot of the sequence is of Stella sitting on the bed in Eunice's apartment, with Blanche cradling her from behind (a reversal of the posture she often adopts with Blanche). Here, for a moment, she looks transfixed by the sound of Stanley's call. She rises and walks a few steps, but when she encounters Eunice halfway across the room, her affect changes. She suddenly looks down as though she is ashamed of herself and grabs her nightgown in her hand as though she is repentant. The camera now moves from Stella to Stanley downstairs, and when we return to the scene of Eunice's apartment, Stella has taken a seat again—a signal that she has decided against going downstairs. But then she rises again, walks toward the door, and exits. When she appears on the balcony, all traces of her faraway look have disappeared, replaced by a very different look—one that shows her palpable anger, hurt, and mistrust. She drops her arm from the railing in what could be read as either a combative or a defeated gesture. She looks down on her husband judgmentally, and her look communicates more weariness of this cycle than arousal by it. The camera moves to a point-of-view shot from Stanley's perspective below, and from this angle, Stella looks like a beaten-down boxer. Hunter wears almost no makeup, and Kazan's shot emphasizes her jaw, which Hunter clenches tightly, as though her mistrust makes it difficult to commence the downward walk. When she does, she takes slow, halting steps: Stella does not run down to her repentant husband. And, as though to emphasize her wavering emotions, Hunter changes sides of the staircase, for a while clinging closely to the wall on her left, and then switching over to grab the railing on her right. Stanley does not come up the stairs to meet her, a fact that recalls Stella Savickas's comment about her veteran husband ("you've got to go a lot farther than halfway with him"). In her descent, Hunter communicates that Stella has to experience and then override deeply painful feelings of anger and shame in order to return to Stanley: she is not simply drawn to him in an unthinking trance.

If Stella may be reaching the end of her ability to ignore Stanley's cruelty, or if Stanley is not able to satisfy her as he once did, then who or what does she desire? Is this simply the case of the honeymoon's end and the coming of a baby, the cramping presence of an in-law, the symptoms of combat fatigue, or might Stanley have a rival? It is here that Hunter's interpretation of Stella diverges most sharply from Kazan's. Alison Lefkovitz's "The Peculiar Anomaly: Same-Sex Infidelity in Post-war Divorce Courts" studies the cases of married women whose wartime experiences had included relationships with women. She reports that courts typically gave generous divorce settlements to husbands whose wives had formed sexual relationships with women during the war, but did not grant the same generosity to women whose husbands had had sexual relationships with men. Women were less likely to be granted full divorces in these cases, and women's adultery was punished in the court as adultery, whereas men's was treated more lightly by the law as "deviance."[35] This meant that men could more easily participate in a "marriage closet" than women. This double standard was part of the strategy to "contain" returning men, on the homophobic belief that as many men as possible should be kept in heterosexual marriages. One of the most interesting aspects of Hunter's performance is that she raises the possibility that Eunice, Stella's upstairs neighbor and landlord, is a rival to Stanley.

At the end of *Streetcar*, Eunice brings Stella a plate of grapes. Between Stanley's carnivorous, Neanderthal offering at the play's opening and Eunice's vegetarian, decadent one, we see embodied a rivalry for the affection of Stella. Though of course grapes are a Dionysian symbol predictive of the tragedy about to befall Blanche, they are also, in their symmetry with the meat at the opening of the play, readable as symbols of Stella's tornness between Stanley and Eunice (a plate of grapes also appears on the table during the scene in which Stella mourns over the photo of Stanley, suggesting Eunice's presence there too). Taking up the clues provided about Stella's relationship with Eunice, Stella appears not so much as a woman hopelessly drawn to an abusive, normative masculinity, but rather as a more complex, possibly bisexual character. This interpretation is emphasized more strongly in the film than the play, perhaps in response to Hunter's developing sense of Stella's resistance. From Eunice's first appearance in the film, she is coded butch, sitting outside drinking a beer, her legs sprawled, both flirting with and acting protectively towards the newly arrived Blanche. Eunice tells Blanche: "she's [Stella] got the downstairs here and I got the up," excluding both her husband and Stanley in her account of their living situation. Her words may indicate that Eunice and Stella have spent the war here together, or simply that Eunice disregards husbands in her description of living arrangements. There is violence at Eunice and Steve's apartment, but there it is Eunice who hits Steve. Threatening to call the vice squad on him for cheating on her, Eunice takes matters into her own hands: in the play we hear the "clatter of aluminum striking a wall" and then Steve appears with a bruise on his forehead. Instead of calling the police, Eunice decides to go for a drink.[36] Perhaps it is not surprising that Stella is drawn to Eunice, who is more than capable of standing up to her husband.

At the beginning of the play it is established that Eunice has not shopped or cooked dinner. She tells Stella, "Tell Steve to get him a poor boy's sandwich 'cause nothing's left here,'" and her friends laugh at this dereliction of household duty.

The screenplay exaggerates Eunice's neglect: she says that she cooked a dinner, but ate all of it herself, so there is nothing left for Steve. Eunice's disdain for her husband stands in contrast to her chivalrous treatment of Blanche, to whom she is solicitous, asking, "What's the matter, honey? Are you lost?" She lets Blanche into the downstairs apartment, offers to get Stella from the bowling alley, and even stays to chat until Blanche dismisses her. Though her husband too is a veteran, Eunice flouts the rules of reintegration. She expresses her scorn for his behavior, and her size and strength allow her to match his violence with violence of her own.

In addition to providing a contrasting case study to Stella—a wife who scorns the official reintegration advice and rules her household—Eunice also provides an example of the kind of woman who was valued during the war but disavowed immediately after. Celebratory images of butchness were widespread in propagandistic efforts to get women to work in factories and other conventionally male jobs. J. Howard Miller's famous "We Can Do It!" features a woman dressed for factory work and showing off her muscles in a manner usually associated with male prowess. Norman Rockwell's *Saturday Evening Post* cover of 1943 goes even further in valorizing female strength in the portrait of a factory woman on her lunch break, eating a ham sandwich, crushing a copy of *Mein Kampf*, wearing a "V for Victory" button, and showing off her bulging arm muscles.[37] Post-war, such a contrast between powerful women and wounded returning men helps to explain why a gender traditionalist like Stanley Kowalski may be in crisis about his masculinity and may be performing increasingly exaggerated and pernicious versions of it. This quick transformation in the proper spheres, roles, and rights of women and men may also help to explain the tension in *Streetcar* between Eunice and Stanley as they fight over Stella and seem to offer her a stark choice between different kinds of futures.

In examining Stella and Eunice's relationship, it worth considering how the discourse of reintegration, designed to ensure normativity, actually created the conditions for homosocial bonds. Other clues point to a potentially queer reading of Stella: her unknown wartime experience, her enthusiasm for Stanley's butch lifestyle, the obliqueness of her speech, and the fact that she ran away from home at 15. In light of all of this, we may ask: is Stella really a figure of unremitting heterosexual obedience? Such "obedience" is challenged a final time in the closing scenes of the *Streetcar* film, as Hunter seems to be constructing the grounds for a new life for Stella. Williams's play had directed Stella to hold on to Eunice's arm during the emotional crisis of Blanche's departure, and in the film Hunter elaborates this stage direction to actually hold Eunice's hand, and, perhaps of greater significance, they hold hands behind Stella's back so that Stanley cannot see (Figure 12.2), and when Blanche is being led away, Stella runs for comfort to Eunice's embrace, not Stanley's (Figure 2.13).

Further, in the scene in which Eunice and Stella help to prepare Blanche for her departure, one of Eunice's lines is modified from the play so that she calls Stella "Baby," the same nickname Stanley uses for her. The same speech is

FIGURE 2.12 Stella holds Eunice's hand behind her husband's back.

FIGURE 2.13 Stella takes comfort in Eunice's embrace.

altered so that she tells Stella "we've got to keep on going" rather than "you've got to keep on going." Further, one of Eunice's lines is revised so that rather than calling Blanche's jacket "blue" as she does in the play, Eunice calls it "lavender" in the film (a color associated both with "lavender marriages"—i.e. heterosexual marriages designed to protect queer people—and "The Lavender Scare"—the campaign to purge queer employees from government service in the 1950s, a form of discrimination that associated homosexuality with Communism and potential security threats.

In the final scenes of the film, Stella and Eunice have displaced Stella and Stanley as the primary couple. Stanley stays on the sidelines and Eunice enters the Kowalski living room as Stella's emotional resource. And at the film's end, once Blanche has exited, rather than returning once more to her cycle with Stanley, Stella tells him decisively "Don't you touch me. Don't you ever touch me again."

Hunter performs the scene standing head to head with Stanley, looking him squarely in the eye, with Eunice backing her up at the side of the frame. Stanley storms off. Then, with tears in her eyes, Stella picks up her baby and turns to look into their apartment where Stanley, off-screen, has started to bellow "Stella! C'mon Stella!" She turns her back on the empty hallway from which she hears his voice, and delivers another newly-written line: "I'm not going back in there again. Not this time. I'm never going back—never." Stanley yells once more—this time in the same tone he had used to call her down the stairs—"Hey Stella! Hey Stella!" but she does not heed him. Instead, she runs decisively up the middle of the staircase to Eunice's apartment with the baby in her arms. Though much attention has been given to the difficult compromises Kazan and Williams were forced to make with film censors, this ending shows how resourcefully they adapted by replacing Stella's original destiny—getting lured back in to the cycle of violence—with a feminist one: escape.

The play's ending had called for Stella to return to Stanley after Blanche's departure. They sit on the staircase together with the baby and Stanley fondles her blouse buttons. Stella has returned once more to the cycle of violence with Stanley, and he is the baby's rival for attention rather than a parent and husband. This ending was frowned upon by the Catholic Legion of Decency because it did not seem to punish Stanley adequately for his rape of Blanche. And certainly, film censorship by the Production Code and the Catholic Legion of Decency was a key factor leading to the film's changed ending. But rather than seeing the new ending as a violation of Williams's artistic integrity, we might see it as possessing an integrity of its own, one that emerges both from Hunter's interpretation of Stella.[38] Williams and Kazan still refused anything that would be recognizable to Hollywood as a happy ending (i.e. Stanley's reformation). Rather than replacing the play's dystopian ending with a happy one, Williams, Kazan, and the cast of *Streetcar* instead replace it with a feminist one—Stella's self-assertion and escape (Figure 12.14). This is not a perfunctory capitulation to censorship but a carefully crafted new ending that owes much to Hunter's presence, insights, and artistry.

The final shot of *Streetcar* is of Eunice at the midpoint of the staircase looking upwards to where Stella has just exited (Figure 12.15). Is Eunice waiting to confront Stanley, or to protect Stella from him if he follows after her? One clue might be found in the meaning of Eunice's name, which is Greek for "Good Victory." An ironic consequence of the victory won by Stanley and his compatriots at Salerno was the rise of the kind of woman who could fight to protect his wife from him back at home. After the shot of Eunice on the stairs, and just before the credits appear, Kazan ends with a still shot of the empty set, one in which the lights are on upstairs at Eunice's, but all is in darkness below.

Reviewers of the *Streetcar* film reacted more favorably to Hunter's performance than those of the Broadway production, often citing her performance as crucial to *Streetcar*'s compelling social realism. *The Baltimore Sun* noticed Hunter's feminist

FIGURE 2.14 Williams's new ending for the film: Stella runs upstairs to Eunice's.

FIGURE 2.15 Closing shot: Eunice waits, looking up to her apartment where Stella has just fled.

interventions and the greater complexity she brought to the character when its reviewer remarked of the relationship between Stella and Stanley that "Even as his body attracts her, his mind causes a feeling of revulsion, and this is one of the many strange relationships superbly mirrored in the film," calling the work "painfully real."[39] Meanwhile, Hunter's hometown paper, the *Detroit Free Press*, called her Stella "warmly sympathetic and filled with pity for Blanche."[40] While not all of these reviews noticed the exact extent and nature of the changes Hunter had wrought on the role, they concurred that she inhabited Stella with sympathy and insight, and their reviews show how far she had taken the part from Kazan's first director's notes. She would win an Academy Award for Best Supporting Actress for the role. But though this high-profile industry recognition went to Hunter (and to Leigh as Blanche, who won the Best Actress prize), Brando's performance would overshadow both of theirs in cultural memory. As Brando eroticized violence as a post-war norm, making it look it bizarrely palatable to several generations of audiences, Hunter decided not to facilitate that narrative, and instead, to forge a feminist realism that resisted the myth of abuse's erotic allure at every point. In 1991, 40 years after the release of the *Streetcar* film, the feminist performance artists of *Split Britches* mounted their own adaptation of *Streetcar*, *Belle Reprieve*. In the show, they spoofed Williams's and Kazan's stage directions for Stella, having their postmodern version of the character remark: "Look, I'm supposed to wander around in a state of narcotized tranquility. That's my part."[41] The Split Britches production was not the first to notice Stella's originally circumscribed role and to rebel against it: Hunter had been there from the start.

Notes

1. Born Janet Cole in Detroit in 1922, Hunter was an alumnus of the Pasadena Playhouse and a veteran of several films before she joined the cast of *Streetcar* and the Actors Studio.
2. Molly Day Thacher Kazan (1906–1963) was a playwright who had been following Williams's career with interest. Before her intervention, Kazan had been inclined to turn down the job of directing *Streetcar* (*Elia Kazan: A Life*, 327).
3. The only major casting change was the replacement of Jessica Tandy, who had played Blanche Dubois, with Vivien Leigh.
4. Kazan was equally established in theatre and film. By the time he came to make *Streetcar* for Warner Bros., he had already won an Academy Award for Best Director for *Gentleman's Agreement* (Twentieth Century Fox, 1947).
5. *Kazan on Directing*, 59.
6. Ibid., 58–59.
7. Ibid.
8. Kim Hunter, Final Acting Script, *A Streetcar Named Desire*. Kim Hunter Papers. Billy Rose Theatre Collection, New York Public Library.
9. In 2013, the Maine Coalition to End Domestic Violence partnered with the Maine Humanities Council and the theatre company Outside the Wire to stage readings from *Streetcar* followed by discussions of intimate partner violence. For more on the patterns of violence in the play, see Susan Coprince's "Domestic Violence in *A Streetcar Named Desire*" *Southern Studies* 7.2-3 (1996), 43–55. For a useful categorization of intimate partner violence, see Michael B. Johnson's *A Typology of Domestic Violence: Intimate Terrorism, Violent Resistance, and Situational Couple Violence* (Lebanon, NH: Northeastern University Press, 2008) and "The Power and Control Wheel" from the National Center on Domestic and Sexual Violence www.ncdsv.org/images/powercontrolwheelnoshading.pdf.
10. Howard Barnes, Review of *A Streetcar Named Desire*, *NY Herald Tribune*, December 4, 1947, 35.
11. Irwin Shaw, "The Brutal Beauty of *A Streetcar Named Desire*," *The New Republic*, December 22, 1947, 34–35.
12. Brando played Sage McRae, a veteran who murders his wife, in Maxwell Anderson's *Truckline Café* (1946) on Broadway (directed by Harold Clurman and produced by Elia Kazan). He made his film debut in Fred Zinnemann's *The Men* (1950) playing a paraplegic veteran grappling with his changed life and marriage in a military hospital.

13 *Tender Comrade* was written by Dalton Trumbo and starred Ginger Rogers.
14 The British Archers film *A Matter of Life and Death*, a World War II paranormal fantasia, was released in the United States as *Stairway to Heaven*. The film starred David Niven as an RAF pilot who crashes and finds himself in a limbo between life and death. Hunter plays June, the telephone operator who responds to his distress call and then becomes his love interest. Hunter herself had been briefly (1944–1946) married to a Marine captain named William A. Baldwin, with whom she had a son (after divorcing Baldwin, Hunter moved to Greenwich Village).
15 See Larry Blades, "The Returning Vet's Experience in *A Streetcar Named Desire*: Stanley as Decommissioned Warrior Under Stress," *The Tennessee Williams Annual Review* 10 (2009), 1–27. Tracing Stanley's participation in the Sicilian Campaign, Blades notes, for instance, that the date on which Stanley rapes Blanche coincides with a war anniversary: September 14 was the decisive Battle of Salerno, which Stanley fought in, and the next day, the day of Blanche's birthday, was the date that Allied Victory was declared (19).
16 *Period of Adjustment* (1960) depicts the reintegration difficulties of two veterans of the Korean war (it became a 1962 film directed by George Roy Hill and starring Actors Studio members Anthony Franciosa, Jane Fonda, and Lois Nettleton). See Chapter 4 for further discussion of this film.
17 According to the reintegration catchphrase "Mom-ism," there was a danger that due to their health, financial stress, or emotional difficulties, veterans would return to dependency on their mothers and never attain adult status. The official advice, therefore, was that despite housing shortages, veterans and their families should avoid living with their in-laws. This isolation of young couples removed not only valuable emotional and financial support, but also deprived them of childcare and a sense of community and connection. Cutting off soldiers from their actual mothers also encouraged a conflation of the roles of wife and mother and perpetuated the expectation that wives would be responsible for the emotional work of mothers. In *Streetcar*'s character of Mitch, who lives with his ailing mother, Williams appears to explore the dynamics of "Mom-ism." Stella and Stanley live without parental support: her parents are dead, and we learn nothing about Stanley's family. This puts the Kowalskis in the situation recommended by reintegration advisors, and the play exposes the risks of this arrangement.
18 J.C. Furnas, "Meet Ed Savickas: A Victim of Combat Fatigue," *Ladies Home Journal* 92 (1945), 142–145. Furnas (1906–2001) was a Harvard-educated social historian who had been a correspondent in World War II. He was best known for his *Reader's Digest* article on automobile safety, "And Sudden Death!" (1935) which influenced Ralph Nader's *Unsafe at Any Speed* (1965).
19 *Selected Letters*, 433.
20 Ibid., 144.
21 Ibid.
22 Susan M. Hartmann, "Prescriptions for Penelope: Literature on Women's Obligations to Returning World War II Veterans," *Women's Studies* 5 (1978), 223–239.
23 Kim Hunter, Acting Script, *A Streetcar Named Desire*. Kim Hunter Papers, New York Public Library, Billy Rose Theatre Collection. T-Mss 1978-003. NCOF + 93–1105.
24 Ibid.
25 Stella asks Stanley not to tell Blanche about her pregnancy, but Stanley tells Blanche anyway; it is his first major violation of Stella's trust depicted in *Streetcar*.

26 The play's stage directions suggest only that "Stella makes a slight movement. Her look goes suddenly inward as if some interior voice had called her name. She begins a slow, shuffling progress from the bedroom to the kitchen, leaning and resting on the back of the chair and then on the edge of a table with a blind look and listening expression" (137).
27 See Angela Jenkins, Simon Millar, and James Robins, "Denial of Pregnancy—A Literature Review and Discussion of Ethical and Legal Issues" for a medical perspective on pregnancy denial. They examine "a continuum of pregnancy denial behaviors, ranging from full awareness of pregnancy with concealment, to suspicion of pregnancy, to full-blown denial." Hunter's performance seems most in line with what they call "Affective denial," a state in which "the woman is intellectually aware of the pregnancy, but makes little emotional or physical preparation for the birth." They suggest that "external stresses and psychological conflicts about pregnancy may lead to denial" and that such denial is a severe health risk (*Journal of the Royal Society of Medicine* 104.7 (2011), 286–291).
28 When Mitch emerges from the bathroom during the poker night scene, he awkwardly hands her his used towel which she cheerfully relieves him of.
29 This German music, which embodies old-world gentility for Blanche, seems a possible trigger for Stanley's PTSD.
30 The stage directions focus on Stanley: "Stanley stalks fiercely through the portieres into the bedroom. He crosses to the small white radio and snatches it off the table. With a shouted oath, he tosses the instrument out the window" (62).
31 Tennessee Williams, *A Streetcar Named Desire* (New York: New Directions, 2004; 1947), 4.
32 Ibid., 19–20.
33 Real-life contemporaries of Stella might have worked at one of New Orleans's seven Higgins factories, for instance, one of which was located a short commute from where the Kowalskis live in the French Quarter. The Higgins factories, which manufactured lifeboats and landing craft vehicles that were used in the D-Day landing at Normandy, had expanded during the war to an operation of seven plants. It was the first plant in New Orleans to bring gender and racial integration to the factory floor. According to Jerry Purvis Sanson, Louisiana women held a range of jobs during the war. They had "became stock board markers at the New Orleans offices of Merrill Lynch, Pierce, Fenner, and Bean; they managed parking lots, drove taxicabs, welded and repaired aircraft, delivered newspapers, worked in machine shops, drove trucks, and managed stores. …In addition, more than 400 Louisiana women applied to the Women's Auxiliary Army Corps Officers School during the first week of open applications in 1942" (*Louisiana During World War II: Politics and Society, 1939–1945*, 270). New Orleans also got its first female streetcar conductors during the war.
34 Betty Friedan, *The Feminine Mystique* (New York: Norton, 2013), 78.
35 Alison Lefkovitz, "The Peculiar Anomaly: Same-Sex Infidelity in Post-war Divorce Courts," *Law and History Review* 33.3 (2015), 665–701, 667.
36 Williams, *Streetcar*, 36.
37 The model for Rockwell's painting, Mary Doyle, said later of posing for the portrait, "I am proud of this painting. It's a symbol of what women did for the war, to do their part, and to give up their nail polish" (Mary Doyle Keefe qtd. in Marcy Kennedy Knight, "Rosie the Riveter," *The Saturday Evening Post*," July/August 2013). This statement suggests that Stella's original stage action of putting on nail polish in the early days of

the theatrical production of *Streetcar* may have had a symbolic resonance as a woman's return from her wartime identity towards the conventional femininity demanded of her after the war.
38 My argument here is indebted to Leonard Leff's "And Transfer to Cemetery: The Streetcars Named Desire." Leff advocates against the notion that there is one "authentic" version of *Streetcar*. *Film Quarterly* 55.3 (2002), 29–37.
39 Donald Kirkley, "The Quality of Terror," *The Baltimore Sun*, 1 November 1951, 14. Other notable reviews include Edwin Schallert, "'Streetcar Named Desire' Powerful Drama on Screen," *L.A. Times*, September 19, 1951, B8, and Bosley Crowther, "Intimate Screen Observation Enhances Current Top-Notch Films," *New York Times*, September 23, 1951, 109.
40 Helen Bower, "Screen 'Streetcar' Exceeds Stage Tragedy," *The Detroit Free Press*, November 2, 1951, 23.
41 Deb Margolin and Peggy Shaw, *Belle Reprieve*, qtd. in Jill Dolan, *Theatre and Sexuality* (London: Palgrave, 2010), 67.

3
PROTEST PERFORMANCES
Actor Rebellion as Feminist Critique

The 1950s opened with a film that invited audiences to consider the status of female actors: Joseph L. Mankiewicz's *All About Eve* (1950). It featured a strong leading performance by Bette Davis as theatre star Margo Channing, a breakout role for Anne Baxter as the fresh-faced talent who seeks to supplant her, and memorable supporting parts for Celeste Holm and Thelma Ritter—all four of whom were nominated for acting Oscars. *All About Eve* also featured a small appearance by Marilyn Monroe as Claudia Casswell, an alumna of the "Copacabana School of Dramatic Arts"—in other words, a showgirl with acting aspirations. Anne Baxter had trained in Stanislavsky-based acting with Maria Ouspenskaya, and the rivalry between the acting generations set against each other in the film vividly dramatizes the "Method wars" of the 1950s. With hushed tones and an elusive character, Baxter plays Eve Harrington, an ambitious young performer who worms her way into the life of a theatre legend of the previous generation. Eventually, through a series of wily manipulations, Eve supplants her predecessor, inching her way from understudy to the star of a new play that had originally been written for Margo Channing.

As Margo, Bette Davis plays a character whose acting style suddenly seems dated. Her charisma is that of the pre-war theatrical star, something like Katherine Cornell's. Margo derisively describes herself as "an old kazoo and some sparkles." Eve belongs to the fascinating new generation of actors. When her exciting talent is discussed by industry professionals, it is in the terms of seeming spontaneity and naturalness that were often used to describe Method actors. This new impression of "naturalness" arose from a change in performance conventions that allowed more of the speech and gesture found in everyday life to enter into the actor's work. One of the characters in the film reports that the playwright whose work

Eve is starring in was blown away by Eve's "lack of pretense" and "strange directness," and how in her mouth the lines "sounded so fresh, so new, so full of meaning."

Fresh, new, full of meaning. In addition to recognizing the allure of this new style of acting on stage, *All About Eve* also wonders what the impact of this kind of acting might be in Hollywood, where Eve's career trajectory seems to be leading her, even though she expresses hesitancy about screen acting. When asked how long she will stay in Hollywood, Eve answers uncertainly, leaving the fate of this new type of acting's cinematic potential unanswered. It is significant that *All About Eve* chooses a female actor to exemplify the new style. *All About Eve* is decidedly ambivalent about the rise of this new type of acting. After all, it was designed as a star vehicle for Bette Davis (Figure 3.1), whose character is described in the script as "a great star, a true star" and one who will "never be anything else." Eve is the ostensible villain. It was one of several roles in the 1950s in which Davis would investigate her own place in the developing media ecosystem. In Stuart Heisler's *The Star* of 1952, she played Margaret Elliot, a declining diva who is careening into personal crisis and is rescued by her return to family life, a role for which she was also nominated for an Oscar.

All About Eve is perceptive about the dynamics surrounding this transformative moment in screen acting, diplomatically paying tribute to the power of the old kind of star while also placing its bets on the new. The film lets Davis's character Margo keep her professional dignity by having her bow out of the part that Eve is trying to steal from her, but the screenplay succumbs along the way to a misogynistic monologue, delivered by Margo herself, in which she reveals her awareness

FIGURE 3.1 Old Hollywood star Bette Davis as Margo Channing and emerging actor Anne Baxter as Eve Harrington face off, with neophyte Marilyn Monroe as Miss Caswell looking on as she contemplates her own future in *Joseph L. Mankiewicz's All About Eve* (1950).

that she will soon be superannuated, and that she will need to find a husband. The film ends with Eve's establishment as a star, a status underlined by the arrival of her own stalker. When it came to Oscar season, Hollywood hedged its bets, nominating both Bette Davis and Anne Baxter in the Best Actress Category (neither won: the award went to Judy Holliday for *Born Yesterday*).

With its fading star and designing understudy, *All About Eve* reanimated a series of backstage drama staples vividly for its cultural moment. In Hollywood's postwar crisis of confidence in its own future, the aging female star became a key metaphor for the studio system's impending demise. In films of the early 1950s, from *All About Eve* to *Sunset Boulevard* (1950) to *Singin' in the Rain* (1952) the aging or superannuated female star represents Hollywood's own decadence, and its fears that it too may be, in the words of Margo Channing, nothing but an old kazoo and some sparkles. Such narratives often depended upon misogynistic tropes—a horror of female aging, and a sense that only young women had a right to be in front of the camera—even while they gave interesting meta-roles to stars like Bette Davis and Gloria Swanson.

To be a young female actor seeking entry to the cinematic medium at this moment was an uncertain proposition. In this chapter, I study several female Method actors who worked in Hollywood in the 1950s and early 1960s. They all played characters associated with "failures" of screen charisma, failures that turn out to be critiques of the particular demands placed upon female actors in Hollywood. In Robert Aldrich's *The Big Knife* (1955), Shelley Winters plays studio bit actor Dixie Evans who protests against the roles available to her in Hollywood. In Henry Cornelius's *I Am A Camera* (1955), Julie Harris plays the aspiring Berlin film actor Sally Bowles, who eventually finds success when she redirects her talents into writing. And in *Sweet Bird of Youth* (1962), Geraldine Page plays the established screen diva Alexandra del Lago who attempts to mount a comeback while her young lover tries to use her connections to launch his own screen career. How might we explain the emergence of the protesting female Method actor in this period? Male Method actors have often expressed a generalized anti-theatricality in which the art of acting itself is viewed as suspect (this is usually related to fears that it is not manly enough), but for female Method actors, protest more often takes the form of industry critique. Acting is not the problem—in fact there is a venerable professional and feminist tradition for women to reach back to as actors, one which they would like to be able to connect with by playing worthy and serious parts on screen. The ideological and industrial conditions under which women are expected to act in Hollywood are the problem.

It is worth considering why female Method actors gravitated to these roles of industry critique. First, it is important to remember that all female actors had good reason to protest the types of roles—both on and behind the camera—available to them in the 1950s, even though the industry was in general transforming in a way that gave more freedom to Hollywood actors than they had had under the studio system. This was, in terms of mainstream media, the era of housewives and helpmeets, Debbie Reynolds and Sandra Dee. The great era of the female star was past. When Eve Harrington's machinations to overthrow her rival are discovered, she is asked by a baffled friend, "You'd do all that—just for a part in a play?" to which her response is, "I'd do much more—for a part that good," a sentiment that speaks to the desperation female actors felt for roles of substance in a Hollywood designed, like the rest of America, to send them back to the kitchen. Eve's response speaks with a grim humor to the roles available to women in the early 1950s.

The protest performances that I study in this chapter are often critiques of the discourse of the aging female star. In the familiar misogynist narrative, the aging star strives to hang on at any cost. In these Method performances by women, female actors challenge the industry's exclusions and express their sense that they are not willing to play by the rules that governed the careers of their elders. The figure of the actress dissatisfied with the roles available to her also signifies the broader contraction of the social and professional roles available to women in the 1950s, so that the trope of the discontented actress becomes part of a larger feminist critique.

Beyond the Bombshell: Shelley Winters

In 1962, Shelley Winters gave an interview to the *Saturday Evening Post* that echoed the generational dynamics of *All About Eve*. Reflecting on the changes that had come over Hollywood in recent years—changes that had given actors greater control over their professional destinies thanks to the breakup of studio monopolies and the rise of independent producer-directors and freelance contracts—Winters suggested that stars who came of age during the studio era might not be worthy of their newfound artistic and professional control. Winters's prime example of a star unsuited for such independence is Elizabeth Taylor. Of Taylor, who had been her co-star in 1951's *A Place in the Sun*, Winters remarks:

> She has no sense of money. The income tax is for everyone else, not for her. When she's in Rome and has a yen for cheesecake, she calls TWA and asks them to fly her a cheesecake from Lindy's in New York. She doesn't know how to go to the grocery store and, if someone didn't bring food to her room, she'd starve to death. All her life people have done things for her and told her what to do.

Winters's comments suggest more than her exasperation with Taylor's diva personality: they reveal the growing resistance to the older model of stardom exemplified by actors like Taylor.

Winters's sense that Taylor was not able to make good choices (however unfair her comment may have been, given Taylor's extraordinary work on screen across the 1950s and 1960s) signals the growing rift between the idea of the star and the idea of the actor. This rift was particularly strong for female Method actors. While

Brando and Clift ended up becoming stars in a quite conventional way, female Method actors of the 1950s and 1960s, even when they played leads, in many ways resembled character actors or supporting actors in their approaches (in these roles there had traditionally been scope for a wider range of female personalities and stories). Method women thereby mounted a more thorough rejection of conventional stardom, one that was often based in feminist ideals.

Winters credited her time at the Actors Studio with leading to the transformation of her Hollywood career. In the 1940s, she was an actor under contract at Universal, playing small parts in films like the 1948 noir *Larceny* and the 1950 Western *Winchester '73*. Winters had signed a seven-year contract with Universal. At the time, she recalls, she had not realized the genre priorities of the studio, nor the extent to which studio management would resist allowing her to move beyond the noir victims and saloon girls that she had been hired to play. She sometimes negotiated loan-outs to foreign, independent, or other studio's films, most notably to Paramount Pictures to appear in George Stevens's *A Place in the Sun* (1951) alongside Montgomery Clift and Elizabeth Taylor (a role for which she received her first Oscar nomination). But when in 1954 she left Hollywood for New York, Universal responded by placing her on suspension. Divorced with a young child, Winters wrote "I was desperately trying to think of a way to get my life together. The newly formed Actors Studio was holding sessions on Tuesdays and Fridays. Sometime in 1948, Elia Kazan had asked me to be an observer. That year, 1954, I began to attend regularly" (15). She recalls witnessing a particularly moving Private Moment exercise, one that gave her renewed confidence in her vocation and loosened her sense of gender distinctions. The exercise, performed by Gerry O'Loughlin, involved a scene in which a young man comes into an apartment and eats take-out chicken standing up, with the lights still off and without removing his coat. "It was the quintessence of loneliness," Winters comments, "I had thought that only women suffered from this kind of loneliness. ... It was one of the most powerful things I had ever seen" (16). After seeing this performance, she reports,

> I left the Actors Studio that day with my depression gone and remembering again that I was an artist. ... No more was I just a rejected wife and an abandoned mother. I was a person in my own right with a responsibility and a life to fulfill. I suddenly realized, too, that I would never be able to do it in California, where I succumbed so easily to the blonde bombshell image.
> *(17)*

Nor was it only Actors Studio sessions featuring male actors that inspired her. She recalled, for instance, the powerful impact of watching Julie Harris's perform a scene from *Victoria Regina* (99).[1]

From here, Winters threw herself into New York's Method community, participating in weekly sessions at the Actors Studio, and engaging Stella Adler as a private coach. Her most rewarding experience with the Method came when she was involved in the workshopping, development, and Broadway production of Michael V. Gazzo's *A Hatful of Rain*, which ran at the Lyceum and Plymouth Theatres from November 9, 1955 to October 13, 1956. Winters played Celia, the wife of a morphine-addicted Korean War veteran (played by Ben Gazzara). In her memoir, she recalls the creative excitement of working with Method actors, and how the Method's collaborative process afforded her opportunities to advocate for her character. While the play was in tryouts, she persuaded Gazzo to add a scene after sensing a gap in the depiction of her character:

> I was putting myself and my unborn baby's life in danger by staying with Ben Gazzara's character, Johnny. In the play, I don't know he's a junkie. I just know he is my husband, sick and stealing everything in sight. I kept trying to get Mike Gazzo to write a scene in which Johnny and I would talk about what our marriage had been like before he had gone to fight in Korea. I wanted the audience to see why Celia is holding on to this man.
>
> *(141)*

Winters describes the playwright's initial resistance to her idea, her persistence until she won the point, and her certainty that "this scene made the whole play work" (141). Winters also relates how she took a feminist Method approach to reshaping the play's set on Broadway:

> on stage right, was a platform, on which stood a dirty sink in a tenement kitchen with old, yellow linoleum. On stage left was the living room, which had an old chaise lounge and a frayed lampshade. The whole apartment looked as if it had never been cleaned. I felt strongly this apartment should look clean and show Celia's efforts to fix it up and make it as much like a home as possible. … Opening night in New York, I made Tony [Anthony Franciosa, who played Celia's brother-in-law] go to Woolworth's with me, and I bought yellow shelving paper, a dark red lampshade, a cheap, nice rug, a patchwork quilt for the chaise lounge, a yellow oilcloth table cover, and a scrubbing brush and a soap pail. At six-thirty opening night on Broadway, I was down on my hands and knees with my hair up in curlers, scrubbing the kitchen side of the stage.
>
> *(140–141)*

Winters describes the propmaster watching her modifications of the set without commenting because he had become used to Method actors (142). Again she notes that her input had at first been resisted, but she ultimately prevailed, and her interpretation was incorporated. In this case, she says that she received a message from scene designer Mordecai Gorelik who conceded that at times "actors know more about a play than anyone else concerned with it" (142).

Using the space the Method allowed for actors to be co-authors, Winters had persuaded Gazzo to allow her to bring more insight, respect, and lines to the play's female lead, and then modified the set in light of her characterization in a way that critically engaged class and gender stereotypes in "kitchen sink dramas" of the 1950s. It was while she was engaged in these theatrical experiences with the Actors Studio that Winters went to Hollywood to play an actress demanding better parts in Robert Aldrich's adaptation of Clifford Odets's *The Big Knife* (1955).

One might be forgiven for thinking that in Robert Aldrich's *The Big Knife* (1955) it is the struggle of the male Method actor against the commercial imperatives of Hollywood that is most at stake. After all, the film's protagonist, Charlie Castle, was modeled on John Garfield (who had played the role on Broadway), and in the film adaptation Jack Palance (Brando's *Streetcar* understudy), took over Garfield's part of the rough-and-tumble star who can not persuade his studio boss to let him out of his contract so he can make socially conscious films. *The Big Knife* follows Castle's difficulties as a noir plot closes in around him, but sympathy for his plight is constrained by the fact that he lost his artistic freedom when he allowed the studio to cover up a car accident in which he was at fault, and in which a child died. To relativize Charlie's sense of victimization, there is another character in the film, an aspiring actor named Dixie Evans played by Winters, who was with Charlie on the night of the accident. At the mid-point of the film, Dixie forcefully reminds Charlie that although he is dissatisfied with his career, at least his artistic compromises have brought leading roles, fame, and a lavish home in Bel-Air. He has been the beneficiary of huge privileges, Dixie tells him, and these have come at the expense of other people's lives and careers. Though she is having trouble breaking out of supporting roles in B movies, Dixie's goal is the same as his: to play meaningful parts in Hollywood. The idea that his success depends on her silencing is made literal when the studio explains to Charlie its plans to murder Dixie (to prevent her from reporting the car accident), and asks him to set her up for the hit with the promise that "she'll go unremembered by the end of the week."

The extended metaphor at work here is hardly subtle: Dixie's determination to talk, to act, and to tell her story is the force that threatens to explode the system on which Charlie's career depends. The scene that unfolds between Charlie and Dixie at the film's mid-point highlights some of the shared problems of artistic self-determination and authorial control facing all actors in Hollywood, but suggests that the problems facing women are much more acute (Figure 3.2). When Dixie presents herself to Charlie, she knows exactly what she wants: a career free from sexual harassment. But what she is currently experiencing feels more like being treated like a sex worker by the studio and powerful men in the industry. Winters, in playing the part, tackles all of the studio's misogynist verdicts on Dixie in order to undo them in her performance and transform the worthless woman they see into a sympathetic character passionate about her art. Winters's performance contains many moments that suggest the difference between Dixie's words

FIGURE 3.2 Shelley Winters as Dixie Evans explodes in career frustration in Robert Aldrich's *The Big Knife* (1955): "Oh that lousy studio—they louse you up, and then they call you a louse!"

and her feelings, her social persona and her inner emotions. Her cautious gestures and concerned facial expressions telegraph Dixie's sense of threat at being caught up in this plot, even as she tries to keep up the silly non sequiturs that characterize her "dumb blonde" persona. Through this complexly layered performance, Winters indicates that Dixie is not synonymous with the role she plays for the studio, but that she has donned a "showgirl" mask to survive. Winters makes it clear that her character's central motive in putting pressure on the studio is to advance her acting career: it is neither a romance with Charlie nor some general notion of power that attracts her.

As Emily Carman has pointed out in "Stardom as Hollywood Historiography," this portrait of film studios as holding a vise grip on their stars was somewhat anachronistic even by the time of *The Big Knife*'s release. Actors like Winters and Palance actually exerted more control over their appearances than the characters they played (the film uses the studio system as a kind of metaphor for film noir's deterministic universe). But even though actors had increasing control over their labor and career decisions, Winters reveals in her memoirs that having more freedom did not mean that robust parts were available for women. If *The Big Knife*'s complaints about studio control were dated, Dixie Evans's problems with typecasting and the availability of fewer significant roles for women were not. In her performance, she brings all of her resources as a Method actor to bear on expressing frustration at the lack of compelling parts available (even in this film, no female actor has screen time or lines comparable to Palance's as Charlie Castle). *The Big Knife*'s model of actor contracts may be obsolete, but its portrayal of the shortage of complex depictions of women in 1950s Hollywood was all too relevant.

The scene of reckoning between Dixie and Charlie at the heart of *The Big Knife* models the kinds of collaborations that tended to make the Method friendly to female actors. Both Winters and Palance might have chosen to play the scene in ways that estranged viewers from Dixie's character and her critiques, but Charlie's patient affirmation of Dixie's points, together with the ways in which Winters nuances Dixie's character, pull feminist meaning out of what might have been played by less engaged actors as a generic noir scene. In her effort to give voice to women in Dixie's situation in Hollywood, Winters conducted her own research, through which she learned about sex work in Hollywood:

> I would get up early in the morning and go have breakfast at Schwab's, where some of the real beautiful Hollywood call girls were having breakfast after having worked all night. They were careful and closed and very reluctant to talk to me about anything. But when I described the role I was researching and Dixie's courage and cunning and the way she was victimized by being told she was a starlet and then used as if she was a prostitute, they understood what I was trying to put on the screen. Then they began to tell me their sad, funny, and terrifying stories...[2]

Winters's conversations at Schwab's were complemented by further work on her acting technique. She traveled back to New York during the making of the film to consult with Strasberg, because she "was having difficulty communicating the nameless fear of this courageous little actress within the limitations of the scene in the film script," turning once more to the Method as a way to stretch and nuance the role in order to do justice to a female character. Winters later reflected: "It was during these times that I finally escaped the dumb blonde-bombshell image Universal and I had created and broke through the crippling sexual double standard that had been imposed on women throughout history" (12).

Within a few years, Winters won two Academy Awards, the first in 1959 for her performance as Mrs. Van Daan in George Stevens' *The Diary of Anne Frank* and the second in 1965 for her role opposite Sidney Poitier in Guy Green's *A Patch of Blue*. Thanks to her drive and resourcefulness, she did find some good parts, but along the way she had to play many supporting roles and do plenty of less distinguished work. She continued to appear in the westerns and noirs that she had left Hollywood to break out of, but which provided a steady paycheck. She also stayed afloat financially through television work, appearing in series like *The United States Steel Hour*, *Wagon Train*, and *Climax!*.

It is worth pausing over Winters' two Oscar-winning performances to see what they reveal about the work of Method women on screen. In the role of Mrs. Van Daan in *The Diary of Anne Frank*, Winters plays a flawed but sympathetic woman who provides the film's most palpable embodiment of the anxiety of life in hiding. Winters' character was based on Auguste van Pels, one of the friends in hiding with the Frank family (she was the mother of Peter, Anne's love interest). Winters uses the Method to play Mrs. Van Daan with great empathy for the agonies of life in hiding. In one scene, she explodes at Anne for spilling milk on a treasured possession, the fur coat her father gave her before he died. In another wrenching scene, her husband forces her to part with the coat because they need to sell it. Winters performance in the film has great range. She is sexually forward, making insinuations about Anne and Peter's adolescent feelings, and at one point asking Otto Frank to admire her legs in front of her husband and everyone in the annex. In what may be her most affecting scene, she has an unexpected emotional reaction to the New Year's cake that is brought by Miep, the Dutch woman who is helping to protect them in hiding. The cake has "Peace in 1943" written on it, and when she recalls that last year's cake had the same hopeful message—"Peace in 1942"—and peace did not come, she is caught off guard by emotion. Near the end of the film there is a particularly compelling scene: after her husband has been caught stealing bread from the general supply, Mrs. Frank tells the Van Daans that they must leave the annex, and Winters's Mrs. Van Daan pleads desperately with her not to evict them, insisting that there is nowhere else for them to go. In another powerful scene, Mrs. Van Daan's husband accuses her of being to blame for their situation, because she would not leave her precious possessions behind to emigrate earlier, and she responds that all of their possessions were obtained only for his comfort. Winters's performance delivers much of the film's tension and pathos.

For her second Oscar-winning Best Supporting Actress performance six years later, Winters again played an overbearing mother, but this time, rather than being the victim of racism, she plays a racist character. In *A Patch of Blue*, she plays the role of Rose-ann d'Arcy, a sex worker whose daughter, who is blind, begins a friendship with a man she meets in a park (a character named Gordon Ralfe played by Sidney Poitier). Winters's role in the film resembles that of a melodrama villain. I have argued that women's Method acting on film often looks different from men's—that many of their performances are characterized by emotional restraint rather than emotional outbursts—but in this case Winters provides an exception. In the opening scenes of *A Patch of Blue* she does a swaggering imitation of Brando's performance style, seemingly in an experiment to find out what would happen if a female actor inhabited this kind of sweaty, uninhibited physicality. She comes home from a long day at work, undresses down to her underwear in front of her daughter and father, grabs a bottle of hard liquor, accuses her father of drinking from it, lashes out at her daughter for spilling the beads she threads to earn extra money, and tells her daughter that her "face is a mess." In *A Patch of Blue*, Winters is the villain against whom the audience roots as romance unfolds between Poitier's character and the daughter Selina played by Elizabeth Hartmann. Winters borrows Brando's pattern of explosive outbursts to embody an oppressive and abusive parent.

If Shelley Winters's experiences of empowerment through the Method contradict stereotypes of women's oppression at the Actors Studio, her status, both during her lifetime and now, is sadly typical of the double standards by which women's Method acting has been measured. Her career paralleled Brando's in many ways, yet while he was deemed epoch-defining, she was described more than once as "blowsy," that is, disheveled or slovenly. Winters dared to inhabit the same terrain as Brando, but while male dirt and slovenliness were sexy, the female equivalent was off-putting. Following her death in 2006, *Entertainment Weekly* deemed her "slightly more a legend in her own mind than in the minds of others," and *Sight & Sound* wrote of her return to Hollywood after her interlude at the Actors Studio, "She returned to the screen having—in every sense—gained in substance"—a dig at her weight. The equally portly Brando's *New York Times* obituary, on the other hand, began with the announcement that he "electrified a generation and forever transformed the art of screen acting."[3] In her own *New York Times* obituary, Winters was left to eulogize herself in a quotation, and the journalist's first comment was a suggestion that she lied about her age.

A feminist re-reading of the Method should challenge the received opinion of Winters as somehow ludicrous and Brando as possessed of authenticity and genius, and might even use Winters's career as a yardstick and an alternative paradigm of the Method's range of tones, strategies, and potentialities. After her sojourn at the Actors Studio and her return to more meaningful roles, Winters certainly still found that some of the parts she was offered were flawed representations of female experience, but from her point of view, as canvases for her artistry they were vast improvements over the clichés she had played in genre films at Universal. She hoped that these new roles even may have helped to open up further opportunities for women on screen:

> Even now I wonder if women's lib arrived too late for women of my generation. When I think of the victim roles that I fought for (and for which I often got nominations and twice Oscars), I hope I was helping to raise the public's consciousness so that the process of rectifying the age-old plight of women could begin. Gloria Steinem and Betty Friedan say that's what I was doing, and I hope they're right.
>
> *(Shelley II, 14)*

In an insightful study of Winters, James Morrison effectively agrees. Morrison provides a rich analysis of the ways in which Winters developed a performance style that allowed her to inhabit her "victim" roles critically, in protest against the status she had been assigned in films—that of being consistently "relegated to the margins." Winters's comments about Hollywood show her critical awareness of the limits she faced, but she credited the Actors Studio with helping her to fight back.[4]

"On Film She's Too Much:" Julie Harris's Queer Method

Julie Harris specialized in performances of failed glamor. In Henry Cornelius's 1955 film adaptation of John Van Druten's play *I Am a Camera* (itself an adaptation of Christopher Isherwood's *Goodbye to Berlin*), Harris plays Sally Bowles, a role she originated on Broadway, and for which she had won the Best Leading Actress Tony Award in 1952.[5] Sally Bowles is an eccentric British expatriate who has come to 1930s Berlin seeking a film career. As she makes the rounds of agents trying to get cast, she sings in a nightclub to make ends meet, and dates a string of men whom she hopes will contribute to her upkeep, inhabiting a circuit of nightclub gigs, sex work, and film work similar to that of Shelley Winters' character Dixie Evans in *The Big Knife*. At one point in Sally's tumultuous friendship with a fellow expatriate, Chris, they find themselves in a restaurant squandering their rent money on champagne and caviar. As the evening progresses, they realize that they have racked up a bill they cannot pay, and Sally proposes that she put her charisma to use in getting them out of it. Chris has little confidence in this maneuver. "Any mess you get into," he tells her, "you try to get out of by using your extremely inadequate sex appeal." Sally is appalled. "My sex appeal inadequate?" she demands. "It's adequate!" They go back and forth. "Inadequate," he repeats. "Adequate!," she counters, until she tells him "Oh Chris, you're so upset or you wouldn't say a thing like that." The humor of the scene resides in the low bar Sally has set for her own attractiveness—it is merely "adequate"—but she will energetically insist on that.

Chris's low opinion of Sally's sex appeal echoes the verdicts of not a few critics responding to Julie Harris's screen work in the 1950s. As one of the least conforming Hollywood screen actors of the 1950s, in terms of both her performance style and her appearance, Harris presented perhaps the strongest challenge to the decade's representational norms of all the actors in this study. And in Sally Bowles, Harris found a role that allowed her to explore what might be done with "inadequate" sex appeal. Harris's first scene in the film, set in a nightclub, alludes to Marlene Dietrich's performance in *Morocco*, but with all conventional star charisma drained from it—an effect achieved by filming Harris from a distance, and by showing the audience members in the café indifferent to her performance rather than enthralled. Harris often risked these kinds of film appearances in roles that allowed her to expose, explore, and evacuate the conventions of cinematic charisma in the service of what might lie beyond it.

Harris's performances across the 1950s offered cinema audiences fascinating alternatives to the norms of Hollywood screen performance. But her contributions have fallen into something close to obscurity because they have often been mistaken for the "failures" they critically investigate. "She was doing a part she shouldn't have been doing *because* she shouldn't have been doing it," said Walter Kerr of Harris's stage performance in *I Am a Camera*, recognizing that

Harris enjoyed working against type and creating counterintuitive, resistant interpretations.[6] Harris often worked from a perceived disjunction between character and role. Ben Brantley has called hers a "presence that seemed tantalizingly at odds with the naturalism of film."[7]

This quality of being "at odds" was precisely what mainstream critics of the 1950s found so troubling about her work. Consider Bosley Crowther's response to Harris's performance in the role of a child in *The Member of the Wedding* (Figure 3.3):

> Julie Harris, who played the restless girl on the stage…is betrayed by the propinquous camera into looking her own grown-up age rather than that of the youngster she is supposed to be. Instead of the unripe features of as 12-year old, we are shown, in close-up, the face of a woman that is mature in expression and form. This discouragement to illusion is aggravated even more by the archness of some of the girlish gestures that the merciless camera reveals.[8]

Though Harris's "archness" and "discouragement to illusion" unsettled Crowther, it was this refusal of absorptive illusion in relation to roles, both social and theatrical, that made Harris's performances a touchstone for queer viewers and critics. Rather than being "betrayed" by the camera, it might be more accurate to say that she betrayed it. Her work, particularly in *The Member of the Wedding*, has long been recognized for its insightful explorations of dynamics of queer historical experience, including the pressure to assume a gender, the resistance to being allowed to choose one's own name, and the effort to create alternative kinship ties in a society governed by the ideology of marriage. In fact, Patricia White opens

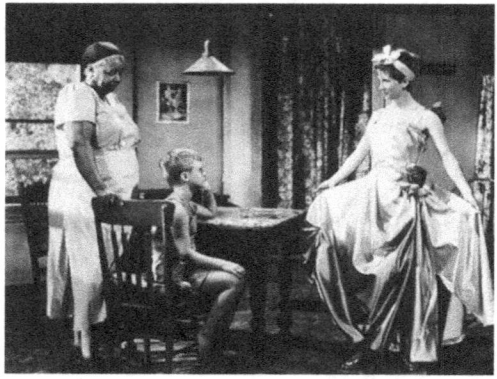

FIGURE 3.3 Ethel Waters as Berenice Sadie Brown delivers the news to Julie Harris as Frankie Addams that an attempt at glamor has failed in Fred Zinnemann's *The Member of the Wedding* (1952).

Uninvited (1999), her foundational study of Hollywood cinema and lesbian representability, with a discussion of Harris's performance in *The Member of the Wedding*, arguing that Harris not only provides an empathetic portrait of a queer child's isolation and search for belonging, but that her performance also becomes an allegory for queer viewership of Hollywood films: Harris's character Frankie "goes 'breaking into weddings' just like we do" and so expresses the "gap between hegemonic representation…and those dispossessed of the image."[9] Harris's queer aesthetic has also been noted by Jack Halberstam"[10] and Hilton Als.[11] Most recently, Rachel Walerstein has suggested that Harris's performances as Sally Bowles and Frankie Addams explore "the affects historically associated with queer longing like loss, despair, anger, shame, and disgust."[12] Investigating the question of why "certain looks signal queerly" (26), Walerstein argues that Harris's performance in *The Member of the Wedding* works against the typical "fetishistic treatment of queer desire" by replacing looks of desire at an object with looks offscreen that signify a longing for recognition or an "elsewhere" where inclusion could be possible, and so directs "us to alternative possibilities against the demands of the camera or even the story" (43). Walerstein's analysis of Harris's achievements is based in theories of the gaze, but a similar case might be made about Harris's challenge to norms of casting in *The Member of the Wedding*. As Nicole Seymour has recently argued, McCullers's novel *The Member of the Wedding* involves a sophisticated examination of temporality and the casting of Harris, an adult actor in the role of a child, contributes to the narrative's refusal of normative understandings of time and development.[13]

In *The Member of the Wedding*, Harris performs a signature moment of failed glamor when her character Frankie, a child who is enthralled with her brother's upcoming wedding, models the bargain basement dress she is planning to wear to the event. She is told by her caregiver Berenice (played by Ethel Waters) that "it just don't do." In other words, Berenice explains to Frankie, she has not been able to achieve the seamless performance of femininity that she aimed at when she put on the dress. As Frankie stands in the baggy satin garment, a bow tied awkwardly around her short-cropped hair, Berenice tries to explain in a gentle way that the ensemble makes her look like "a human Christmas tree," and then attempts to make some improving alterations while Frankie stands mystified and disheartened by the prospect that the gown will not make the impression she desires at the wedding.

In her work of adapting the role of Frankie from stage to screen, Harris strongly championed Frankie's queerness and gender noncomformity and attempted to guard them against attempted erasures. Returning to *The Member of the Wedding*'s production files reveals the extent to which Harris fought to express her character's contours, including Frankie's gender expression. In her correspondence with Fred Zinnemann while the film script was in development, she defended Frankie's use of profanity and asked Zinnemann to cut lines in the script that seemed designed to bring the part into line with conventional femininity.

For instance, Harris protested against the line: "Tell us how you met Jarvis and Winterhill. It is so romantic," and of "Sister-in-law, doesn't that sound wonderful," Harris insisted: "This is not Frankie Addams" (Harris lost this battle, but managed to deliver the line so unexpectedly that she might be said to have won). Harris's remarks to Zinnemann also sought to protect Frankie's masculinity, a value which she made clear in her objection to the removal of the motor that sat in Frankie's room in the stage production. When she writes to Zinnemann about adapting the play into a film, she wonders where the motor has gone:

> The properties as listed in this script do not include the motor. The motor is one of the things in Frankie's room as described in the book; and everytime Frankie comes into the room, she turns the motor on using it for various purposes, to sharpen her pencils, to file her nails, or just for general action and noise. The motor can be any old one she could have picked up in a scrap yard or put together as kids frequently do.

For Harris, the motor was an essential part of her characterization of Frankie. Harris also objected to a moment in the script in which Frankie leaves the honeymooners' car of her own accord, rather than having to be wrenched from it. She proposes that the scene be written and played as follows:

> Instead of Frankie leaving the car voluntarily, why should she not be dragged out of the car? For example she could get into the front seat and when they tried to take her out of the car, she could grab the steering wheel and hold on until her grip was broken. When she is finally removed from the car bodily, she could fall into the dust of the road crying "Take me, take me." This would be better than "I want the world to die." She has not had time to realize that she wants the world to die. All she knows is that she wants her brother and sister-in-law to take her at this particular moment. (File 102)

In the manuscript of the letter, Zinnemann has written next to Harris's suggestion "rehearsal," to suggest trying it out. Ultimately, Harris's interpretation prevailed: in the film, Frankie is dragged out while gripping the steering wheel. For Harris, the action of gripping the wheel was an essential part of Frankie's emotional crisis—a desperate effort to be in the driver's seat, to exert the kind of control also shown when Frankie chooses a new name and makes plans to run away. In Harris's insistence on showing Frankie being "removed from the car bodily," she sought to represent the violent social order and normative gender regimes that are perpetually exerted on Frankie. Not only in her correctives to the script, but also in her physical interpretation of the role, Harris claimed the right to refuse to perform norms of feminine decorum. For instance, in one scene she removes a sliver from her foot with a knife. She sits with her legs apart, half dressed, wearing a boy's undershirt under her petticoat, in a conspicuous refusal of ladylikeness.

Harris's own seeming gender fluidity was a subject of notice in the media coverage of *The Member of the Wedding*. Giving some sense of just how much Harris's looks challenged the kind of beauty and femininity that Hollywood typically sought in its actresses, one *Life* magazine journalist described her as follows:

> Many actors look like actors. Julie looks like a 12-year-old boy who has been taking Lionel Strongfort's bodybuilding exercises for a long time with no success. She is 26, very small (5 feet 4 inches, 105 pounds) and her silhouette is almost flat. Her hair is short (for the play), literally titian. She… smiles often but not always with warmth.[14]

Cosmopolitan remarked on her "reddish hair" and "rabbity face," noting that "on the street she goes around lipstickless" and is a "frail, plain-faced girl."[15] Meanwhile, in 1952, Hedda Hopper confessed to having developed a "warm professional crush" on Harris because "she exudes an extreme sensitivity. There's an elfin quality about her thin, pointed face, her slightly pouting mouth and dark eyes that seem to feel they're revealing too much of her inner nature."[16] When Hopper asked Harris what kind of stories she would like to see produced, Harris mentioned Faulkner's *Light in August* ("It's about a girl who's going to have a baby, but the man deserts her. So she travels through the South, getting rides with various people, until she finds him") and the Joseph Conrad story "Freya of the Seven Isles," choices to which Hopper could only respond, "I must say you have some offbeat ideas for pictures." Though Hopper did not necessarily mean it as a compliment, "offbeat" was a fitting way to describe Harris's career in the 1950s as a hipster, intellectual, and personality, one who often seemed to cultivate a non-conformist image in order to distinguish herself from the average starlet. Harris tells Hopper that she lives in New York, in a third-floor walk-up and that "when I have children, I want to keep on working." For its part, the press consistently emphasized Harris's boyishness. In a 1955 article, "Joan of Arc in Jeans," the *Miami Herald* gave a vignette of Harris as a tomboy, like her character Frankie Addams in *The Member of the Wedding*, rehearsing the part of Joan in denim.[17] Harris broke important new ground for women on film in the 1950s with the bohemian soft butchness of her performances.

There remains a significant gap between the insight and appreciation queer critics have brought to Harris's work and the more general critical reception of these performances, which ranges from perplexity to neglect. Method acting historian Foster Hirsch describes her performance in the film version of *The Member of the Wedding* as "strange," "exhaustingly intense," "overwrought," and possessed of an "almost startling homeliness," and concludes that "on film she's too much" (319). Instead of her iconoclastic performance in *The Member of the Wedding*, he prefers her more docile one in *East of Eden*, where she is "luminous and yielding as she plays quietly against James Dean's raw intensity" (320). But it was the insistence on being "at odds" that Brantley saw in Harris that was perhaps her most significant contribution.

Beyond Hirsch, little of the scholarship on Julie Harris identifies her as a Method actor. Yet Harris was a committed Actors Studio member, appearing in the Studio's first Broadway production, *Sundown Beach*, as a young war bride in 1948 and again their 1963 production of June Havoc's *Marathon '33* as a Depression-era vaudevillian fallen on hard times.[18] She gravitated to the ensemble values of the Studio, and she regularly attended sessions and performed scenes. Harris associated the Method with a democratization of performance values after World War II. She sought purposely, she said, not to cultivate the kind of worshipful adulation that stars like Katherine Cornell and Laurence Olivier had enjoyed in the 1940s, remarking that "I think our generation wanted it to be more democratic. If we had the talent and the opportunity I don't think we would have become that kind of star. It was a little old-fashioned ... There was no place for kings and queens at the Actors Studio."[19] Of Strasberg and Kazan, she commented, "I loved them both as teachers, very exciting," and if she distinguished between them by calling Strasberg more classical and cerebral, and Kazan more contemporary, she nonetheless noted that at the end of the day "they both wanted the same thing from the result of the acting, which was truth and reality and a certain amount of theatricality." She mentions the importance of the improvisations and exercises at the Studio to the development of her craft, as well as the value of the movement classes offered by Anna Sokolow. The need for an actor to be able to play a wide range of roles, and to resist being typecast, was a value that had been instilled in Harris by her work at the Actors Studio, where members were frequently encouraged to develop the parts of their craft that did not come easily to them. But as her work in *The Member of the Wedding* (and later, in *Reflections in a Golden Eye*) suggests, Harris did not always use the Method to create performances of absorptive naturalism that are so often associated with Method acting. And in addition to her interest in anti-naturalistic styles of film acting, Harris's performances of the 1950s and beyond show a deep commitment to investigating questions of desire and protesting against the roles assigned to women.

In Robert Wise's *The Haunting* (1962), Harris plays Eleanor Lance, the protagonist of Shirley Jackson's novel *The Haunting of Hill House* (1959), a character whom Emily Nussbaum has described as "a true-blue weirdo. She's Emily Dickinson, she's Jane Eyre—a dangerously needy oddball, but also one who's funny, observant, and full of rage." "She's a mess," Nussbaum continues, "but she's a specific mess," appreciating the character's "granular eccentricity."[20] Jackson's novel—which has been recognized by literary critics for its fiercely satirical turning of the Gothic genre to the task of conveying the experience of a woman's suffocation by post-war domesticity—was adapted for the screen by Wise and is considered both a horror classic and a milestone in queer cinema for its inclusion of a lesbian character (Theodora, played by Claire Bloom). Its experimentalism and feminism may be apparent now, but *The Haunting*'s original reception was a more uncertain affair. Pauline Kael described what she perceived as the hostility of the audience at the screening she attended, and postulated that it was the film's psychological and restrained approach to the genre, its shortness of gore, that displeased the audience, writing that "In their terms, they were cheated. Nothing happened. And of course they missed what was happening all along." Some measure of the hostility Kael witnessed may also have come from the film's deep plunge into the psyche of a woman who feels invisible and marginalized and is suffering a breakdown after 11 years of caring for her mother. Harris's performance, as Richard Armstrong has noted in *The Rough Guide to Film*, has "an intensity that is frightening in itself."[21]

As the film opens, an agitated Eleanor pleads with her sister's husband for the use of the car so that she can travel to Hill House, where she has been selected to participate in "psychic research" under the direction of a professor named Dr. Markway (Figure 3.4). Eleanor, we soon learn, is suffering from caregiver fatigue. While her breakdown might be absorbed into a psychoanalytic reading, the opening scene in the film underlines Eleanor's own certainty that her crisis has social and economic sources: she draws attention to the uncompensated labor she has performed and her crucial contributions, as an unmarried sister, to the family's finances. Resisting her sister's claim to control her mother's inheritance because she is married and has children, Eleanor perches on the edge of the family couch (that also serves as her bed) neatly dressed in pumps, her hair pulled back in a bun. Though her dress and manner are those of an adult, her tone and request are adolescent: "You've just got to let me have the car. There's no other way of getting there and I'm expected." The family has clearly cast her as neurotic, and her niece chants "Auntie Nell is blinking! Auntie Nell is blinking!" in response to one of her nervous ticks. Her brother-in-law counsels her, "Calm down, Eleanor." But her request to use the car is a reasonable one: as she repeats more than once in the film, it's "half mine." She also challenges her brother's diagnosis of her hysteria, asking

FIGURE 3.4 Julie Harris as Eleanor Lance pleads with her family for the use of the car in Robert Wise's *The Haunting* (1962).

98 Protest Performances

"Why shouldn't I be nervous? My first chance at a vacation in all my life, and you won't let me take it?" As Harris smashes her hand into a pillow, she delivers a visual retort that underscores her suppressed rage. Eleanor's brother-in-law comments that her demand to leave their family home is so urgent that it seems like "a jail break." She explodes at her family, "Get out! Get out all of you! You happen to be in my bedroom and I pay a good part of your rent for it!" When she takes the car against family orders, she thinks to herself in voiceover: "At last I am going someplace where I am expected and where I am being given shelter, and I shall never have to come back. I hope, I hope, I hope this is what I've been waiting for all my life. I'm going, I'm really going, I'm finally taking a step." And when she reaches Hill House, she confesses to the leader of psychic research, "I must be more tired than I thought. My mother died two months ago," as she touches her forehead and eyes in gestures of fatigue. And she later confesses, "For the past eleven years, I've been walled up alive." Across the course of her career, Harris contributed many portraits of characters "walled up alive."

"Actress and Star"? Geraldine Page

I opened this chapter with a discussion of *All About Eve*, a 1950 film that proposed a bitter rivalry between the old kind of star and the new kind of actor. The decade closed with a play by Tennessee Williams that fused the two: a play in which a Method actor, Geraldine Page, was cast as Alexandra del Lago, a Hollywood star fearing that her career may be over because of her age.[22] The characters in Tennessee Williams's *Sweet Bird of Youth*—particularly Chance Wayne, the young hustler seeking to exploit del Lago, vocalize some of the decade's harsher verdicts on the older actress, but the play also responds to them forcefully and ends by asserting the rights and power of the great performer at any age. *Sweet Bird of Youth* (1959) was first directed by Elia Kazan on Broadway, and then adapted to film by

FIGURE 3.5 Geraldine Page as Alexandra del Lago asserting the rights of the female actor in Hollywood.

Richard Brooks (1962), with Page playing the lead in both versions. Alexandra del Lago, fatigued by Hollywood's age hysteria, flees from Los Angeles to Florida after the release of her latest film, which she believes has been a flop. In a flashback to the filming of the supposed debacle, we are given a glimpse of the degradations that have led her to lose confidence and forsake her career. The flashback begins with a close-up of a movie camera, with a man's hand positioned to adjust it. Del Lago descends a staircase in period dress, leaning over the railings to have her cigarette lit by an actor in uniform standing below. Then the film cuts suddenly to the director who says "no, no" and cringes over the way the light is falling on her neck. "I told you I want a shadow right here on her neck," the director tells the lighting crew. As the lighting is adjusted, he leans patronizingly over to del Lago to say "it's not your fault, sweetie. Terrific!" as she examines herself in her compact mirror anxiously. To communicate del Lago's insecurity, Page often touches her neck, as though to express her anxiety about its preservation. And in this scene we hear her speaking in voiceover, describing her sense of the predatory nature of the camera: "the camera dollies in, and you, your head, your face, are caught in the frame…and all your terrible history screams while you smile."

When she returns to this scene in memory, she explains to her gigolo companion, Chance Wayne (played by Paul Newman), that her capacities as an actor and Hollywood's objectifications are at odds: "Oh, I had it. I had the will and the talent to go with it. But the camera—the camera doesn't know how to lie." She continues: "There is a thing, god help us, called a close-up." Del Lago is worried that she looks too old for the character she is playing. And for a time, the audience is led to believe that she is right: that del Lago is the has-been she believes herself to be as she flops in a hotel bed, drinks, smokes hashish, dons an oxygen mask, receives massages, and otherwise tries a variety of strategies to keep herself afloat. But even during this period of abjection, she has not entirely forgotten who she is or the career she has built. In one scene, as Chance languishes on the floor trying to bully her into using her clout to get him an acting contract, she towers over him, asking "Do you have any talent?" and warning him that "Baby, there is no easy way to the top." Williams's narrative asserts the rights of the female actor at any age even more strongly when del Lago receives a phone call from Walter Winchell that delivers the unexpected news that her performance has in fact been acclaimed as a triumphant comeback. As del Lago listens to Winchell's encomium and the news that she is now in demand again, she delivers lines that express her incredulity: "They want me? They really want me? For what part?" As Chance tries to insert himself into the conversation with Winchell, demanding that she tout him as her new discovery, she pushes him away with her foot as she continues her incredulous reactions: "The New Yorker praised it? It's broken box office records?" From the debauchery of her hotel room, she rises from the ashes, her confidence restored, to defend herself as an artist of worth. It is at this moment of her triumph that Chance becomes enraged by her success and his own lack of it, and tries to humiliate her by reminding her of her age. He drags her to the mirror,

FIGURE 3.6 Opening credits of Richard Brooks's *Sweet Bird of Youth*, "Starring Paul Newman."

trying to shame her in the way that the director did. "What do you see?" he asks her violently, as he confronts her with her image. But his words have no power over her: she stretches her arms out to the mirror, affirming her identity: "I see me. Alexandra del Lago—artist and star." By asserting her right to stay in the spotlight, and allowing her a box office triumph, Williams's script asserts the ageless relevance of the actress (Figure 3.5).

As she brushes Chance off as both lover and chauffeur, she tells him: "I climbed up alone, and I will climb back alone—back to where I belong. I will live alone and I will work alone." As a final salvo, she refers to Hollywood as a "gold-plated hell," even in the wake of her triumphant comeback. In this scene, two Actors Studio members, and one of the studio's definitive playwrights, work together to dramatize resistance to the hegemony of the male Method actor in the cultural imagination, and to the misogynist discourse of the aging female star, and in doing so clear a space for the female Method actor like Page to occupy the screen.

But ironies compound. The plot of *Sweet Bird of Youth* asserts the dominance of the actress, yet it is Newman who has top billing in the film's credits (Figure 3.6). And these credits are delightfully undermined. First we see the words "Starring Paul Newman," and a shot of what appears to be the solo male Method star cruising down the highway oozing autonomous cool—but then, in the next shot, as Geraldine Page's name appears with second billing, she rises from the back seat (Figure 3.7) of the car that Newman is driving. In fact it is her car, and he is her chauffeur. Wielding a bottle of liquor, she addresses him: "Hey, whoever you are…." The insouciance of her opening address to Chance suggests that the film is self-aware that its theme—an assertion of the actress's perpetual relevance—comes at the end of a decade in which the male Method actor has ascended to the centrality that the female star once held in Hollywood as the object of the gaze and the definitive star type. Despite Newman's star billing, *Variety*'s reviewer asserted

FIGURE 3.7 Geraldine Page as Alexandra del Lago rises from the back seat of her car to address Paul Newman's Chance Wayne: "Hey, whoever you are…."

that "this is Page's picture. She draws the best, wittiest, and most acid lines and the most colorful character and what she does with this parley is a lesson in the art of acting."[23] Even Bosley Crowther, though somewhat horrified by the sexual appetite and debauchery Page showed in the role, was won over by her performance to the extent that he thought she was too good for the film:

> Miss Page's drunken Hollywood has-been—she's a shatteringly frightful grotesque, clawing the walls and the bare shoulders of her male companion with equal wild distress. Miss Page makes her a brilliant lot of fiendish femininity….But what's she doing in this provincial mess? Mr. Williams has dragged her into it…[24]

Crowther notices the sexual hunger and ambition of Page's performance, as well as her loose and defiant performance style, which, like Harris's in *The Member of the Wedding*, might be seen as betraying the camera rather than being betrayed by it. Page's performance brilliantly walks the line between sincerity and aging-actress camp in a way that allows her to both cultivate sympathy for her heroine and make some fun of her plight (sometimes, she speaks with elevated elocution, while at other times she participates in the more guttural and vernacular speech associated with Method acting). But Page's strongest challenge to the decorum of screen acting may be her hostility to the camera itself. Even as a voice in the film announces that "Alexandra del Lago is the sex symbol of America," we see Page's refusal to perform this kind of star quality in *Sweet Bird of Youth*. She first appears wearing dark sunglasses, avoiding making eye contact with the camera. For much of the time she is on screen, her mascara is smudged and at one point in the film, she pulls off her fake eyelashes, conspicuously documenting her discarding of a certain kind of film beauty. We see her fall over tables and collapse in bars due to drunkenness—the kind of performance of dishevelment usually reserved for male Method actors. She ignores the camera, much in the way that actors at the Moscow Art Theatre turned their backs to play scenes. Just as del Lago meets the camera on her own terms, so too does Page, with a performance that thematizes her refusal to play by the rules of Hollywood.

Notes

1. Winters had developed an admiration for Harris after being present at the opening night of Carson McCullers's *The Member of the Wedding*: she called the performances given by Harris and Ethel Waters "a pinnacle of theater acting" (100).
2. Winters, Shelley. *Shelley II: The Middle of my Century* (New York: Simon and Schuster, 1989), 66.
3. Ty Burr, "*EW* Remembers Shelley Winters," *Entertainment Weekly* (20 January 2006); Philip Kemp, *Sight & Sound* 17.3 (March 2007).
4. James Morrison, "Shelley Winters: Camp, Abjection, and the Aging Star," *Hollywood Reborn: Movie Stars of the 1970s*, ed. James Morrison (New Brunswick: Rutgers University Press, 2010), 120–137, 121.
5. Harris remarked in later years on how disappointed she was that due to censorship the film could not address feminist issues more squarely: "Well, there again, the year that film was made they were trying to skirt the abortion issue and get a seal of approval from the censor, so they made a lot of compromises … We didn't do the real story" (Margaret Herrick Library, folder 183, SMU collection of Ronald L. Davis oral histories on the performing arts, transcript of interview by Ronald L. Davis with Julie Harris, taped at the Adolphus Hotel in Dallas, February 10, 1989, 23–24). Though Harris felt that the filmmakers had compromised too far, Bosley Crowther opined that they had not compromised enough when he wrote that "the capstone of cheap contrivance and tasteless indelicacy" in the film is "a climactic joke about a postponed abortion and what turns out to be a false pregnancy. It was undoubtedly because of this improvisation that the film has been denied a Production Code seal," Bosley Crowther, August 9, 1955, New York Times, *Screen: I Am a Camera*.
6. Walter Kerr, *Journey to the Center of the Theatre*. New York: Knopf, 1979, 222.
7. Ben Brantley, "Luminous Julie Harris, Close Up and Afar," *The New York Times*, August 25, 2013. Accessed 26 January 2020: www.nytimes.com/2013/08/26/theater/luminous-julie-harris-close-up-and-afar.html
8. Bosley Crowther, "Stanley Kramer's Production of 'The Member of the Wedding' has Preview at Sutton," *New York Times*, December 31, 1952.
9. Patricia White, *Uninvited*, xii. White also devotes a chapter of the book to the meanings of Harris's performance as a "latent, not necessarily, not yet, lesbian" in *The Haunting*, arguing that the film's use of the Gothic genre's key epistemological question "Is it really there?" becomes a trope for lesbian desire in Hollywood cinema. White, *Uninvited*, 88.
10. Jack Halberstam, *Female Masculinity*. Durham: Duke UP, 1998, 7, 189, 191–2.
11. Hilton Als, "Post-script: Julie Harris," *The New Yorker*, August 25, 2013.
12. Rachel Walerstein, "'It Just Don't Do' (What You Think it Does): The Periperformative Possibilities of Julie Harris's Face," *The Journal of the Midwest Modern Language Association* 51.1 (2018), 25–53.
13. Nicole Seymour, "Somatic Syntax: Replotting the Developmental Narrative in Carson McCullers's *The Member of the Wedding*," *Studies in the Novel* 41.3 (2009), 293–313.

14 "Julie Harris: Fame Touches a Skinny, Intent Actress whose feet get hot when she's nervous," Robert Wallace, *Life*, April 7, 1952, 156.
15 Allen Churchill, "The New First Lady of the Theatre," *Cosmopolitan* 1952, 22.
16 Hedda Hopper, "Julie Harris Not Only "Member of Wedding" but Pixie of Theatre," Hedda Hopper., *L.A. Times*, August 24, 1952, 1-12, Column 1.
17 *Miami Herald*, "Joan of Arc in Jeans," 1955.
18 Howard Taubman lauded Harris's performance in *Marathon '33* as a former vaudevillian reduced to performing in a Depression-era dance marathon (a character based on playwright June Havoc's own experiences), writing that Harris "has rarely given a more convincing performance": "she is fighting for her dignity courageously"; "she is trusting and then savage" as "the lost, ardent creature who has stumbled into the dregs of show business and who nevertheless keeps her heart pure and her ambitions high" (Howard Taubman, "Julie Harris in June Havoc's Realistic *Marathon '33*, *New York Times*, December 23, 1963, 20).
19 Margaret Herrick Library, folder 183, SMU collection of Ronald L. Davis oral histories on the performing arts, transcript of interview by Ronald L. Davis with Julie Harris, taped at the Adolphus Hotel in Dallas, February 10, 1989.
20 Emily Nussbaum, "Netflix's Soul-Dead Version of 'The Haunting of Hill House'," *The New Yorker*, November 12, 2018.
21 Richard Armstrong, *The Rough Guide to Film*, p. 609.
22 The part of del Lago was written for Tallulah Bankhead, who played it in the Florida tryout, and the character also bears resemblances to stars like Joan Crawford, Bette Davis, and Gloria Swanson in the 1950s.
23 *Variety* staff review of *Sweet Bird of Youth*, 31 December 1961. Accessed online 26 January 2020 https://variety.com/1961/film/reviews/sweet-bird-of-youth-2-1200420100.
24 Bosley Crowther, "Sweet Bird of Youth," *The New York Times*, 29 March 1962, 28.

4
JANE FONDA
Method Auteur

As a New Hollywood ingenue, French New Wave sex symbol, and actor-producer of successful and significant films including *Coming Home* (1978), *The China Syndrome* (1979), *9 to 5* (1980), and *On Golden Pond* (1981), Jane Fonda's career has been long, accomplished, and diverse. She has been nominated for Academy Awards for Best Actress seven times and won twice (for *Klute* (1971) and *Coming Home* (1979)). She is also well-known for her political activism on behalf of a variety of progressive causes. In 2005 she co-founded the Women's Media Center (with Gloria Steinem and Robin Morgan), an organization that seeks "to raise the visibility, viability and decision-making power of women and girls in media … ensuring that their stories get told and their voices are heard."[1] Most recently, she has emerged as a climate activist, Netflix star, and venerated film industry elder.[2] Over the course of six decades, Fonda's film career and public life have often reflected, represented, and interpreted the transformations in American women's lives. In 2018 she was the subject of a documentary, Susan Lacy's *Jane Fonda in Five Acts*, which highlighted her unique achievements as an actor, producer, public figure, and activist.

Fonda is also a major figure in the history of Method acting, one whose film work has often been concerned with remaking that tradition on feminist terms. She has frequently chosen roles that allow her both to assert her identity as a Method actor and also to expand the Method's feminist insight and potential. And she has engaged and transformed the Method's recurring themes and values in a variety of ways, including undertaking a feminist reorientation of the Method's relationship to psychoanalysis, moving the figure of the veteran's wife to center stage, making explicit the politics of Method women's stylistic refusal of affect and emotional display, and producing her own films, which foreground questions of women's labor and representation.

In her autobiography *My Life So Far* (2005), Fonda describes her first encounter with Method acting as a turning point in her life. Fonda met Lee Strasberg in Los Angeles, and then began taking private classes with him in New York. When she performed for the first time before her fellow students, she felt that

> in that moment my life did a flip-flop, though I didn't understand at the time why it had such a powerful effect on me. When I walked outside after the class, the city felt different, as if I now owned a piece of it. I went to bed that night with my heart racing, and when I woke up the next morning I knew why I was alive, what I wanted to do.
>
> *(121)*

Method acting helped Fonda to gain a sense of artistic vocation and authority. She explains that her father (Henry Fonda, the iconic actor venerated for his roles in films like *The Grapes of Wrath* and *12 Angry Men*) thought emotions were "disgusting" and that in her family and immediate social circle she was "unaccustomed to people expressing themselves, even to the point of looking ridiculous" (121). She emphasizes that the permission the Method and its preparation practices gave her simply to have and to reveal feelings was liberating in itself. Fonda clarifies that this prohibition on feeling had not been local to her household, but was a broader cultural imperative: "Sally Field captured what acting did for girls like us who grew up in the fifties when she said, 'I guess it was a way for me to express all the feelings that I had in some acceptable terms'" (122). Acting in the context of Strasberg's New York classes allowed Fonda to "probe new parts of myself—sorrow, anger, joy—and feel safe exposing them. I felt I was appreciated for the fullness of my self rather than some 'good girl's' proper façade" (122). The young Fonda also appreciated the intellectual inquiry that the Actors Studio fostered, including long hours "engaged in endless discussion, being asked for and giving opinions" (122).

But while Fonda credits the Method with having been vital to her career, she was never an unthinking acolyte of Strasberg. If we study the course of her career, we can recognize a conscious feminist re-making of the Method. Sharing the Method's investment in realism, but expanding the purview of that realism by attending to women's lives, the peace movement, and other contemporary social themes, Fonda consistently sought to play multi-dimensional, challenging female characters in leading roles, and as she gained more control over her film appearances, she was able to express herself in ever more visible ways as a feminist interpreter of the Method.

In Paolo Sorrentino's *Youth* (2015), Fonda seems to cast a retrospective glance at her own career when she plays Method movie star Brenda Morel in a brief cameo that resembles the protesting performances I considered in my third chapter. In Sorrentino's film, Fonda has just one scene. *Youth* focuses primarily on the artistic neuroses of male characters, especially that of a creatively blocked director played by Fonda's fellow Method actor Harvey Keitel. But though her role is small, it is powerful, and it closely resembles Shelley Winters's explosion of artistic frustration as Dixie Evans in *The Big Knife*. In Fonda's scene in *Youth,* a story of male artistic discontent is challenged by an embedded feminist critique. In Brenda Morel, Fonda plays a character who is in part biographical. Like Fonda, Morel was a member of the Actors Studio, has been a star for decades, and wields great power in Hollywood. But unlike Fonda, she is purely an actor, rather than an actor-producer. Sorrentino's characterization of Morel vacillates between depicting her as a castrating antagonist and a much-needed reality check for Keitel's character, Mick Boyle, who is struggling to get his latest film off the ground. Fonda's appearance provides a forceful corrective to the film's fragile male artistic egos.

In *Youth*, Morel's plot function is simple: to ring the death knell of Mick's film by withdrawing from it. At first he thinks she is quitting because her vanity is wounded by the quasi-autobiographical role he has scripted for her as "ugly, feeble, a pale shadow of [her] former beauty." But Morel is in fact offended by the very suggestion that her ego would be so fragile as to compromise her artistry, and she responds with a string of profanities, before divulging her true motive for the visit: she has dropped out of his film in favor of a TV series in which she will be playing "an alcoholic grandmother who's had a serious stroke. A character with real balls." Not only does she prefer this lively role as a tough survivor to Mick's offer to embody "a pale shadow" of her former self, but doing so will also bring in the money she needs to support her family. Mick tries to shame her with appeals to artistic prestige—"Television's shit!," he wails—but she responds that she is actually saving him by putting a stop to his film: "The real shit is this film of yours, Mick. I understand cinema, you know I do. You're the one who doesn't understand it anymore. Because you're old, you're tired, you don't know how to see the world anymore ... you risk nullifying all the beautiful films you've already made." In her brief cameo, Fonda's character asserts her industry clout, talent, work ethic, the autonomy of her body, and the authority of her critical judgment: it is a one-woman feminist Method tour-de-force.[3] It is also a powerful reminder of the strength with which Fonda has engaged and repurposed the central themes and techniques of the Method. In what follows, I explore these engagements across her career, beginning with the tradition's most fraught affiliation from a feminist perspective, its relationship to psychoanalysis.

Fonda and Psychoanalysis

As I mentioned in the Introduction and Chapter 1, most feminist critics of the Method have understood Method acting as being primarily characterized by its investment in psychoanalysis, which they have often viewed as an inevitably misogynistic practice. I have mentioned earlier, too, that this close focus on the Method's psychoanalytic investments can sometimes obscure the sociological concerns that drove the work of Method women—their industry critiques, their resistance to normative gender roles, and their broader concern for social justice. But even if psychoanalysis was not their sole interest nor the only thing they took away from their immersion in the Method, it is also important to recognize the ways in which Method women were as critically engaged and resourceful in their relationship to Freud as their feminist contemporaries in other disciplines.[4] Jane Fonda's career provides an exemplary model of the ways in which feminist Method actors interrogated and revised psychoanalysis, testing its potential to be transformed to feminist uses.

Fonda began her career during the great midcentury boom in psychoanalysis, as Freud's ideas and those of his interpreters made their way into the American mainstream and the therapeutic profession expanded. Her status as the daughter of a famous father meant that she was sometimes typecast as a character with "daddy issues": in *Period of Adjustment* (1962), for instance, her character calls her father in tears from her honeymoon, and in *The Chapman Report* (1962), she is told by a sexologist that "you've got to break away from all this, and your father—you can't go on being daddy's little girl." In her earliest roles, the arc of her performance is generally the development of her character from identification as her father's daughter to identification as her husband's wife, after working through some Freudian bumps and hang-ups along the way. And while we might glean in these performances occasional flickers of resistance, including a sincerity that sometimes seems to verge on camp, in general the young Fonda externally complies with the demands of these films' scripts. As the virginal young woman coming to the city to gain experience in Peter Tewksbury's *Sunday in New York* (1963), and as Robert Redford's screwball hippie spouse in Gene Saks's *Barefoot in the Park* (1967), Fonda played naïve, idealistic, "repressed" but sexually curious, and slightly risible types—it was not always certain if she was the source or the butt of the joke. In the late 1960s Fonda moved to France to make films with New Wave director Roger Vadim, garnering comparisons to another of Vadim's frequent collaborators, Brigitte Bardot. This phase of her career culminated in Vadim's *Barbarella* (1968), a camp classic science fiction movie in which she plays a Barbie doll-like superwoman from the future.

In George Cukor's *The Chapman Report* (1962), a film based on Irving Wallace's novel (which was inspired in turn by the Kinsey Reports), four women's lives become case studies for a visiting researcher with a Freudian bent. Shelley Winters plays a middle-aged wife having an affair with her local community theatre director. Glynis Johns plays a bohemian intellectual who falls for a sporty young stud, while Claire Bloom is cast as a "nymphomaniac," and Fonda as "frigid," two poles of female sexuality according to the clinical parlance of the day. Fonda's character Kathleen Barclay is a wealthy young widow. She attends a lecture by the Kinseyesque sexologist, George C. Chapman, who announces his coolly detached, scientific approach. He tells his female audience that "four out of five women" have "too little knowledge of sexuality," and that "the subject of sex remains under the table—back room, back street. Suppressed, unknown, and always indecent." He tries to recruit the women to participate in his study by explaining that by becoming "fact-finders," and not "appraising, assessing" their sexuality in moral terms, they will be liberated "from needless repression and guilt." Consenting to aid in this research, Fonda's Kathleen goes to Chapman's office where she is interviewed anonymously, behind a screen, by Chapman's assistant Radford.

Shortly before her visit, we learn from a flashback that she is struggling to make sense of her sexual history. We are shown a scene in which she is unable to have sex with her husband, and then the stony discussion in which he calls her a "femme de glace" ("woman of ice") and cruelly suggests that there's nothing that can be done to help her. Skipping back to the present, Kathleen arrives for her interview arrayed in virginal white, and at first seems to submit calmly to the questions from Radford about her sexual history. However, when he turns to the matter of whether she enjoyed sex with her husband, she becomes distraught. When he presses for details on "how much time was devoted" to "preliminary sex play," she at first responds defensively—"a long time!" to which he follows up, "How long?" at which point she says "what?" confusedly and scrambles under the table to rescue a cigarette she has dropped. A later-career Fonda would likely have played this scene more definitively as feminist comedy—feigned shock at the idea of men understanding foreplay—but in this early film she plays it more earnestly, becoming visibly distressed, crying, and fleeing the interview room in consternation. The presence of such emotional earnestness in a comedy of manners led one reviewer to remark that "Jane Fonda, as the frigid young widow, is oddly out of place."[5] On her next meeting with Radford (who has broken with the compact of scientific anonymity by coming to her house, and who will become her love interest), she accuses him of traumatizing her and insists, "I'm not a pathological case."

Tonally, *The Chapman Report* seems to waver between finding sex funny and light on the one hand, and giving hints of a troubling culture of misogyny and sexual violence on the other. These more troubling glimpses undercut Chapman's assurances about the future of sexual liberation. This becomes clearest when Claire Bloom's "nymphomaniac" character is raped, and Fonda's character comes to her assistance, a feminist plot event that shifts the emphasis from Bloom's supposed pathology onto her assailant's crime. *The Chapman Report* is filmed like a lush comedy, but its visual style ultimately cannot contain its unsettling undertones, and at the end we find a rather perplexing attempt to reconcile sexology's findings with conventional marriage (Fonda falls in love with Radford, the sexologist who interviewed her, as he comes to embrace the value of traditional concepts of romantic love). While the film cannot be said to have a decisively feminist attitude, it does contain hints of defiance and stirring consciousness. Shelley Winters's character, describing her sense of entrapment in her marriage, quotes Madame Bovary's feeling that "the future was a dark corridor," and Fonda's Kathleen, who has been put in charge of revising her deceased husband's memoir (he was a military hero), says "I want to re-write everything" but admits that "it's hard when you're used to telling a story in a certain way…it's so hard to tell that same story in a different way," a line that registers both Kathleen's desire to correct her husband's views and to break free of limiting cultural scripts, but also foreshadows her difficulty in identifying a new story beyond remarriage.

The second—and much higher-profile—Fonda performance which requires mention as a milestone of her early career was her role as the title comic book character Barbarella in the 1968 science fiction film. The aesthetic of Roger Vadim's *Barbarella*'s could not be further removed from the realist terrain of the Method: it is self-consciously tacky and campy, reveling in its pulpy performances, cheap costumes, and bad special effects. In one particularly notorious scene, Fonda's Barbarella is enclosed in a contraption called the Excessive Pleasure machine (Figure 4.1), which has been designed to make her have orgasms until she dies. In this scarcely disguised pornscape, the film's villain pushes Barbarella ever closer to orgasm by playing an organ (pun intended?) that is attached to the bottom of the machine, while close-ups of Fonda's face show her in mounting, glamorously coiffed ecstasy. The Excessive Pleasure machine has been designed to kill her, but because she is a superhero, she burns it out, proving herself capable of attaining greater and greater heights of pleasure as the machine' starts to fizz and burn around her. From the "frigid" wife of *The Chapman Report* to the unconsenting and multi-orgasmic Barbarella, Fonda's performances in the 1960s shuttled between the poles of vulgar Freudian lingo. But her appearance in *Barbarella* seems to have been a final straw, instigating in Fonda a commitment to presenting female psychology and sexuality in a different way, one grounded in the realist values of the Method as well as the insights of second-wave feminism.

Fonda's rebellion began in 1971, when she repudiated her passive, yielding, and highly sexualized image, cut her hair, and emerged in Alan J. Pakula's *Klute* as a feminist anti-hero. From that time, Fonda would subject the misogynist tropes

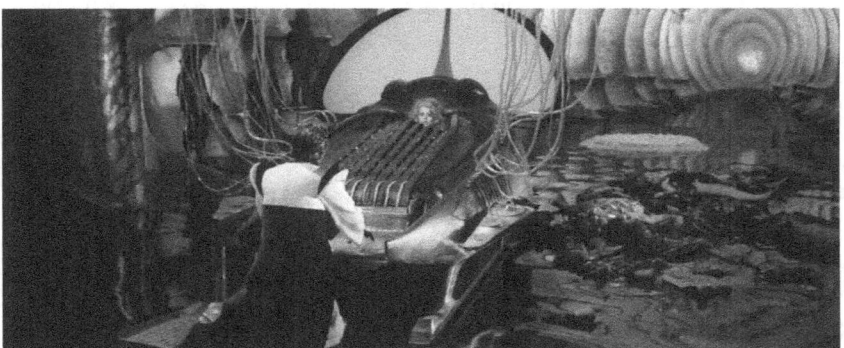

FIGURE 4.1 Jane Fonda in the Excessive Pleasure Machine in Roger Vadim's *Barbarella* (1968).

of her earlier career to visible scrutiny and opposition. This change coincided with her political radicalization and her increasingly public commitments to the peace movement, feminism, anti-racism, labor and other civil rights and left-wing struggles. It was at this moment that Fonda broke away from roles of objectification and began to forge her own path as a politically engaged feminist Method actor. A critique of psychoanalysis was a significant strand of Fonda's burgeoning feminism, and *Klute* provided her first opportunity for a searching inquiry into the authority of Freud.

Klute is a hard-boiled drama, the first film in what would become known as Pakula's "Paranoia Trilogy" (which also features *The Parallax View* (1974) and *All the President's Men* (1976)). *Klute* was an early example of the wave of neo-noirs beginning in the 1970s that foregrounded urban crime and took an interest in "deviance" with an emphasis on Foucauldian ideas of surveillance and social control (others included Scorsese's *Taxi Driver* (1976) and William Friedkin's *Cruising* (1980)). In *Klute*, Fonda plays Bree Daniels, a sex worker who is also a model and aspiring actor. She is drawn into an investigation while helping the detective Klute, who is played by Donald Sutherland, to capture the murderer of one of her colleagues. As they pursue the killer, a process that involves exposing Bree to great danger as a kind of bait, Bree and Klute become romantically involved. Though *Klute* is named for Sutherland's character, it was Fonda's performance—tough, intellectual, skeptical—that sparked greatest interest among audiences and critics. *Klute* is remembered as a breakthrough film for her. In perhaps its best-remembered scene, Fonda as Bree is in the middle of having sex with a client, faking an orgasm while subtly looking at her watch behind his back. Bree's faked orgasm might be read as a protest against Barbarella's forced ones, as well as a declaration of a change in point of view, one in which women's experiences of and attitudes about sex matter.

Related to both its murder plot and its politics of female orgasm, *Klute* features what we might call an investigation into the uses and limits of psychoanalysis. Through the scenes that Fonda improvised and that depict Bree in her therapist's office, *Klute* mounts a substantive challenge to psychoanalysis, and also, through Bree's experiences as a struggling actor, to the permeation of psychoanalysis into acting. In *Klute*, the language of needing to cast off "repression," which had been dispensed so confidently by the sex researchers of *The Chapman Report*, is subjected to intense scrutiny and critique. *Klute*—and Fonda's performance in it—suggest that very serious consequences could follow from unleashing libidos in a culture before addressing that culture's inherent misogyny.

In scenes with her rarely speaking therapist, Bree examines her supposed neuroses. Bobbie Goldstone, who reviewed the film in 1971 for the feminist journal *Off Our Backs*, thought that it affirmed the Freudian perspectives it explored, because it suggested that Bree had become a sex worker not "because of economic need or lack of choice but rather because of her inability to form deep personal relationships" and that the film viewed sex work as "an illness curable through a combination of analysis and the right man's love."[6] But I would argue that in *Klute*, and particularly in Fonda's improvised therapy scenes, we find not only a more skeptical approach to psychoanalysis but also a pronounced sociological view of sex work. Fonda was deeply involved in the development of the therapy scenes, and even before filming began, she requested that these scenes be filmed last, when she felt that she would have the most insight into Bree's character. The role of the therapist went to Fonda's fellow Method actor Vivian Nathan.[7] Fonda improvised her scenes with Nathan, and her approach to psychoanalysis shows a mixture of resistance and curiosity, as well as an effort to pursue a feminist version of the process.

The initial scene between Bree and Nathan's character (who is described in the script only as "Psychiatrist") opens with a gesture of resistance. The first thing Bree says is, "I'm not going to be able to come back any more," to which Nathan's character responds, with therapeutic neutrality, "Oh, I'm sorry," and Bree follows up by saying "because I just can't afford it," but only after a pause long enough to have made it seem like something else was the cause, and in a tone that still makes it seem that something else might be the cause. The camera cuts to Nathan who asks, "Did I fail you, Bree?" Bree suddenly asks, "Why do I still want to trick?" and her therapist responds, "Did you think I had some magic potion? You'd come and tell me what your new problem was and I'd just take it away?" By the film's end, Bree seems just as mistrustful of the process as she was at the beginning: *Klute* ends equivocally with her saying again that she is quitting, this time because she is leaving town, even as she admits that she'll probably only be gone a week. Structurally, the scenes set in the therapist's office seem to hold out the promise of revealing Bree's interiority, but they ultimately refuse to do so, as Bree continues to resist the idea that it would be healing or safe to divulge her feelings about her experiences (it is worth noting the influence of the Anti-Psychiatry movement in addition to feminist critiques of psychoanalysis on *Klute*: Anti-Psychiatry raised questions about the discipline's complicity in oppression and social control).

Klute alternates between scenes that show Bree as a sex worker, actor, model, and therapy patient, suggesting that the boundaries between them are porous and their parallels are worthy of investigation. For instance, Bree wonders why she is so at ease "acting" as part of sex work (there, she calls herself "the best actor in the world") when she has such difficulty acting in theatrical scenes. And when Bree's therapist tells her that "I charge by the hour just like you do," she draws a provocative connection between therapy and sex work. In another blurring of boundaries, when Bree has an appointment with one of her clients, Mr. Goldfarb, a garment district manager, he does not hire her to have physical contact with him but rather to perform an elaborate theatrical scene (Mr. Goldfarb is played by an actor named Morris Strassberg).

A thread that seems to unite the film's interest in sex work, acting, and therapy is the question of how much self-investigation and self-revelation each respectively demands. Bree tells her therapist how easy she finds sex work because the self-expression required comes from her clients. Bree finds sex work easier than acting because it doesn't involve her own interiority, and she tells her therapist that "for an hour I'm the best actress in the world and the best fuck in the world." Her therapist probes: "Why do you say you're the best actress in the world? At that time," to which Bree responds, "Oh, because it's an act. That's what's nice about it. You don't have to feel anything. You don't have to care about anything. You don't have to like anybody. You just, uh, lead them by the ring of their nose." Bree's therapist tells her, "You're a successful call girl. You're not a successful…" leaving the word "actress" hanging in the air unsaid. While the comment seems intentionally provoking, it is true that Bree's attempts to progress professionally as an actor have been deeply demoralizing. In one scene, Bree attends an audition and performs a scene from George Bernard Shaw's *Saint Joan*. Here, she adopts an Irish accent like Siobhan McKenna's (who had made a success in the role on Broadway). The director for whom she is auditioning cuts her off mid-monologue and comments dismissively, "very interesting accent." In another scene, she meets with a prospective agent. In a series of questions that seem designed to belittle her, he asks what she's done, and whether it was "Broadway or Off-Broadway." "Well, I studied with George Tater," she tells him, "and appeared in two of his productions." He reminds her that these were "workshop productions" rather than professional ones, and that there were merely "a good place to begin." He then enquires about her ideas about acting, and particularly whether she places any priority on introspection: he asks her if she knows herself. Bree resists this invitation to interiorize. She brushes off his questions, responding that she knows herself "As much as anybody," and when he asks her if the process of acting allows her to know herself better, she responds, "I forget myself when I'm acting."

Why does *Klute* give so much attention to Bree's resistance to exposing or exploring "interiority?" It is certainly possible that the film is trying to suggest that Bree is not a good actor, and that she cannot hope to become one until she faces her own inner conflicts and demons. But the film could also be inviting an alternate interpretation more aligned with Bree's own attitudes: a critique of the fetishization of interiority and the sharing of personal affects with an audience. Everyone in the film who is pushing Bree to emote seems somehow sadistic. Also, the film's concern with themes of surveillance and the prevalence of violence against women suggests that it is not so much that Bree needs to look inward, but that she needs to retain her survivalist instincts by looking outward: she cannot afford therapy's invitations to let her guard down.

Bree prefers the role of sex worker to those of therapy patient and actor because as a sex worker she is the one inviting the release of revelations, emotions, and desires from others. Even though she resists it for herself, she sells to her clients a vision of release from what has been repressed. The film's critique of psychoanalysis is apparent in the fact that it is the most cynically proffered line of Bree to her client that speaks the cliché of overcoming repression: "I think the only way that any of us will ever be happy is to let it all hang out. Do it all." This is one of the opening lines of *Klute*: it plays on an audio tape of Bree speaking to a client.

In her autobiography, Fonda was clear about where the center of her character's experience lay for her, and why Bree was resistant to self-examination—because it obscured the violence enacted from outside. Instead of learning more about herself, Fonda's Bree becomes a feminist witness to the violence enacted upon women. In one scene, Bree hears a tape documenting the murder of her colleague by a john. Fonda prepared for this scene with research:

> At my request, Alan [J. Pakula] arranged for me to visit the actual city morgue, where I was allowed to look through the case files. What I saw remains with me to this day: hundreds and hundreds of color photographs of battered and bruised women who had been killed by husbands, lovers, johns. I had to excuse myself, go to the bathroom and throw up. It's not that I hadn't known that violence against women was widespread, but the reality of it had not dawned upon me until I saw face after face. This experience is what informed the scene toward the end of the film when Bree finds herself confronted by the murderer.[8]

In the crucial confrontation scene, Fonda listens to the tape that documents the murder, and while doing so, realizes that the murderer intends to kill her too. It is only in this scene—the scene of witnessing the violence against her colleague—that Bree emotes: she starts to cry. Fonda writes that she had not intended to have Bree cry in this scene, but that she was "overwhelmed" by sadness:

> It was sadness for my friend, sadness for all the women who are victims of men's rage, sadness at our vulnerability. It felt...inevitable. I began to cry—for all the victims. Soon the tears came from my nose as well as my eyes. For an audience, it didn't matter what caused the tears. What mattered was that it was so unexpected, and the unexpected reality brought an electricity to the scene that wouldn't have been there had I simply been "scared." Lee Strasberg once said, "Don't plan. Be."[9]

It is when faced with violence that Bree emotes, rather than in the therapeutic situation. In fact, revelations of the therapist's office are consistently withheld, especially in Bree's second scene with her therapist, in which she explains:

> I had tried to get away from a world that I had known, because I don't think it was very good for me. I found myself looking up its ass, and seeing people that I used to know and that I liked a lot, that were my friends, sort of, girls, and uh, they could have been me. I mean I know I'm not stupid...uh well I guess I just realized that...I don't really give a damn.

At this point she throws her hands up. The scene cuts from Bree to her therapist, then to an elevator with two men in it as we hear Bree's comment: "All I'd like to do is be faceless and bodiless and left alone." In her improvised therapy scenes, and in her performance throughout the film, Fonda engages in a complex engagement with psychoanalysis, one that invites us to consider sociological and political interpretations of Bree's situation as well as psychological ones. Fonda articulated this in her biography: "I understood then that my expanding consciousness as an activist could broaden my understanding of people and why they behave as they do—from (rhetorical, but it's true) a purely Freudian, individualist perspective to one that includes historical, societal, economic, and gender-based factors" (253). In other words, in *Klute* Fonda drew on but also critically questioned and subjected to feminist sociological analysis what she had learned from Strasberg about the value of psychoanalysis and self-revelation.

Fifteen years later, Norman Jewison's *Agnes of God* (1985) gave Fonda another chance to explore the potential of an explicitly feminist psychoanalysis, this time in the role of an analyst. As in *Klute*, she acted alongside a fellow Method actor—Anne Bancroft. In the film, a young nun, Agnes, has been charged with manslaughter after her newborn baby is found dead. Fonda plays Dr. Martha Livingston, the court-appointed psychiatrist responsible for determining whether Agnes is fit to stand trial. *Agnes of God* is an idea-driven film in which psychiatry is measured against religion as a route to understanding the world. Most reviewers felt that the film, like the play it was based on, was a bit schematic, with its characters being asked to serve as mouthpieces for abstract ideas. But reviewers also agreed that the performances of Fonda and Bancroft elevated the work beyond the limitations of the script. Their characters engage in a thoughtful dialogue and build a friendship as they grapple with how best to serve Agnes and the demands of justice, and with whether Agnes most urgently needs protection from the court system, psychiatry, or the church.

The film is set in Montreal at a religious community called Les Petites Soeurs de Mary Magdalene. When Fonda, a sophisticated professional woman, arrives at the convent smoking a cigarette (her version of Freud's cigar), the nun at the gate stares at her as though she is an unwelcome intruder. Dr. Livingston extinguishes her cigarette. When she is admitted to meet the Mother Superior (played by Bancroft), she finds a woman who once liked to smoke herself, and who ceremonially lights Fonda's next cigarette (throughout the film cigarettes become mutable symbols of feminism, religious illumination, skepticism, rebellion, intellectual and analytic power, sexual abuse, and erotic connection). The exchange between Fonda and Bancroft begins calmly as Fonda's character presents Bancroft's with a series of questions: "Who knew about Agnes's pregnancy?" "Who's the father?" "Why haven't you asked her?" Along the way, when it seems that Mother Miriam is leading her toward her own interpretation of what happened, and trying to establish the convent's innocence by insisting on a particular version of events,

Dr. Livingston stops her with the words, "I'm the doctor. I'm the one who is going to decide," a statement of her professional assurance and authority.

The character over whose fate they debate, Agnes (played by Meg Tilly) has lived in the convent all her life and was abused by her mother as a child. Dr. Livingston's work involves winning Agnes's trust, with the ultimate goal of determining whether she is fit for trial. On a walk through the convent grounds, they discuss the biology of child-bearing, and Dr. Livingston, in response to a question from Agnes about children, tells her "I can't have them anymore. I've stopped menstruating." But although Dr. Livingston represents the rational scientific view, the woman who is seemingly removed from the complications of maternity, she turns out to have her own stake in stories like Agnes's. She is a lapsed Catholic herself, we learn, and her sister died in a convent. We also learn that Fonda's character has had an abortion in the past. In a similar deepening of backstory, we learn that though Bancroft's character is a nun, she was once a wife and mother, well acquainted with the world beyond the convent's walls, and that Agnes is her niece. And she too, it turns out, is versed in the language of psychoanalysis. These details break down the binaries between sacred and secular, nun and psychiatrist, and suggest that each woman is imbricated in both worlds. After Dr. Livingston has interviewed Agnes, Mother Miriam tells her, "I know what you're thinking—she's a hysteric, pure and simple." Dr. Livingston concedes the diagnosis and defends its worth, and then accuses Mother Miriam of having an ulterior motive—protecting Agnes's religious faith. As the scene escalates, Dr. Livingston speaks bluntly against what she implies is Mother Miriam's effort to protect church ideology and hierarchy: "I'm fighting for this woman's life. Not some bloody bishop's."

The film includes sensationalistic, gripping, horror-genre-adjacent scenes that involve Dr. Livingston leading Agnes through reenactments of her previous traumas. These scenes appear partly like sessions of psychoanalysis, partly like exorcisms (and partly like the most unfavorable accounts of Strasberg's work with female actors). In one, Dr. Livingston takes on the role of Agnes's mother. The scene ends with Agnes and Dr. Livingston saying "I love you" to each other in a moment of mutual healing. Next, Dr. Livingston announces to Mother Miriam that she has gotten the court's permission to hypnotize Agnes. She wants Mother Miriam's permission as well. The two women deepen their engagement, with Bancroft telling Fonda, "I can smell an ex-Catholic a mile away," and Dr. Livingston sharing that "it wasn't sex" that drove her out of the church. "My sister died in a convent, and it's her voice I hear."

In one of the film's most memorable scenes, Dr. Livingston and Mother Miriam smoke a cigarette together on one of their walks around the convent grounds. Their conversation wends to the question of whether the saints might have smoked. They joke that the stuffy St. Paul would have smoked a pipe, but that Mary Magdalene would have chosen Virginia Slims—at which point Fonda archly remarks, "You've Come a Long Way, Baby," associating Mary Magdalene with the self-declared brand of women's liberation. In the same scene, Mother Miriam expresses her own religious doubts and wonders if there is still "room for miracles" in the modern world. The scene ends with an uncertain image as Fonda drops the lit cigarette on the ground and walks away without putting it out. Following this scene, the tension between psychiatrist and Mother Superior reaches a peak as Fonda accuses Miriam of using religious language to cover up sexual abuse in the convent: "you won't face the fact that she was raped, or seduced, or did the seducing." *Agnes of God* foregrounds two Method women in dialectical performance, testing the limits of both psychoanalysis and religion. Across the course of her career, Fonda moved from playing a character who was the docile subject of psychological research, to one who was a rebellious therapy client, to one who was herself a feminist psychoanalyst.

Remaking the Veteran's Wife

If *Klute* and *Agnes of God* gave Fonda opportunities to forge feminist responses to psychoanalysis, elsewhere she reckoned with another recurring aspect of the Method tradition—the figure of the veteran's wife whose template was the character of Stella Kowalski that Kim Hunter had played so memorably in *A Streetcar Named Desire*. Fonda first played a variation on this figure when she appeared in the film adaptation of Tennessee Williams's *Period of Adjustment*, directed by George Roy Hill (1962). Two decades later, Fonda would produce a film of her own, *Coming Home* (1978), which brought further feminist insight to the figure of the soldier's wife, as well as making her a figure of burgeoning anti-war consciousness. To study these two films is to recognize Fonda's crucial transformation of the trope of the veteran's wife.

In *Period of Adjustment*, Tennessee Williams revisits some of the themes of *A Streetcar Named Desire*. Both plays concern a veteran's attempts to return to civilian life. But beyond plot similarities, there are notable differences between the works. There is of course the difference of chronology—*Period of Adjustment* is set after the Korean War (1950–1953), not World War II. But perhaps more importantly, rather than the tragic drama of *Streetcar*, which treated mental illness, intimate partner violence, and sexual assault, *Period of Adjustment* considers the stresses and strains of a veteran's marriage in a more hopeful register, depicting relationships that seem possibly repairable. In fact, *Period of Adjustment* was billed as a comedy (Fonda was nominated for a Golden Globe for Best Actress in a Comedy or Musical). The sadistic Stanley Kowalski's counterpart in *Period of Adjustment* is George Haverstick, whose tantrums seem childlike and not physically threatening to others, nor is there a haunting, tragic character parallel to Blanche Dubois, a change that allows the veteran's wife Isabel to assume the leading female role.

Isabel, a student nurse, meets George in a hospital where he is being treated for a nervous condition developed during the war. The opening credit sequence shows light-hearted vignettes of the two falling in love. Fonda's Isabel appears

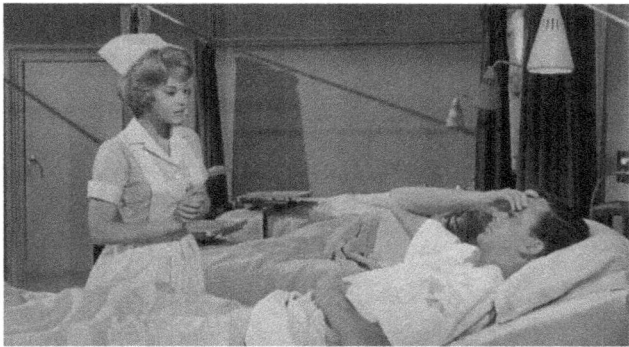

FIGURE 4.2 Fonda's Isabel comes when summoned to tend to her patient in George Roy Hill's *Period of Adjustment* (1962).

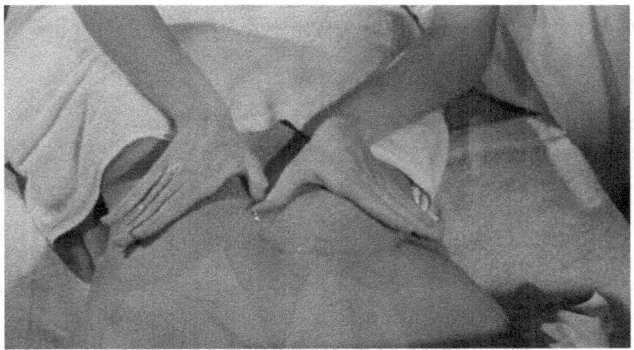

FIGURE 4.3 Isabel gives her patient a therapeutic back rub.

as a nubile fantasy version of a nurse. To syncopated, lively music, the first shot of the film shows George's hand reaching out for a glass of water on his bedside table. He accidentally knocks it over. After the spill he pushes his call button again and again to summon help. Fonda's Isabel immediately and gracefully responds (Figure 4.2), floating into the room in pristine professional attire, hair perfectly coiffed. She imparts sympathy as he touches his head to indicate pain. After he points to the spilled glass, Isabel obligingly pours a new one, helps him take a pill, and gets him settled again. Next, we see her giving him a back rub while batting her eyes (Figure 4.3). Then, we see him telling her a war story (Figure 4.4), using his hand to mime a plane's flight: she smiles and listens, then intercepts his hand lovingly to kiss it.

Isabel and George marry, but their rosy relationship ends as soon as the wedding is over. Once Isabel is no longer George's professional caregiver, he

FIGURE 4.4 Isabel listens to George's war stories with interest.

immediately transforms into a petty tyrant, making unilateral decisions. He quits his job without discussing it with her, and they set off from St. Louis to Miami in the car he has bought (an old hearse) because he has decided they will settle down there. Along the way, they check into a wretched motel during a rainstorm, and a bedraggled Isabel contemplates her future with despair. More drama ensues when they stop at the home of one of George's war buddies, Ralph, and his estranged wife Dorothea (played by Actors Studio members Anthony Franciosa and Lois Nettleton). Here, George abandons Isabel for several hours, during which time she makes plans for what she will do if he never returns. He does however return, and through a series of conversations he is educated and seemingly reformed. Through discussions with Ralph, George learns that for a man, "It's alright to have needs and weaknesses," and that "A woman is a human being, just like us." Meanwhile, Ralph assures Isabel that her husband was not promiscuous while in the army, and George that his sexual performance problems are something he can get over. By the end of the film, a temporary accord has been reached by the newlyweds, and we see them preparing to go to bed on Ralph's fold-out sofa. But despite the education George has received both in his wife's rights and his own need for emotional flexibility, a terrible ambivalence lingers in the closing words of the film, in which the newlyweds realize that in marriage, "nothing has to depend on just one day" because "there's so much time," a verdict that suggests either that there is potential for positive change—or that marriage is a life sentence (Figure 4.5). The body language of the newlyweds, sitting back to back, seems to suggest the latter.

Coming a decade and a half later in Williams's career, perhaps it is not surprising that *Period of Adjustment* contains more explicitly feminist language than *Streetcar*. When George assures Isabel that their fights are normal, he uses the official language of reintegration that has been quoted to him: "It's just an adjustment period." Fonda's Isabel instantly replies with a defiant refusal very different from Kim Hunter's portrayal of a veteran's wife walking on eggshells: "Adjustment to

FIGURE 4.5 The final scene of *Period of Adjustment*: Isabel and George with their backs to each other, contemplating the length of marriage.

what? Humiliation? No thank you!" In another scene, when George asks, "Aren't you being just a bit unreasonable?," Isabel responds, "Is it unreasonable to want to be treated as if I lived? Existed?" This acknowledgment of the difficulties facing post-war marriages and the attempt to reeducate men might be partly expected from a film with Tennessee Williams as writer, Isobel Lennartas screenwriter, and Cheryl Crawford as producer.[10]

But there are two regards in which *Period of Adjustment* seems not as socially conscious as it might be: one is the depiction of nursing and the question of Isabel's professionalism; the other is its attitude about war. During a fight, Isabel tells George that the care she gave him in the hospital was nothing more than her professional duty: "It was my job. I had to. I did not touch your body except as a nurse, hired to do it." Here, she defends herself as a professional, and draws attention to the difference between compensated and uncompensated labor. But we also learn along the way that Isabel's dreams of being a nurse have been crushed: she did not leave her job—she was in fact "politely dismissed" after she fainted at the sight of blood in her first operation. She reports that this was quite a blow for "a girl who has her heart set on being a Florence Nightingale" and "establishing clinics in the Upper Amazon." The characterization of Isabel as lacking the competence to qualify as a nurse seems gratuitous and sexist. Fonda tries to work against the script by showing Isabel to be perfectly skillful in her hospital scenes (this is something that she would return to with purpose in *Coming Home*). The second underdeveloped area is the film's stance on the war itself: *Period of Adjustment* mostly treats the war as backdrop, a kind of given with which the characters must now deal. As she became an activist, Fonda would develop the story of the veteran's wife to include anti-war resistance as well.

Describing the transition in her career from actor to producer during the period of her increasing political work in the late 1960s and early 1970s, Fonda wrote that "my relationship to my profession had changed. I was beginning to feel

I could be in control of the content of my films, and this made me care more and want to go deeper as an actress."[11] Sixteen years after *Period of Adjustment*, working with her own production company (IPC Pictures, with producing partner Bruce Gilbert), and with her commitments to the peace movement, civil rights, and feminism inseparable from her public image, Fonda made *Coming Home* (1978), a film that foregrounded the figure of the veteran's wife and made her both committed to the values of nursing and also a burgeoning member of the anti-war movement. She would also develop Tennessee Williams's coordinates to emphasize the related considerations of sexuality and disability that were a recurring element of "reintegration" dramas featuring Method actors. And in *Coming Home*, Fonda transformed Williams's Isabel, an aspiring professional nurse who is deemed an amateur, into Sally Hyde, a volunteer nurse whose resembles that of a professional.

Coming Home took several years to develop and it marked the deepest integration yet of Fonda's artistic and political work. Her commitment to a cinematic realism that in many ways resembled Fred Zinnemann's was part of an effort to disseminate her values to the widest possible audience. Fonda said of the films she produced during this period that she wanted to depict "ordinary people going through personal transformation."[12] In developing and creating *Coming Home*, she turned to the practices of sociological research and scene improvisation that she had inherited both from the Actors Studio and from feminist Method actors before her.

Fonda and her production team conducted interviews with Vietnam veterans and their spouses with the intention of telling a story that emerged from a range of personal experiences.[13] The characters they created blended various people's experiences, but they drew especially upon the narratives of a real-life couple named Bill and Terry Hager. While Bill was deployed, Terry became involved in the anti-war movement. Historian Jerry Lembcke suggests that it was Terry's point of view on events, rather than her husband's, that the filmmakers cleaved to most closely as they developed the script. Terry became one of several models for Sally Hyde, a marine captain's wife who married young and who becomes caught up in a love triangle with two Vietnam soldiers. One of them is her husband (Captain Bob Hyde, played by Method actor Bruce Dern), who is, in Fonda's description, "unable to let go of the militaristic myths of what a man should be," and the other, who becomes her lover, is a paraplegic vet in a military hospital (Luke Martin, played by Method actor Jon Voight), who is "angry but able to shed the old warrior ethos and free his mind."[14] Through Luke, and through her work in a VA (Veterans Affairs) hospital, Sally becomes drawn to the anti-war movement. It is not difficult to see in the character of Sally echoes of nineteenth-century dramatic heroines, including Nora in Ibsen's *A Doll's House*, whose intellectual and political awakening leads her away from her husband (Fonda had played Nora in a 1973 film version of Ibsen's play directed by Joseph Losey). One of the key lines of *Coming Home* is Sally's statement about her husband that could have been uttered by Nora herself: "He's not going to like the fact that I've changed…

and I have changed." In addition to tracing a woman's radicalization, one of the goals of *Coming Home* was to draw public attention to the neglectful treatment of returning Vietnam veterans in American military hospitals. While they were taking oral histories, Fonda notes, "The guys from the paraplegic ward told me how their urine bags weren't emptied and were always overflowing on the floor."[15] This detail was incorporated into the script for the first meeting between Sally and Luke. In their first scene together, Luke's urine bag spills on the floor, an encounter between nurse and patient which transforms the meet-cute scenario from the comically saccharine opening credits of *Period of Adjustment* into a much more realistic portrait of hospital life.

From this awkward start, Sally and Luke develop a friendship, a shared political cause in the peace movement, and then a romance, one that causes Sally to wonder how she can remain with her controlling and conventional spouse. Bruce Dern's character Captain Bob Hyde is connected to the rigid husband of *Period of Adjustment* through various scenes of Sally giving him back rubs, scenes which allude to the conflation of nurse and wife in the earlier film. At one point, he grows jealous while she is touching him, asking "Is that the way you massage the basket cases in the hospital?," a line that shows his difficulty respecting his wife's hospital work. Sally's husband does not approve of her volunteering at the hospital, telling her explicitly, "I don't want you to work." But after his deployment at the beginning of the film, Sally builds a new life. It begins when she forms a friendship with another serviceman's girlfriend who becomes her roommate in an apartment away from the base, and progresses to her beginning to volunteer at the hospital, meeting Luke and falling in love with him, attempting to politicize other military wives, and ultimately, participating in a climactic scene involving her husband and lover that was improvised by the three Method actors.

Along the way, *Coming Home* features an important love scene that has become the subject of extended commentary both by Fonda herself and by feminist film scholar Linda Williams. Fonda has said that it was important to her that the sex scene between Sally and Luke did *not* suggest penetration. As Fonda described it in her autobiography, she wanted "a dramatic way to redefine manhood beyond the traditional, goal-oriented reliance on the phallus to a new shared intimacy and pleasure my character had never had with her husband. But Hal [director Hal Ashby] didn't see it that way…penetration was definitely where he was headed with the scene." Instead, Fonda wanted to depict "the semblance of oral sex" to "create a groundbreaking love scene." She knew that Ashby had already filmed scenes that suggested penetration with her body double, and so in her own version of these scenes, Fonda describes going to great lengths, with the support of her co-star Voight, to avoid entering any position that looked like penetration so that Ashby would not be able to edit her scenes together with those of the body double. Fonda describes Ashby storming off the set, and still trying to edit the footage in a way that undermined her conception, but Fonda's maneuvers succeeded: the

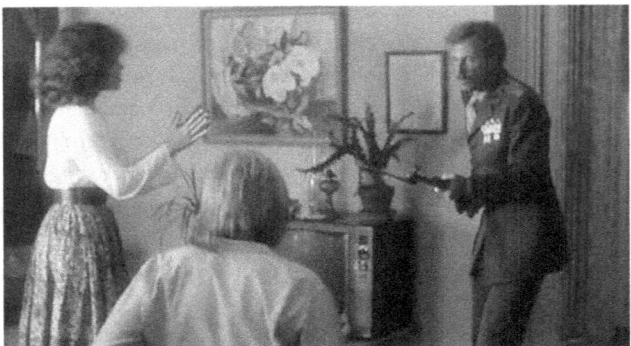

FIGURE 4.6 The improvised scene in which Fonda's Sally and Jon Voight's Luke attempt to reason with Sally's husband (played by Bruce Dern) in Hal Ashby's *Coming Home* (1978).

scene that ended up in the film is clearly one in which Fonda's character reaches orgasm via cunnilingus.[16]

Of Fonda's success in remaking the love scene, Linda Williams suggests that it was an important milestone in the representation of sex on screen, one in which Fonda expresses "the dramatic convergence of a pro-sex, antiwar ethic." Williams lauds her for being perhaps the first woman in Hollywood "to play characters whose orgasms mattered" (165). And Williams suggests that Fonda's anti-war ethos and her politics of female pleasure are interconnected—that the shift away from phallic sexuality is related to the turn away from war. But while a feminist critic like Williams was able to recognize Fonda's achievements, the first reviewers of the film seemed to miss the point entirely, seeing the emphasis on Sally's sexuality as a self-indulgent distraction from the war plot.[17] Reviewers who did not like the film also thought it was overly didactic: "she seems to have substituted a role model for a role," and is nothing more than "an ideological Before and After poster," complained Gary Arnold of the *Washington Post*, who found Fonda's orgasm "cliché," yet praised Voight's "glowing, robust masculinity" and "overwhelmingly sexual presence." With no insight into Fonda's attempts to deepen and complicate the Freudian stereotypes to which she had been subjected in her earlier career, Arnold could only call Sally "prim, frigid, innocuous."[18]

Similarly inclined to put Fonda in her place, Vincent Canby of *The New York Times* commented facetiously that what he had thought would be a war film "is really about the wife's first fully satisfying orgasm," and says he can't tell if the portrayal of a character with a disability as a good lover is meant to be "ironic." He also disliked the film's anti-war politics. But he saved special mockery for a scene in which the lovers confront the husband. Canby wrote that "the central triangle is resolved with a sequence that should get an appalled laugh from any movie historian." This is a scene in which the three characters in the love triangle—Sally Hyde, Captain Hyde, and Luke Martin—discuss the situation together, with Voight's character trying to empathize with Dern's, and to discuss with him the war and his experiences beyond their roles as rivals for the same woman. It is not certain why Canby found this scene so risible, or why he thought that movie historians should think so (Figure 4.6).

Clearly, these critics were riled by Fonda's opinionated filmmaking and the idea that gender and sexual politics were related to war. It is a point that *Coming Home* insists upon throughout, with the connection between militarism and misogyny made particularly clear in one scene in which Sally and her roommate (played by Penelope Milford) spend a night out drinking with some soldiers, and as they get drunker the men start telling misogynist jokes. No doubt the skeptical reviews of critics like Arnold and Canby stung less after the film triumphed at the Oscars, winning awards for Best Original Screenplay and Best Actress and Actor for Fonda and Voight. *Coming Home* was recognized as a powerful film questioning the Vietnam war, but it has not necessarily been recognized as a film in which Fonda both continued and transformed the Method tradition's interest in the figure of the veteran's wife. However, the way she built the film around research and improvisation, engaged so strongly with her director and co-star to make a feminist point in the film's key love scene, and alluded to previous Method performances (her own in *Period of Adjustment* and Hunter's in *Streetcar*, as well as Brando's in *The Men*) all suggest that Fonda was deeply indebted to her Method roots when she made *Coming Home*.

Fonda has often acted alongside other Method actors—Anthony Franciosa in *Period of Adjustment*, Marlon Brando in *The Chase*, Harvey Keitel in *Youth*. In Martin Ritt's *Stanley and Iris* (1990), she appears opposite Robert DeNiro in a film which makes a concerted effort to incorporate feminist awareness into Method acting. By casting these two leading Method actors alongside each other, Martin Ritt—who had led sessions at the Actors Studio and directed notable Method screen performances such as Joanne Woodward and Paul Newman's in *The Long, Hot Summer* and Paul Newman and Patricia Neal's in *Hud*—created an opportunity for Fonda and De Niro to form a new kind of relationship between male and female Method performers.

Stanley and Iris is a realist drama about an assembly-line worker, Iris (played by Fonda) and a cafeteria worker at her factory, Stanley (played by De Niro). While both characters struggle with family and money problems (Iris has recently been widowed and is supporting two children alone, and in the course of the film her teenage daughter becomes pregnant; Stanley has an aging father whom he is finding difficult to care for), they develop a bond that begins when Iris, realizing that Stanley cannot read, offers to teach him. During their sessions, they develop a friendship that slowly evolves into love. De Niro's character may be named Stanley, but he is a far cry from Brando's Stanley Kowalski. A lonely character whose pride makes it difficult for him to accept help, De Niro's Stanley is ultimately able, with the help of Fonda's Iris, to find love through the refusal of machismo.

The film is full of dialogue that reflects on feminist themes, as well as on Fonda's own career. At one moment, when Stanley hesitates to divulge something to Iris, she jokes "This is not going to be in an FBI file"—something with which Fonda was all too familiar, thanks to her anti-war activism. And in educating her son, Iris tells him that he should be "putting the toilet seat down for us ladies." In a heart-to-heart chat with her pregnant daughter, Iris frankly (and with curlers in her hair) discusses her own maternal ambivalence and the difficulties of being a mother. But the film is most pointedly self-reflexive in a pedagogical scene in which Fonda's Iris teaches De Niro's Stanley how to read while she stands ironing her family's clothes. This is a scene in which her character is frustrated and overwhelmed with her responsibilities. Stanley is sitting at the kitchen table with his reading materials, but when he realizes how overwhelmed she is, he stands up to listen to her problems, from the financial (tax bill) to the personal (no sex life). When he offers to help her out with her sex life, she demurs, but she is happy to instruct him on how he can help in ironing her clothes (Figure 4.7). This scene of his domestic labor lays the groundwork for their relationship to move from friendship to love and, more importantly, refuses the longstanding association between the Method, violence, and masculinity inaugurated by Brando's performance in *Streetcar Named Desire* and continued by De Niro's in *Taxi Driver*. Here, De Niro's character allows himself to be educated by Fonda's into a different model of masculinity. This scene might be taken as something of an emblem for Fonda's transformative feminist engagements with the Method across her career.

In a variety of ways—through her frequent practice of working with other Method actors, her return to the themes and preoccupations of the Actors Studio and her predecessors' performances, her investment in research and improvisation—Fonda has consistently demonstrated her affiliation with the Method tradition and

FIGURE 4.7 Robert De Niro's Stanley offers to help Jane Fonda's Iris with the ironing in Martin Ritt's *Stanley & Iris* (1990).

also her desire to re-shape it to feminist purposes. I have given several examples of this work here, but others remain to be explored. For instance, in *They Shoot Horses, Don't They?*, for which Fonda was nominated for her first Academy Award, she played a Depression-era dance contest competitor, a version of a character that Julie Harris had played in the Actors Studio production of June Havoc's *Marathon '33*. Fonda's only appearance opposite Brando, in Arthur Penn's *The Chase* (1966), is also worthy of study. Fonda said of that experience that it was one of the few times in her career that she was thrown off balance by another performer. Perhaps Fonda's difficulty acting with Brando in 1966 came from the fact that she had not yet fully learned how to take possession of the feminist Method strategies that would make her his equal as a cultural force. But as Linda Williams has suggested, Fonda would soon become "an actor whose sexual performances were as crucial to the 1970s cinematic knowledge of sex and perhaps as important and influential in their own female sphere as Marlon Brando's animal sexuality was in that of the male" (180). While Williams does not mention their shared roots at the Actors Studio when drawing this connection, it is increasingly clear that one of the most important contributions of Fonda's body of work has been her feminist remaking of the Method: she has consistently shown herself able to match, meet, deconstruct, and reimagine the powerful specter of Method masculinity in order to make room for herself and other women in the tradition.

Notes

1 "About Women's Media Center": https://womensmediacenter.com/about Accessed August 23, 2020.
2 See Maria Pramaggiore, "Jane Fonda: From Graylist to A-List," in *Hollywood Reborn*, edited by James Morrison (New Brunswick, NJ: Rutgers University Press, 2010), 16–38.
3 Fonda's performance in *Youth* also alludes to her performance in *The Morning After* (1986) as the alcoholic actor Alex Sternbergen (aka Viveca Van Loren). In Stanley Lumet's noir, Fonda's character wakes up after a one-night stand to find that her lover has been murdered. In the ensuing drama, she inhabits the role that typically belongs to noir's "fall guy" while also rebelling against her fate as an actress in Hollywood. In one scene, she quotes from *On the Waterfront* as she tells her boyfriend that in her acting career, "I coulda been a contender." As in Morel's monologue in *Youth*, which includes the detail that she cleaned toilets so that she could support herself while honing her craft at the Actors Studio, Fonda's character in *The Morning After* writes herself into the Method genealogy even while protesting at how she has been excluded from it.
4 In the 1970s, feminism reexamined psychoanalysis. Juliet Mitchell's *Psychoanalysis and Feminism* (1974) argued for repurposing the concepts of psychoanalysis to feminist ends. Mitchell's book reviewed previous, largely negative, feminist responses to Freud (by Beauvoir, Friedan, Greer, and others) and argued that feminism could not afford to be without the concepts developed by Freud, and that these concepts were not meant to be prescriptive but rather, analytical.
5 "Chapman Report: Adaptation of Wallace Novel Opens Here." *New York Times,* October 18, 1962, p. 47.

6 Goldstone, Bobbie. "Klute, Again," *Off Our Backs* 2.2 (1971), p. 34. Despite Goldstone's critiques, she did credit Fonda with an ability to make "cliched identity-crisis lingo like 'I'm used to feeling numb' believable."
7 In her autobiography *My Life So Far* Fonda says that she requested a female therapist for Bree, because she did not believe that Bree would confide in a male therapist, and in a 1975 interview she says it was Pakula's idea ("I Prefer Films that Strengthen People": An Interview with Jane Fonda. *Cinéaste* 6..4 (1975), 2–9). Vivian Nathan had been a founding member of the Actors Studio and had appeared in the Broadway productions of *The Rose Tattoo* (1951) and *Camino Real* (1953). She also served as a session moderator at the studio and eventually joined its board of directors.
8 Jane Fonda, *My Life So Far*, 252.
9 Ibid., 253.
10 Isobel Fredrika Hochdorf, born in 1915, attended Smith College and NYU and moved to Los Angeles in 1937, where she changed her name to Lennart and began working on scripts at MGM. In 1941, she received her first screen-writing job at Twentieth Century-Fox and sold her first screenplay, *The Affairs of Martha*, which led to a successful film. She was hired by MGM on a full-time basis. Lennart joined the Communist Party in 1939, left it after the German-Soviet Nonagression Pact, and rejoined in 1940 after Germany invaded the Soviet Union. Her final departure from the party came after the 1945 Duclos Letter. She said she knew little of the party's set-up, its leadership, or funding, and had joined uncritically. After being named in September 1951, Lennart appeared before the Committee on Un-American Activities. She named 21 people whom she believed had already been named, apparently because MGM executives told her they could not protect her if she did not cooperate and her feelings towards the party had changed. She later expressed deep regret at her cooperation. Her last film script was *Funny Girl*, the Fanny Brice biopic starring Barbra Streisand. See Larry Ceplair, "Isobel Lennart and the Dynamics of Informing Hollywood," *Historical Journal of Film, Radio and Television* 274, (Oct. 2007), 513–529.
11 *Jane Fonda: My Life So Far*, p. 148.
12 Ibid.
13 Fonda's production team, at the film's inception, included Waldo Salt, John Schlesinger, and screenwriter Nancy Dowd, though Schlesinger and Dowd would eventually be replaced by screenwriters Robert C. Jones and Rudy Wurlitzer and Schlesinger succeeded by Hal Ashby. The interviews done while researching the film have been considered by historians of Vietnam. See Jerry Lembcke, "From Oral History to Movie Script: The Vietnam Veteran Interviews for *Coming Home*," *The Oral History Review*, 26.2 (1999), 65–86.
14 *Jane Fonda: My Life So Far*, 345. Luke Martin was partly based on Ron Kovic, whose 1976 autobiography would be adapted into the film *Born on the Fourth of July* (Oliver Stone, 1989).
15 *Jane Fonda: My Life So Far*, p. 349.
16 Fonda's account of her struggle with Ashby over the matter of penetration is given in *Jane Fonda: My Life So Far*, 370–374.
17 It is worth mentioning that verdicts on Fonda's work from the 1970s should be understood within the context of the immense ire Fonda had unleashed when she protested against the Vietnam war and was deemed "Hanoi Jane" by those who disagreed with her.
18 Gary Arnold, *Washington Post*, April 12, 1978.

5
EPILOGUE
Barbara Loden's *Wanda* (1970)

Across the chapters of this book, I have shown how a group of women associated with the Actors Studio worked to change the depiction of women's lives on film. They did so, I have suggested, by forging their own mode of Method acting, one that was built upon what they learned at the Actors Studio, but which was different from the work of male actors because it engaged with the roles, traditions, and concerns of female actors as well as with contemporary developments in feminist thought. These women found much of what they needed to make feminist choices within the Method and its creative practices. The Method's validation of personal experience as the grounds for making art dovetailed naturally with feminism's ethos of the personal as the political. Sometimes, though, as the cases of Kim Hunter, Shelley Winters, Julie Harris, Geraldine Page, and Jane Fonda have shown, the tradition did not go far enough for them or contain everything they needed, and so they grappled with it, transforming it from the inside. They also protested against the range of roles available to them in Hollywood, inscribed that protest in their performances, and forged new roles.

Rather than being the marginal figures they have sometimes appeared in previous critical histories, these women expanded and energized the Method through their feminist transformations. Often, realism looked different in their incarnations, and rather than being "hysterical" (the style that has been attributed to them), or "explosive" (the style associated with many male Method actors), Method women often gave performances of subdued emotion and anti-glamorous affect. I have referred to these kinds of performances, and to others by women of the Actors Studio that offered realist depictions of women's experiences animated by feminist consciousness, as feminist Method acting. To attend to these remarkable performances is to build not only a fuller understanding of the history of the Method, but also of film history more broadly, by illuminating women's work in ways that have at times been eclipsed by attention to the riotous, attention-grabbing style of many male Method actors.

The 1970s brought two important developments to this history. First, in the 1970s feminism became a mainstream social movement, and it was finally possible for female Method actors to inhabit the role that Pauline Kael had attributed to Marlon Brando in the 1950s—that of the "representative type" of their society, the one who "really strikes a nerve," and whose conflicts and concerns embodied widely shared political and social questions. In films like Martin Scorsese's *Alice Doesn't Live Here Anymore* (1974) and Martin Ritt's *Norma Rae* (1979), as well as the films produced by Fonda, female Method actors helmed mainstream Hollywood projects that addressed feminist issues squarely. Second, beginning in the 1970s, directors and actors began to develop historical perspective on the influence of the Method on American cinema. As a second generation of male actors associated with the Method (Dustin Hoffman, Robert DeNiro, Al Pacino, Harvey Keitel, etc.) became stars, films like Sydney Pollack's *Tootsie* (1982) and Robert Altman's *Come Back to the Five and Dime, Jimmy Dean, Jimmy Dean* (1982) investigated the legacies and dynamics of the Method, including its gender politics.

In *Tootsie* (1982), a male Method actor who cannot get any jobs because of his reputation for being difficult to work with reinvents himself as a woman, adopting a practical, no-nonsense middle-aged wardrobe and acting persona something like Patricia Neal's. The film, though it contains an element of anti-feminist backlash (in that it suggests that there are no good parts for men anymore) nonetheless offers an affectionate tribute to the style of the female Method tradition as Hoffman transforms from Michael Dorsey to Dorothy Michaels. And in Robert Altman's *Come Back to the Five and Dime, Jimmy Dean, Jimmy Dean* (1982), which features Method actor Sandy Dennis alongside an ensemble cast including Cher and Kathy Bates, the legacy of James Dean is revisited at the 20-year reunion of a James Dean fan club in Marfa, Texas. Sandy Dennis's character Mona, who had long believed that her child was fathered by James Dean, learns that the true parent is in fact her friend Joanne, who had been living as Joe in the 1950s before going through gender confirmation surgery. By casting Method actor Sandy Dennis in the role of Mona, and by questioning the "straightness" of Dean's legacy, the film queers genealogies of the Method, asking audiences to revisit, rethink, and rebuild them. Both films belong to what we might call the "meta-Method" or (borrowing a prefix from neo-noir) "neo-Method" period of the 1970s and 1980s.

An important female filmmaker who investigated the Method's legacies in this period was Actors Studio member Barbara Loden. Her film *Wanda* (1970) is now considered a foundational work of women's independent cinema (it was released by the Criterion Collection in 2010). Shortly before making the film, Loden had played the role of Mona in *Come Back to the Five and Dime* in the Off-Broadway production directed by Altman. *Wanda* explores the issues of self-expression and artistic authority Loden faced as an artist, one whose career path resembled those of some of the characters we have encountered in this book, including Shelley Winters's chorus girl Dixie Evans in *The Big Knife* and Jane Fonda's model and aspiring actor Bree Daniels in *Klute*. As Maya Montañez Smuckler writes, Loden "detested" the "dumb blonde" roles she was cast in in Hollywood, and eventually realized that her destiny as an artist would have to be found elsewhere, by becoming a filmmaker herself, and one not beholden to the pressures of Hollywood.[1]

Loden came from a working-class background in North Carolina. She moved to New York and used modeling as a way to make a living while studying art and acting. In the late 1950s, she met Elia Kazan, had a child with him while he was still married to Molly Thacher, and played roles in two of his films, *Wild River* (1960) as Betty Jackson (the secretary of Montgomery Clift's character) and *Splendor in the Grass* (1961) as Ginny Stamper (the sister of Warren Beatty's character). On stage, Loden won a Tony award in 1964 for playing Maggie, a character based on Marilyn Monroe, in Arthur Miller's play *After the Fall*, a role Loden related to deeply, and for which she drew on her own experiences. Her own career arc, from model to Method actor to successful Hollywood performer to groundbreaking feminist independent director, makes hers a fitting story with which to conclude this book, one which exemplifies the trajectory of Method women's careers toward ever-greater artistic self-determination both within and beyond Hollywood.[2]

Wanda depicts episodes in the life of a woman from Pennsylvania coal country after she leaves her husband and their children. With verité-style camerawork by Nicholas Proferes, the use of non-professional actors, and the structure of a road movie, it traces Wanda's journey as she borrows money from a friend, appears at a court date to yield custody of her children and grant her husband a divorce, tries to get work, and wanders around shopping malls, streets, and movie theatres. Along the way, she gets involved with a man named Mr. Dennis (played by Michael Higgins), a criminal who is planning a bank robbery. With echoes of *Bonnie and Clyde* (the Arthur Penn film that had revolutionized Hollywood three years before, and which *Wanda* could be read as a feminist engagement with) Wanda becomes Mr. Dennis's accomplice, assistant, and companion.

Loden got the idea for her screenplay from a newspaper article she read about a woman who had been an accomplice to a robbery similar to the one depicted in the film, and upon being sentenced to 20 years, thanked the judge. Loden was curious about what could have made this woman seemingly relieved or grateful for her sentence. She responded to this detail in the news story because she recognized elements of her own experience in it. Loden mentioned in interviews that she too had once drifted through life, giving herself over passively to relationships and situations that others seemed to want or demand, without being guided by her own will, ambitions, and intentions. Building a bridge between herself and the role in Method fashion, in *Wanda* Loden investigated passivity and acceptance of abuse. When Loden described the character, she said that Wanda was "ill-equipped," with no "preparation for life," "came from poor working-class people, married young, had several children." "She drifted from one situation to another, from one man to another," until she became involved with an "authoritarian figure," one who was "dominating her" but, in her view "at least it was a form of attention" and "he told her what to do and what not to do."

Wanda is recognizably a Method-influenced film, and one that demonstrates Loden's facility with its approaches, techniques, and styles. At the film's center—and the film is unimaginable without it—is Loden's virtuosic Method performance, one that draws on her own experiences and makes use of Method approaches for developing physical naturalism. She employs the restraint and flat affect of the feminist Method tradition (one critic called Loden's performance "implosive," a term that nicely captures the reversal of energy and refusal of explosiveness in this tradition).[3] Like *Klute*, which was made the following year, the film does not give audiences easy access to its female protagonist's interiority: both Loden's script and performance rebuff attempts to understand, diagnose, pathologize, or place what is going on inside Wanda, who speaks few words and whose body language is defensive (she often stands with her arms crossed).

By the time she made *Wanda*, Loden was married to Kazan, and the film can be read as a reflection on her own development of artistic autonomy in her personal and professional relationship with him. Loden said in an interview at the AFI that the relationship between Wanda and Mr. Dennis in the film drew on the early years of her relationship with Kazan, to whom she at first felt artistically inferior and submissive. Loden invokes Kazan's work so that she can carve out her own cinematic alternative to it: the opening of *Wanda* might even have caused some viewers to wonder if they were in for a replay of Kazan's *A Streetcar Named Desire*. *Wanda* begins in a Polish-American household full of domestic stress, with a crying baby, a frazzled mother, and an angry husband. We are briefly led to believe that these are the characters the film will be centrally concerned with. Externally, they resemble the Kowalskis. But then the camera, directing our attention to the main story which had only seemed to be at the margins of that one, pans from the kitchen to the couch, where another woman is sleeping. This is Wanda Goronski, blonde and disheveled. She wakes up, seemingly stiff, tired, and weary. She tells the woman with the baby (who may be her sister) in reference to the man of the house, "He's mad because I'm here," and then we see Wanda remove herself from the *Streetcar*-evoking set, and enter the world of an industrial northeastern town.

In addition to being a surrogate for Kazan, the man she pairs up with, Mr. Dennis, also becomes an allegorical embodiment of the objectifying film culture through which Loden rose. In one scene, Mr. Dennis asks her about the messy bun she pulls her hair into every day, "Why don't you do something about your hair? Looks terrible" (Figure 5.1). He shames her for wearing the same scruffy shirt and pants every day, and tells her, "I thought I told you to get a dress. No slacks. When you're with me, no slacks. No hair curlers. Makes you look cheap. You wanna look cheap?" Mr. Dennis's comments establish the baseline expectations for female

Epilogue: Barbara Loden's *Wanda* (1970) **131**

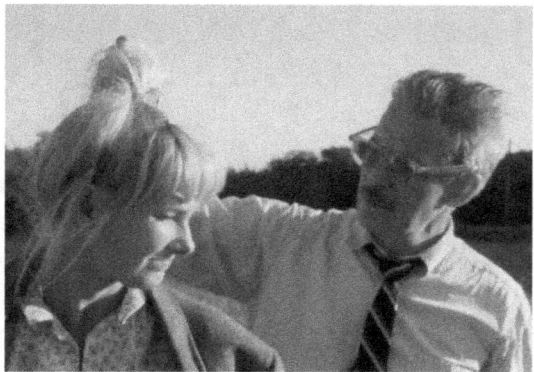

FIGURE 5.1 Mr. Dennis opines on Wanda's appearance in Barbara Loden's *Wanda* (1970): "Why don't you do something about your hair? Looks terrible."

performers, expectations that Loden refuses at every turn in *Wanda*. As Wanda, Loden makes very few costume changes, and she openly defies the prohibition on curlers in the opening scenes of the film when she goes to her court date in the scruffy shirt and pants and a set of rollers in her hair.

In one of the film's most pointed metatheatrical scenes, Mr. Dennis tries to prepare Wanda for the bank robbery. Wanda appears wearing a maternity top, visibly showing a bump. Mr. Dennis hands her a piece of paper—the script for the heist, it turns out. "I wrote it down step by step. Memorize it," he tells her. "Mr. Dennis, I can't do this," she informs him, refusing to step into the part he has created for her. He punches her pregnant stomach, a shocking moment. Again, she calmly asserts her refusal: "No, Mr. Dennis, I really mean it. I can't do it." Her maternity costume resembles the one worn by Kim Hunter in *A Streetcar Named Desire*. To underline her refusal, Wanda lifts the shirt and pulls a red pillow out from under her shirt—the prop pregnancy bump. He shakes her by the shoulders. "You can do it. Now here, you take this and memorize it." Wanda grows progressively more agitated as she protests that she is unwilling to carry out the demands of the script. This scene conflates performance anxiety, maternal ambivalence, and feminist rage as we see Wanda become nauseous at the prospect of being forced into the role of a pregnant wife (Figure 5.2).

Despite Wanda's refusals, she does end up participating in the crime. But she re-scripts it, because she must: the event throws up unexpected moments to which she must respond. In one, Mr. Dennis loses control of his gun and she fights with the victim to get it back. In this case, her unscripted action helps Mr. Dennis. But during the next phase of the heist, another unforeseen event arises: while Mr. Dennis is riding with the manager to the bank, Wanda is following in the getaway car. She is pulled over by police and asked for her license. In the time that is lost during the police stop, Mr. Dennis's heist goes awry. The police arrive and shoot him dead.

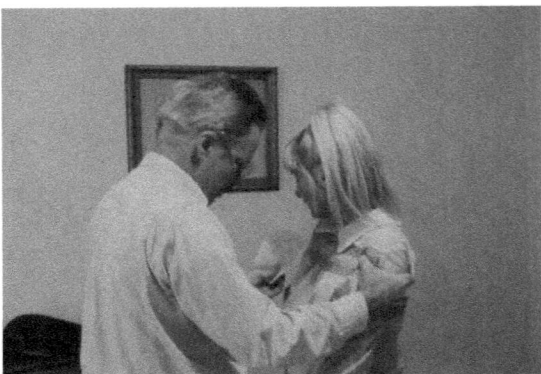

FIGURE 5.2 Mr. Dennis hands Wanda the script she must learn for the bank heist in which she is posing as his pregnant wife.

After Mr. Dennis is killed, Wanda stands outside the bank, alongside a curious crowd, looking straight ahead with a difficult-to-interpret expression on her face. Her improvisations have had unexpected effects: one of them saved her "director;" the other killed him. The loss of Mr. Dennis forces Wanda once more to write her own script, to make her own choices within the narrow set of options available to her. And while the film certainly does not conclude by solving Wanda's problems, particularly her economic precarity, it does end with a scene in which she asserts herself more decisively than we have seen her do before. We see her drinking in a bar with a man in uniform. Then we see them drive in his convertible to a deserted area. He begins to kiss her, and then he becomes violent as he tries to go further than she wants to go. She begins to protest, to scream, and to resist. Eventually, she hits him with the empty purse that she has carried throughout the film and runs away, escaping into the woods, falling and crying.

In the next scene, we see Wanda approaching a house that is lit up in the night. A kind woman comes out and says to her, "Honey, you waiting for somebody?" a line that recalls Eunice's question to Blanche at the beginning of *A Streetcar Named Desire*, "What's the matter, honey? Are you lost?" Wanda is taken in at the house. Her future is uncertain, but for this night she has shelter. The film's final shot is an ambiguous one of her listening to live music at a table full of raucous men and the women who are showing them a good time. Musicians play passionately on the stage, and the aura is merry, but Wanda merely sits numbly, perhaps replaying the violence from which she has escaped, perhaps wondering what she will do next. It is not a triumphal scene, but it is one in which Wanda has survived another day, and in which she has escaped two abusers.

In 1980, the feminist documentarian Katja Raganelli made a film about Loden, *I Am Wanda*. In it, Loden speaks about her multiple vocations as actor, acting teacher, and director. In scenes in which she is shown working with her students, she models a feminist pedagogy, counseling a couple who are playing a love scene along conventional lines, "let's find some different things to do instead of just groping each other." When Loden discusses the values that drive her work, she speaks of trying to find a way to give voice to underrepresented parts of women's experiences. She describes caring for her mother at the end of her life, and her hopes that "through what I do I might be able to help to express some of the things that my mother wasn't able to express in her lifetime and some of the things she went through." Loden emphasizes that she is no longer intimidated by older, more powerful artists. She remarks on how Kazan's comments had helped her in the making of *Wanda*: "we have a lot of the same viewpoints…where we differ is helpful also." She describes a time when she asked Kazan how he thought a particular scene in *Wanda* should go, and when he answered, she realized it was not at all what she had envisioned: "by his making a statement that I didn't agree with, it made me more clear about what I really did want to achieve in that scene."

Four years later, the influence of Loden's *Wanda* on Hollywood film could be strongly felt in Martin Scorsese's *Alice Doesn't Live Here Anymore* (1974). *Wanda's* qualities could be seen in the film's style, its plot (a road movie about a woman who is suddenly alone and trying to survive), and its searching feminist Method performance, much of which was developed and improvised by Ellen Burstyn. Of course, Hollywood's penchant for happy endings meant that Alice finds her footing more decisively by the film's end than Wanda ever does. But both films, in their different registers, showed how thoroughly compatible feminist perspectives could be with Method acting.

I have tried to show in this book that the Actors Studio encouraged feminist artistry because of how it empowered actors more generally. It asked its members to bring their full selves their performances, gave them a sense of entitlement to intervene in scripts and advocate for their characters, trained them to find and tell stories between the lines, and invited them to engage with pressing intellectual ideas and political struggles and to draw strength from each other as a non-profit community of artists engaged in a shared realist tradition. For the female actors I have studied in this book, the Actors Studio provided space for thought and helped them to emerge as conscious, passionate, and self-respecting artists across the three decades (1950s to 1970s) during which Hollywood transformed alongside, and partly because of, their work. While I have not been able to analyze every notable feminist Method performance in a book of this scope, I hope I have provided some tools with which the tradition as a whole might be approached and an invitation to consider other works it contains. Good places to go from here might be to Kim Stanley's performances in *The Goddess* and *Séance on a Wet Afternoon*, Lee Remick's in *Days of Wine and Roses*, Carroll Baker's in *Something Wild*, Sandy Dennis's in *Whose Afraid of Virginia Woolf?*, Marilyn Monroe's in *The Misfits*, and Jo Van Fleet's in *The Rose Tattoo*. Writing from the perspective of an acting teacher, Elizabeth C. Stroppel posed the question that has long defined feminist inquiry in relation to the Method: "Is the Method inherently antithetical to feminist thought and praxes, or can it be instilled with feminist consciences?"[4] (114) Through case studies of a variety of female actors who worked hard to carve places for themselves in the Method and on the screen, I have argued not only that this tradition can be a feminist one, but that thanks to their work, it already is.

Notes

1. Maya Montañez Smuckler, *Liberating Hollywood: Women Directors and the Feminist Reform of 1970s Cinema* (New Brunswick, NJ: Rutgers University Press), 97.
2. Loden is today something of a cult figure: recently the French writer Nathalie Léger wrote *Suite for Barbara Loden*, a poetic appreciation of Loden's film alongside Léger's own memoirs about researching Loden's life. See Smuckler, *Liberating Hollywood*,. 96–102, for a more detailed account of Loden's career.
3. Comparing Loden's style to that of John Cassavetes, Adrian Martin and Cristina Álvarez López note that *Wanda* functions as the inverse of films like *A Woman Under the Influence* (1974): where Cassavetes' style is explosive and hysterical, Loden explores a sullen, implosive energy. www.filmcritic.com.au/reviews/w/wanda.html
4. Elizabeth C. Stroppel, "Reconciling the Past and the Present: Feminist Perspectives on the Method in the Classroom and on the Stage," *Method Acting Reconsidered: Theory, Practice, Future*. David Krasner, ed. New York: Palgrave Macmillan, 2000, pps. 111-123 (p. 114).

BIBLIOGRAPHY

Adler, Stella. *The Art of Acting*. New York: Applause Books, 2000.
Adler, Stella. *Stella Adler on America's Master Playwrights: Eugene O'Neill, Thornton Wilder, Clifford Odets, William Saroyan, Tennessee Williams, William Inge, Arthur Miller, Edward Albee*, edited by Barry Paris. New York: Vintage, 2013.
Adler, Stella. *Stella Adler on Ibsen, Strindberg, and Chekhov*, edited by Barry Paris. New York: Vintage, 2000.
Affron, Charles. *Star Acting: Gish, Garbo, Davis*. New York: Dutton, 1977.
Als, Hilton. "Unhappy Endings." *New Yorker*, 3 December 2001, 94–104.
Artaud, Antonin. *The Theatre and its Double*. 1938. New York: Grove, 1994.
Baker, Aaron. "Robert De Niro: Star as Actor Auteur." In *Acting for America: Movie Stars of the 1980s*, edited by Robert Eberwein, 19–35. New Brunswick: Rutgers University Press, 2010.
Baker, Carroll. *Baby Doll: An Autobiography*. New York: Arbor House Publishing Co., 1983.
Barnes, Howard. "Review of *A Streetcar Named Desire*." *The New York Herald Tribune*, 4 December 1947, 35.
Barnhisel, Greg. *Cold War Modernists: Art, Literature, and American Cultural Diplomacy*. New York: Columbia University Press, 2015.
Baron, Cynthia. *Modern Acting: The Lost Chapter of American Film and Theatre*. London: Palgrave, 2016.
–. "Stage Actors and Modern Acting Methods Move to Hollywood in the 1930s." *Cinémas* 251 (2014): 109–129.
Baron, Cynthia and Sharon Marie Carnicke. *Reframing Screen Performance*. Ann Arbor: University of Michigan Press, 2008.
Baron, Cynthia, Diane Carson, and Frank P. Tomasulo. *More Than a Method: Trends and Traditions in Contemporary Film Performance*. Detroit: Wayne State University Press, 2004.
Barsam, Richard and Dave Monahan. *Looking at Movies: An Introduction to Film*. New York: Norton, 2015.
Batiste, Stephanie. *Darkening Mirrors: Imperial Representation in Depression Era African American Performance*. Durham, NC: Duke University Press, 2011.

Beck, Dennis C. "The Paradox of the Method Actor: Rethinking the Stanislavsky Legacy." In *Method Acting Reconsidered*, edited by David Krasner, 261–282. New York: St. Martin's, 2000.

Bernstein, Robin. *Racial Innocence: Performing American Childhood from Slavery to Civil Rights*. New York: New York University Press, 2011.

Black, Gregory D. *The Catholic Crusade Against the Movies, 1940–1975*. Cambridge: Cambridge University Press, 1998.

Blades, Larry. "The Returning Vet's Experience in *A Streetcar Named Desire*: Stanley as Decommissioned Warrior Under Stress." *The Tennessee Williams Annual Review* 10 (2009), 1–27.

Blum, Richard. *American Film Acting: Stanislavski Heritage*. Ann Arbor: UMI Research Press, 1984.

Björklund, Jenny, "Playing with Pistols: Female Masculinity in Henrik Ibsen's *Hedda Gabler*." *Scandinavian Studies* 88.1 (2016), 179–200.

Bolte, Charles G. *The New Veteran*. New York: Reynal and Hitchcock, 1945.

Bowne, Henrietta and Hornell Harte. "Divorce, Depression, and War." *Social Forces* 22.2 (1943), 191–193.

Breuer, Bessie. *Sundown Beach*. 1948. New York: Grindstone Press, 1973.

Brooks, Peter. *The Melodramatic Imagination: Balzac, Henry James, Melodrama, and the Mode of Excess*. New Haven, CT: Yale University Press, 1995.

Brustein, Robert. "America's New Culture Hero: Feelings Without Words." *Commentary* 25, February 1958, 123–129.

Brustein, Robert. *Revolution as Theatre*. New York: Liveright, 1970.

Byars, Jackie. *All That Hollywood Allows: Re-Reading Gender in 1950s Melodrama*. Chapel Hill: University of North Carolina Press, 1991.

Califia, Pat. "I Love Butches." In *The Persistent Desire: A Femme-Butch Reader*, edited by Joan Nestle, 420–422. Boston: Alyson Publications, 1992.

Callahan, Vicki. *Reclaiming the Archive: Feminism and Film History*. Detroit: Wayne State University Press, 2010.

Carman, Emily. *Independent Stardom: Freelance Women in the Hollywood Studio System*. Austin: University of Texas Press, 2015.

Carnicke, Sharon Marie. *Stanislavsky in Focus: An Acting Master for the 21st Century*. New York: Routledge, 1998.

Carr, Virginia Spencer. *The Lonely Hunter: A Biography of Carson McCullers*. Athens, GA: University of Georgia Press, 1975.

Case, Sue-Ellen. *Feminism and Theatre*. New York: Routledge, 1988.

Child, Irvin L, and Marjorie Van de Water, eds., *Psychology for the Returning Serviceman*. Washington, DC: Infantry Journal Press, 1945.

Cima, Gay Gibson. *Performing Women: Female Characters, Male Playwrights, and the Modern Stage*. Ithaca: Cornell University Press, 1993.

Cleto, Fabio. *Camp: Queer Aesthetics and the Performing Subject*. Ann Arbor: University of Michigan Press, 1999.

Cohan, Steven. *Masked Men: Masculinity and the Movies in the Fifties*. Bloomington, IN: Indiana University Press, 1997.

Cohen, Lola, ed. *The Lee Strasberg Notes*. New York: Routledge, 2010.

Cope, Virginia H. "A Multiethnic Streetcar Named Desire: We've Had this Date from the Beginning." *Modern Drama* 57.4 (2014), 493–512.

Counsell, Colin. *Signs of Performance: An Introduction to Twentieth-Century Theatre*. Abingdon: Routledge, 1996.

Crawford, Cheryl. *One Naked Individual: My Fifty Years in the Theatre.* Indianapolis, IN: Bobbs-Merrill, 1977.
Crawford, Christina. *Mommie Dearest.* New York: William and Morrow, 1978.
Davidson, Bill. "Geraldine Page: Diamond Who Likes it Rough." *Saturday Evening Post,* 17 November 1962, 30–31.
Davidson, Bill. "Shelley Winters, Headlong Talker." *Saturday Evening Post,* 11 August 1962, 32–33.
De Cordova, Richard. "A Case of Mistaken Identity: Class and Generational Difference in Three Family Melodramas." *Home is Where the Heart Is: Studies in Melodrama and the Woman's Film.* London: British Film Institute, 1987.
Denker, Henry. *The Actress.* London: W.H. Allen & Co./Penguin Random House, 1979.
Desjardins, Mary. *Recycled Stars: Female Film Stardom in the Age of Television and Video.* Durham, NC: Duke University Press, 2015.
Diamond, Elin. *Unmaking Mimesis: Essays on Feminism and Theatre.* New York: Routledge, 1997.
Dolan, Jill. *Theatre and Sexuality.* New York: Palgrave, 2010.
Dolan, Jill. *Utopia in Performance: Finding Hope at the Theatre.* Ann Arbor: University of Michigan Press, 2005.
Dombrowski, Lisa. *Kazan Revisited.* Middletown: Wesleyan University Press, 2011.
Dos Passos, John. "The Death of James Dean." *Esquire,* October 1973, 157, 382–386.
Dowling, Ellen. "The Derailment of *A Streetcar Named Desire.*" *Literature/Film Quarterly* 9.4 (1981), 233–240.
Doyle, Jennifer. *Sex Objects: Art and the Dialectics of Desire.* Minneapolis: University of Minnesota Press, 2006.
Edgerton, Alanson. *Readjustment or Revolution: A Guide to Economic, Educational, and Social Readjustment of Our War Veterans, Ex-War Workers, and Oncoming Youth.* New York: Whittlesey House, McGraw-Hill, 1946.
Elsom, John. *Cold War Theatre.* New York: Routledge, 1992.
Enelow, Shonni. *Method Acting and its Discontents: On American Psycho-Drama.* Evanston: Northwestern University Press, 2015.
Ewing, Sherman. "Wanted: More Stars, Less 'Method.'" *Theatre Arts,* January 1961. In *Theatre Arts on Acting,* edited by Laurence Senelick, 280–284. New York: Routledge, 2008.
Flint, Peter B. "Stella Adler, 91, Actress and Teacher of the Method." *New York Times,* December 22, 1992.
Frome, Shelly. *The Actors Studio: A History.* Jefferson, NC: McFarland and Co., 2001.
Furnas, J.C. "Meet Ed Savickas: A Victim of Combat Fatigue." *Ladies Home Journal* 92 (1945), 142–145.
Fuss, Diana. *Identification Papers: Readings on Psychoanalysis, Sexuality, and Culture.* New York: Routledge, 1995.
Gainor, J. Ellen. "Rethinking Feminism, Stanislavsky, and Performance." *Theatre Topics* 12.2 (2002), 163–175.
Gallagher-Ross, Jacob. "Mediating the Method." *Theatre Survey* 56.3 (2015), 291–313.
Gaut, Berys. *A Philosophy of Cinematic Art.* Cambridge: Cambridge University Press, 2010.
Gerstner, David A. and Janet Staiger, eds. *Authorship and Film.* Routledge: AFI Film Readers, 2002.
Gilbert, James. *Men in the Middle: Searching for Masculinity in the 1950s.* Chicago: University of Chicago Press, 2005.
Girelli, Elisabetta. *Montgomery Clift, Queer Star.* Detroit: Wayne State University Press, 2013.
Gledhill, Christine. *Home is Where the Heart Is: Studies in Melodrama and the Woman's Film.* London: British Film Institute, 1987.

Gledhill, Christine and Linda Williams, eds. *Reinventing Film Studies*. New York: Bloomsbury Academic, 2000.
Goldberg, Jonathan. *Melodrama: An Aesthetics of Impossibility*. Durham, NC: Duke University Press, 2016.
Golding, Sue. "James Dean: The Almost Perfect Lesbian Hermaphrodite." In *Stolen Glances: Lesbians Take Photographs*, edited by Tessa Boffin and Jean Fraser, 197–202. London: Pandora 1991.
Goffman, Erving. *The Presentation of Self in Everyday Life*. New York: Random House, 1959.
Gross, Robert. "Hello Stanley, Good-bye Blanche." *Cercles* 10 (2004), 74–85.
Guthrie, Tyrone. "Is There Madness in the Method?" *New York Times Magazine*, 15 September 1957, 23, 83–82.
Halberstam, J. Jack. *Female Masculinity*. Durham, NC: Duke University Press, 1998.
Harrop, John. *Acting*. London: Routledge, 1992.
Hartmann, Susan M. *The Home Front and Beyond: American Women in the 1940s*. Boston: Twayne Publishers, 1982.
Hartmann, Susan M. "Prescriptions for Penelope: Literature on Women's Obligations to Returning World War II Veterans." *Women's Studies* 5 (1978), 229–239.
Havighurst, Robert, Walter H. Eaton, John W. Baughman, and Ernest W. Burgess. *The American Veteran Back Home: A Study of Veteran Adjustment*. New York: Longmans, Green and Co., 1951.
Hirsch, Forster. *A Method to their Madness: The History of the Actors Studio*. Boston: Da Capo Press, 1984.
Hollinger, Karen. *The Actress: Hollywood Acting and the Female Star*. London: Routledge, 2013.
Hollinger, Karen. *Feminist Film Studies*. London: Routledge, 2012.
Hooper, Michael. "Warring Desires: Sex, Marriage, and the Returning Solider." *The Tennessee Williams Annual Review* 10 (2009), 31–39.
Hornby, Richard. *The End of Acting*. New York: Applause Books, 2000.
Humm, Maggie. *Feminism and Film*. Bloomington: Indiana University Press, 1997.
Jarvis, Christina S. *The Male Body at War: American Masculinity During World War II*. DeKalb: Northern Illinois University Press, 2004.
Jewett, Chad M. "'Somehow Caught:' Race and Deferred Sexuality in McCullers's *The Member of the Wedding*." *The Southern Literary Journal* 45.1 (2012), 95–110.
Kael, Pauline. "The Current Cinema: Tango." *The New Yorker*, 28 October 1972, 130-138.
Kael, Pauline. "Marlon Brando: An American Hero." *The Atlantic Monthly*, March 1966, 72–75.
Kael, Pauline. "The Glamour of Delinquency." *The Age of Movies: Selected Writings of Pauline Kael*, edited by Sanford Schwartz. New York: Library of America, 2011, 25-39.
Kaplan, E. Anne, ed. *Feminism and Film*. Oxford: Oxford University Press, 2000.
Kazan, Elia. *Elia Kazan: A Life*. New York: Knopf, 1988.
Kazan, Elia. *Kazan on Directing*. New York: Vintage, 2010.
Kerr, Walter F. "Earnest Players." *New York Herald Tribune*, 17 June 1956, 1.
Kitching, Howard. *Sex Problems of the Returned Veteran*. Verplanck, NY: Emerson Books, 1946.
Konkle, Amanda. *Some Kind of Mirror: Creating Marilyn Monroe*. New Brunswick: Rutgers University Press, 2019.
Kouvaros, George. *Famous Faces Not Yet Themselves: The Misfits and Icons of Postwar America*. Minneapolis: University of Minnesota Press, 2010.
Krampner, Jon. *Female Brando: The Legend of Kim Stanley*. New York: Back Stage Books, 2006.

Krasner, David. *Method Acting Reconsidered: Theory, Practice, Future*. New York: St. Martin's Press, 2000.
Krauss, Kenneth. *Male Beauty: Postwar Masculinity in Theatre, Film, and Physique Magazines*. Albany: State University of New York Press, 2014.
Lee, Hyung Shik. "Violence against Women in American Drama: A Feminist Comparison of *A Streetcar Named Desire* and *The Conduct of Life*." *Journal of Modern British and American Drama* 16.2 (2003), 197–224.
Lefkovitz, Alison. "'The Peculiar Anomaly': Same-Sex Infidelity in Postwar Divorce." *Law and History Review* 33.3 (2015), 665–701.
Lewis, Robert. *Method – or Madness?* New York: Samuel French, 1958.
Lhamon, W.T. *Deliberate Speed: The Origins of a Cultural Style in the American 1950s*. Cambridge, MA: Harvard University Press, 1990.
Lindner, Robert M. *Rebel Without a Cause: The Hypnoanalysis of a Criminal Psychopath*. New York: Random House, 1944.
Love, Heather. "Doing Being Deviant: Deviance Studies, Description, and the Queer Ordinary." *differences* 26.1 (2015), 74–95.
Malague, Rosemary. *An Actress Prepares: Women and "the Method."* New York: Routledge, 2012.
Mamet, David. *True and False: Heresy and Common Sense for the Actor*. New York: Vintage, 1997.
Margolin, Deb. "Mining My Own Business: Paths between Text and Self." In *Method Acting Reconsidered: Theory, Practice, Future*, edited by David Krasner, 127–34. New York: St. Martin's Press, 2000.
Mariano, John. *The Veteran and His Marriage*. New York: Council on Marriage Relations, 1945.
Marowitz, Charles. *The Method as Means: An Acting Survey*. London: Herbert Jenkins, 1961.
Marowitz, Charles. *The Other Way: An Alternative Approach to Acting and Directing*. New York: Applause, 2006.
Marsh, John. "It's Not Easy Being Red: The Rise and Fall of the Literary Left." *American Literary History* 25.3 (2014), 605–615.
Martin, Pete. "Hollywood's Blonde Pop-off," *Saturday Evening Post*, 28 June 1952, 22–23, 122–123.
May, Elaine Tyler. *Homeward Bound: American Families in the Cold War Era*. New York: Basic Books, 2008.
McConachie, Bruce. "Method Acting and the Cold War." *Theatre Survey* 41.1 (2000), 47–67.
McCullers, Carson. *The Member of the Wedding*. 1946. New York: Mariner Books, 2004.
McDonald, Kathlene. *Feminism, the Left, and Postwar Literary Culture*. Jackson: University of Mississippi Press, 2012.
McGarry, Eileen. "Documentary, Realism, and Women's Cinema." *Women and Film* 2.7 (1975), 50–59.
McGinley, Paige. "Reconsidering 'the American Style:' Black Performers and Black Music in *Streetcar* and *Cat*." *Theatre Journal* 68.1 (2016), 1–15.
Mercer, John and Martin Shingler. *Melodrama: Genre, Style, and Sensibility*. New York: Columbia University Press/Wallflower Press, 2005.
Michel, Sonya. "American Women and the Discourse of the Democratic Family in World War II." In *Behind the Lines: Gender and the Two World Wars*, edited by Margaret Randolph Higonnet, Jane Jenson, Sonya Michel, and Margaret Collins, 154–167. New Haven, CT: Yale University Press, 1987.
Michel, Sonya. "Danger on the Home Front: Motherhood, Sexuality, and Disabled Veterans in American Postwar Films." *Journal of the History of Sexuality* 3 (1992), 109–28.

Mizruchi, Susan L. *Brando's Smile: His Life, Thought, and Work*. New York: Norton, 2015.
Moi, Toril. *Henrik Ibsen and the Birth of Modernism: Art, Theater, Philosophy*. Oxford: Oxford University Press, 2006.
Morrison, James. "Shelley Winters: Camp, Abjection, and the Aging Star." In *Hollywood Reborn: Movie Stars of the 1970s*, 120–137. New Brunswick: Rutgers University Press, 2010.
Mulvey, Laura. "Visual Pleasure and Narrative Cinema." In *Film Theory and Criticism: Introductory Readings*, edited by Leo Braudy and Marshall Cohen, 833–844. New York: Oxford University Press, 1999.
Murphy, Brenda. *Congressional Theatre: Dramatizing McCarthyism on Stage, Film, and Television*. Cambridge: Cambridge University Press, 1999.
Murphy, Brenda. *Tennessee Williams and Elia Kazan: A Collaboration in the Theatre*. Cambridge: Cambridge University Press, 2006.
Nadal, Alan. *Containment Culture: American Narratives, Postmodernism, and the Atomic Age*. Durham, NC: Duke University Press, 1995.
Naremore, James. *Acting in the Cinema*. Los Angeles: University of California Press, 1988.
Naremore, James. "Authorship and the Cultural Politics of Film Criticism." *Film Quarterly* 44.1 (1990), 14–23.
Neal, Patricia. *As I Am*. New York: Simon and Schuster, 1988.
Nelson, Deborah. *Tough Enough: Arbus, Arendt, Didion, McCarthy, Sontag, Weil*. Chicago: University of Chicago Press, 2017.
Nissen, Axel. *Actresses of a Certain Character: Forty Familiar Hollywood Faces from the Thirties to the Fifties*. Jefferson, NC: McFarland & Company, Reprint edition, 2011.
O'Malley, Suzanne. "Can the Method Survive the Madness?" *New York Times*, October 7, 1979.
Pfau, Ann G. "Allotment Annies and Other Wayward Wives: Wartime Concerns About Female Disloyalty and the Problem of the Returned Veteran." In *The United States and the Second World War: New Perspectives on Diplomacy, War, and the Home Front*, edited by G. Kurt Piehler and Sidney Pash, 99–128. New York: Fordham University Press, 2010.
Pierpont, Claudia Roth. "Method Man." *New Yorker*, October 27, 2008.
Plant, Rebecca Jo. "The Veteran, His Wife and Their Mothers: Prescriptions for Psychological Rehabilitation After World War II." In *Tales of the Great American Victory: World War II in Politics and Poetics*, edited by Diederik Oostdijk and Markha G. Valenta, 95–100. Amsterdam: Vrije University Press, 2006.
Prime, Rebecca. *Hollywood Exiles in Europe: The Blacklist and Cold War Film Culture*. New Brunswick: Rutgers University Press, 2014.
Pratt, George K. *Soldier to Civilian: Problems of Readjustment*. New York: McGraw Hill, 1944.
Pullen, Kirsten. *Like a Natural Woman: Spectacular Female Performance in Classical Hollywood*. New Brunswick: Rutgers University Press, 2014.
Quart, Leonard and Albert Auster. "The Wounded Vet in Postwar Film." *Social Policy* 13.2 (1982), 24–31.
Robins, Elizabeth. *Ibsen and the Actress*. 1928. New York: Haskell House, 1973.
Robinson, Harlow. *Russians in Hollywood, Hollywood's Russians: Biography of an Image*. Boston: Northeastern University Press; Hanover, NH: Published by University Press of New England, 2007.
Ross, Andrew. "Containing Culture in the Cold War," In *No Respect: Intellectuals and Popular Culture*, 1989, 42–64.

Rubin, Gayle. "Of Catamites and Kings: Reflections on Butch, Gender, and Boundaries." In *The Persistent Desire. A Femme-Butch-Reader*, edited by Joan Nestle, 466–482. Boston: Alyson, 1992.
Salome, Lou. *Ibsen's Heroines*, edited and translated with an introduction by Siegfried Mandel. Redding Ridge, CT: Black Swan Books, 1985.
Savran, David. *Communists, Cowboys, and Queers: The Politics of Masculinity in the Work of Arthur Miller and Tennessee Williams*. Minneapolis: University of Minnesota Press, 1992.
Scheeder, Louis. "Strasberg's Method and the Ascendency of American Acting." In *Training of the American Actor*, edited by Arthur Bartow, 3–16. New York: Theater Communications Group, 2006.
Sears, James. *Lonely Hunters: An Oral History of Lesbian and Gay Southern Life, 1948–1968*. New York: Basic Books, 1997.
Senelick, Laurence. *The Changing Room: Sex, Drag, and Theatre*. New York: Routledge, 2000.
Shaw, Irwin. "The Brutal Beauty of *A Streetcar Named Desire*." *The New Republic*, 22 December 1947, 34–35.
Schneider, Molly. "Televisions Tortured Misfits: Authenticity, Method Acting, and Americanness in the Midcentury 'Slice of Life' Anthology Drama." *Journal of Film & Video*. Fall/Winter 68.3/4 (2016), 30–50.
Silverman, Kaja. *Male Subjectivity at the Margins*. New York: Routledge, 1992.
Singer, Ben. *Melodrama and Modernity: Early Sensational Cinema and Its Contexts*. New York: Columbia University Press, 2001.
Strasberg, Susan. *Bittersweet*. New York: G.P. Putnam's Sons, 1980.
Strasberg, Susan. *Marilyn and Me: Sisters, Rivals, Friends*. New York: Grand Central Publishing, 1992.
Solomon, Alisa. *Re-dressing the Canon: Essays on Theatre and Gender*. London: Routledge, 1997.
Sontag, Susan. "Notes on 'Camp.'" *Against Interpretation and Other Essays*. 1966. New York: Picador, 2001, 275–292.
Stacey, Jackie. *Star Gazing: Hollywood Cinema and Female Spectatorship*. London: Routledge, 1994.
Stamp, Shelley. *Lois Weber in Early Hollywood*. Berkeley: University of California Press, 2015.
Stanislavski, Konstantin. *An Actor's Work*. Translated by Jean Benedetti. New York: Routledge, 2008.
Stanislavski, Konstantin. *Creating a Role*. Translated by Elizabeth Reynolds Hapgood. New York: Routledge, 1961.
Strasberg, Lee. *Strasberg at the Actors Studio: Tape-Recorded Sessions*. New York: Theatre Communications Press, 1965.
Stokes, John and Maggie B. Gale. *The Cambridge Companion to the Actress*. Cambridge: Cambridge University Press, 2007.
Stryker, Susan and Stephen Whittle. *The Transgender Studies Reader*. New York: Routledge, 2006.
Thompson, David. *Why Acting Matters*. New Haven: Yale University Press, 2015.
Trask, Michael. *Camp Sites: Sex, Politics, and Academic Style in Postwar America*. Stanford, CA: Stanford University Press, 2013.
Trask, Michael. "Patricia Highsmith's Method." *American Literary History* 22.3 (2010), 584–614.
Waller, Willard. *The Veteran Comes Home*. New York: The Dryden Press, 1944.
Waller, Willard. *War and the Family*. New York: The Dryden Press, 1940.
Wecter, Dixon. *When Johnny Comes Marching Home*. Boston: Houghton Mifflin Company, 1944.

Weiss, Margot D. *Techniques of Pleasure: BDSM and the Circuits of Sexuality*. Durham, NC: Duke University Press, 2011.
Wexman, Virginia Wright. *Creating the Couple: Love, Marriage, and Hollywood Performance*. Princeton, NJ: Princeton University Press, 1993.
Wexman, Virginia Wright. *Film and Authorship*. New Brunswick, NJ: Rutgers University Press, 2003.
White, Patricia. *Uninvited: Classical Hollywood Cinema and Lesbian Representability*. Bloomington, IN: Indiana University Press, 1999.
Whyman, Rose. *The Stanislavsky System of Acting*. Cambridge: Cambridge University Press, 2008.
Willett, Julie. "Behaving like Brando: Transgressing Race and Gender in *The Wild One*." *International Journal of Motorcycle Studies* 5.1 (2009). Retrieved 14 February 2021 from http://ijms.nova.edu/Spring2009/IJMS_Rndtble.Willett.html.
Williams, Tennessee. *Sweet Bird of Youth; Period of Adjustment; The Night of the Iguana*. New York: New Directions, 1972.
Williams, Tennessee. *A Streetcar Named Desire*. 1947. New York: New Directions, 2004.
Winters, Shelley. *Shelley II: The Middle of My Century*. New York: Simon and Schuster, 1989.
Wojcik, Pamela Robertson. *Guilty Pleasures: Feminist Camp from Mae West to Madonna*. Durham, NC: Duke University Press, 1996.
Wojcik, Pamela Robertson . *Movie Acting, The Film Reader*. London: Routledge, 2004.
Yellin, Emily. *Our Mothers' War: American Women at Home and at the Front During World War II*. New York: Free Press, 2005.
Zinnemann, Fred. *Fred Zinnemann: An Autobiography*. London: Bloomsbury, 1992.

INDEX

Actors Studio: democratic ethos 96, 105, 133; empowerment of actors 13–14, 15, 133; as feminist space 15, 22–24, 33–39, 43, 90, 100, 127, 133; Fonda and 105, 120, 124, 125; Harris and 96; history of 8–10; leftist politics 7; Loden and 128; realist values 2, 3; sexism in 11, 13, 32–34; stereotypes of 39; television and 20n21, 133–134; Winters and 84–86
Adler, Stella 8, 9, 10, 19n15, 20n19, 67, 85
Affron, Charles 12
After the Fall 129
Agnes of God 114–116
Ahmed, Sarah 17
Aldrich, Robert 19n18, 85
Alice Doesn't Live Here Anymore 6, 14, 17, 41, 43–44, 128, 133
All About Eve 80–82, 83, 98
All the President's Men 110
Allen, Woody 18n5
Allison, Nathan D. 25–26
Als, Hilton 93
Altman, Robert 127
Anderson, Maxwell 76n12
Anti-Psychiatry movement 111
Armstrong, Richard 97
Arnold, Gary 122, 123
Awake and Sing 19n18
Ashby, Hal 121, 126n13

Baker, Adam 14
Baker, Carroll 17, 43, 133
Balcerzak, Scott 13
Bancroft, Anne 1, 5, 114–116
Bankhead, Tallulah 103n22
Barbarella 107, 109
Barefoot in the Park 107
Barranger, Milly S. 7
Bastién, Angelica Jade 46
Baxter, Anne 80
Beauvoir, Simone de 31, 32, 125n4
Beckett, Samuel 24
Belle Reprieve 76
Benedek, László 9, 24, 28
Best Years of Our Lives, The 53, 68
Big Knife, The 86–88, 91, 106, 129
Big Lift, The 28
Blades, Larry 77n15
Bloom, Claire 96
Body and Soul 29
Boleslavsky, Richard 9
Bonnie and Clyde 6, 129
Brando, Marlon 11, 14, 27, 28, 36, 45n10, 76n12, 84, 90, 123, 128; brooding masculinity 1, 5, 39, 53, 89, 124, 125; emblematic of Method acting 3, 5, 23, 24, 29–30; rebellion 14, 24, 44; *Streetcar* 5, 15–16, 29–30, 41, 49, 68, 75, 124
Brantley, Ben 92, 96
Breakfast at Tiffany's 1
Breuer, Bessie 23
Brooks, Richard 99
Burstyn, Ellen 6, 14, 17, 41, 42, 43–44, 133

144 Index

Cahiers du Cinéma 13, 25
Camus, Albert 24
Canby, Vincent 122–123
Carman, Emily 12, 87
Case, Sue-Ellen 32–33, 35
Cassavetes, John 134n3
Catholic Legion of Decency 38, 74
Chapman Report, The 107–109, 110
Chase, The 125
Chekhov, Anton 9, 18n5, 35
Chekhov, Michael 8
Cher 128
China Syndrome, The 104
Clift, Montgomery 3, 5, 6, 23, 24, 27, 28, 29, 41, 44, 45n10, 46n13, 84, 129
Clurman, Harold 23
Cobb, Lee J. 4
Cohan, Steve 26, 43, 44, 45n4
Come Back to the Five and Dime, Jimmy Dean, Jimmy Dean 128
Coming Home 6, 14, 104, 119, 120–123
Conrad, Joseph 95
Conroy, Marianne 26
Cool Hand Luke 17
Cornelius, Henry 91
Cornell, Katherine 26, 80, 96
Counsell, Colin 41
Crawford, Cheryl 10, 14, 23, 39, 119
Crawford, Joan 12, 20n25, 103n22
Cromwell, John 18n5
Crowther, Bosley 1, 3, 5, 92, 101 102n5
Cruising 110
Cukor, George 107

Davis, Bette 12, 25, 80, 81, 103n22
Days of Wine and Roses 133
De Niro, Robert 1, 5, 14, 36, 46n14, 123–124, 128
Dean, James 3, 5, 6, 11, 23, 24, 25, 39, 41, 44, 48n36, 95, 128
Dee, Sandra 83
Dennis, Sandy 6, 9, 18n5, 19n15, 127, 133
Dern, Bruce 44, 120–123
Diary of Anne Frank, The 6, 88–89
DiCaprio, Leonardo 46n14
Didion, Joan 17
Dietrich, Marlene 91
Doll's House, A 9, 20n21, 120–121
Douglas, Kirk 2
Doyle, Mary 78n37
Du Barry Was a Lady 10
Dunne, Irene 12

Duse, Eleonora 31, 32, 36–37, 39
Dymtryk, Edward 28, 68

East of Eden 5, 10, 17, 24, 28, 96
Edwards, Blake 1
Eisenberg, Emma Copley 17
Enelow, Shonni 9, 26, 33, 38
existentialism 24, 25, 39

Face in the Crowd, A 1, 40
Far Country, A 47n30
Faulkner, William 95
feminism: domestic violence 52, 76n9; mainstreaming in 1970s 128; post-war period 30–32; Ratings Code and 2; second-wave 2, 3, 4, 15, 68, 109; "toughness" 17; *see also* Method acting, feminist
Field, Sally 14, 44, 105
Fonda, Henry 105
Fonda, Jane 6, 14, 42, 77n16; *Agnes of God* 114–116; career 104; *Chapman Report* 107–109; *The Chase* 125; *Coming Home* 120–123; introduction to Method 105; *Klute* 109–114, 126n7, 129; *Period of Adjustment* 116–119; political activism 104, 110, 119, 122, 123, 124, 126n17; psychoanalysis and 106–116; *Stanley and Iris* 123–124; *They Shoot Horses, Don't They?* 125; as veteran's wife 116–124; *Youth* 105–106, 123, 125n3
Foote, Horton 9
For Me and My Gal 10
Foucault, Michel 110
Franciosa, Anthony 28, 77n16, 85, 118, 123
Freed, Arthur 10
French, Samuel 25
Freud, Sigmund 4, 23, 38, 47–48n30, 107, 110, 114, 125n4
Friedan, Betty 31, 32, 44, 68, 90, 125n4
Friedkin, William 110
From Here to Eternity 28, 46n11, 46n12
Fugitive Kind, The 17
Furnas, J.C. 55–56, 67, 77n18
Fury 46n14

Gaines, Jane 11
Gallagher-Ross, Jacob 9, 26, 34
Garfield, John 10, 19n18, 86
Gaynor, Janet 12
Gazzo, Michael 28, 85
Gentleman's Agreement 76n4
Ghosts 37

Goddess, The 14, 18n5, 133
Goffman, Erving 27
Golden Boy 29
Goldstone, Bobbie 110–111, 126n6
Gorelik, Mordecai 85
Graduate, The 1
Grapes of Wrath, The 105
Greer, Germaine 44, 125n4
Group Theatre 7, 10, 19n17, 23

Hagen, Uta 8, 19n15, 31–32
Hager, Bill and Terry 120
Halberstam, Jack 93
Harris, Julie 10, 14, 18n5, 20n21, 23, 28, 29, 38, 84, 91–98, 101, 102n1, 102n5, 103n18, 125
Hartmann, Elizabeth 89
Hartmann, Susan 57
Hatful of Rain, A 3, 18n5, 19n15, 28, 85
Haunting, The 96–98
Havighurst, Robert V. 54
Havoc, June 125
Hays Code 2
Heisler, Stuart 81
Hellman, Lillian 7
Higgins, Michael 129
Hill, George Roy 77n16, 116
Hirsch, Foster 6, 39, 95
Hoffman, Dustin 128
Hollinger, Karen 5
Holm, Celeste 80
Hondo 7, 22
Hopper, Hedda 95
Horowitz, Daniel 31
House Un-American Activities Committee 7, 126n10
Hud 5, 18n2, 40–41, 123
Hunter, Kim: feminism 10; *Matter of Life and Death* 77n14; Oscar 5, 7, 11; political activism 7; *Requiem for a Heavyweight* 18n5, 38; *Streetcar* 10, 29, 40, 49–76, 116, 123; wartime women roles 53

I Am a Camera 91, 102n5
Ibsen, Henrik 9, 20n21, 36, 37, 120
In Harm's Way 1, 2
Inge, William 9
Interiors 18n5
Isherwood, Christopher 91

Jackson, Anne 23
Jackson, Shirley 7, 96
Jane Fonda in Five Acts 104

Jewison, Norman 114
Johns, Glynis 107
Johnson, Lesley 18n6
Johnson, Nunnally 4

Kael, Pauline 24, 46n11, 97, 128
Kazan, Elia 45n10; Actors Studio and 10, 23, 27, 32, 84, 96; Communist Party and 7; creative collaboration 36; *East of Eden* 24, 28; *Face in the Crowd* 1; *Gentleman's Agreement* 76n4; Group Theatre and 9–10; Loden and 129, 130, 133; *On the Waterfront* 24; sociological concerns 9, 39; *Streetcar* 9, 11, 28, 49–52, 54, 58, 59, 60, 62, 65, 66, 67, 68, 70, 71, 74, 75, 76, 130; *Sweet Bird of Youth* 98; toxic masculinity 28; *Wild River* 3, 14; women, work with 11, 14, 28, 44
Kazan, Molly Thacher 49, 76n2, 129
Keitel, Harvey 106, 123, 128
Kerr, Walter 91
Kinsey Reports 107
Klute 6, 104, 109–114, 126n7, 129, 130
Konkle, Amanda 37–38
Krampner, Jon 14–15
Kurosawa, Akira 24

Labeouf, Shia 46n14
Laboratory Theatre 9
Lacy, Susan 104
Lady from the Sea, The 36–37, 39
Larceny 84
Lefkowitz, Alison 71
Léger, Nathalie 134n2
Leigh, Vivien 19n18, 57, 75, 76n3
Lembcke, Jerry 120
Lennart, Isobel 119, 126n10
Leto, Jared 46n14
Lewis, Robert 10, 23, 25
Lloyd, Justine 18n6
Loden, Barbara 128–133
Lombard, Carole 12
Long Hot Summer, The 123
Losey, Joseph 120
Lumet, Stanley 125n3
Lupino, Ida 12

Macbeth 36
Malague, Rosemary 33, 38
Malden, Karl 23, 27
Maltby, Richard 26
Mankiewicz, Joseph L. 80
Mann, William J. 14

Marathon '33 96, 103n18, 125
Matter of Life and Death, A 53, 77n14
McCarthysim 7, 30–31
McConachie, Bruce 45n3
McCullers, Carson 7, 14, 28, 93
McDonald, Kathlene 31
McDonald, Paul 12
McQueen, Steve 23
"Me Too" movement 17
Mean Streets 14
Meisner, Sanford 19n15
Member of the Wedding, The 14, 28, 29, 92–95, 96, 101
Men, The 27, 53, 68, 76n12, 123
Method acting: affective memory 34, 38, 47n24; definition of 8–9; disruptive power of 25–26; masculinity and 26–30, 46n14; "Method PTSD" 29–30; misconceptions of 16–17, 22–23, 25, 39, 41; "natural" acting 80–81, 96; "neo-Method" 128; rebellion and 24–25, 44, 45n3; social concerns of 38–39; *see also* Actors Studio
Method acting, feminist: anti-industry critique 82–84, 86–88, 107; awards 5–6, 19n10; critical inattention to 3, 5, 13, 14–15, 24, 29, 42; flat affect 40, 130; genealogies of 1, 4, 19n15, 128; inhospitable environment for 2, 6; midlife ethos 3; ordinary lives 3, 15; politics off-screen 7–8, 11; psychoanalysis and 4, 33, 38, 106–116; Strasberg and 32–39; style of 39–44, 127
Milford, Penelope 123
Miller, Arthur 7, 9, 33, 38, 129
Miracle Worker, The 5
Misfits, The 37, 133
Mitchell, Juliet 125n4
Mizruchi, Susan L. 14
Monroe, Marilyn 14, 18n5, 33, 37–38, 80, 129, 133
Morgan, Robin 104
Morning After, The 125n3
Morocco 91
Morrison, James 90
Moscow Art Theatre 9, 102
Murray, Don 28

Naremore, James 12, 39, 42
Nathan, Vivian 111
Neal, Patricia 1–2, 3, 5, 17, 18n2, 23, 40–41, 43, 123, 127
Nelson, Deborah 17

Nelson, Ralph 18n5
Nettleton, Lois 77n16, 118
Never Fear 12
Newman, Paul 5, 18n2, 40, 99, 100, 123
Nichols, Mike 1
Niven, David 77n14
Norma Rae 128
North, Alex 70
Nussbaum, Emily 96

Odets, Clifford 10, 19n18, 29, 85
Olivier, Laurence 26, 96
O'Loughlin, Gerry 84
On Golden Pond 104
On the Waterfront 5, 9, 24, 46n11, 125n3
One-Eyed Jacks 14
Ouspenskaya, Maria 9, 10, 19n18, 80
Outrage 12

Pacino, Al 128
Page, Geraldine 3, 7, 9, 18n5, 19n15, 22–23, 30, 42, 98–102
Pakula, Alan J. 109, 110, 113, 126n7
Palance, Jack 86
Parallax View, The 110
Parsons, Estelle 6
Patch of Blue, A 6, 88, 89
Penn, Arthur 125, 129
Period of Adjustment 53, 77n16, 107, 116–119, 121, 123
Place in the Sun, A 24, 41, 83, 84
Poitier, Sidney 88, 89
Pollack, Sydney 127
Preminger, Otto 1, 2
Prince and the Showgirl, The 38
Production Code 2, 10, 38, 64, 74, 102n5
Proferes, Nicholas 129
psychoanalysis 4, 8, 10, 17, 26, 38, 97, 106–116, 125n4

queerness: Harris, Julie 95; *Haunting* 96; *Member of the Wedding* 92–93; *Streetcar* 7, 71–73

Raganelli, Katja 132–133, 134n2
Raging Bull 14, 46n14
Rashomon 24
Ratings System 2
Ray, Nicholas 24, 25
Rebel Without a Cause 24, 25, 41
Reflections in a Golden Eye 96
Remick, Lee 133
Requiem for a Heavyweight 18n5, 38

Revenant, The 46n14
Reynolds, Debbie 37, 83
Ritt, Martin 9, 11, 14, 18n2, 28, 44, 123, 128
Ritter, Thelma 80
Rockwell, Norman 72, 78n37
Rogers, Ginger 68, 77n13
Roosevelt, Eleanor 30
Rose Tattoo, The 133
Rossen, Robert 29

Saint, Eva Marie 3, 5, 18n5, 28
Saks, Gene 107
Sartre, Jean-Paul 39
Savickas, Ed and Stella 55–56, 64, 67, 68, 70
Scorsese, Martin 14, 36, 41, 46n14, 110, 128, 133
Séance on a Wet Afternoon 133
Search, The 27
Seaton, George 28
Selznick, Irene 49
Seymour, Nicole 93
Shaw, George Bernard 112
Shaw, Irwin 10
Singin' in the Rain 82
Smuckler, Maya Montañez 129
Smyth, J.E. 12
Sokolow, Anna 96
Something Wild 17, 133
Sontag, Susan 17
Sorrentino, Paolo 105–106
Splendor in the Grass 129
Split Britches 76
Stamp, Shelley 11
Stanislavsky, Konstantin 8, 9, 10, 19n17, 25, 31, 32, 80
Stanley, Kim 9, 14–15, 18n5, 41–42, 47n30, 133
Stanley and Iris 123–124
Stapleton, Maureen 18n5, 23
Star, The 81
Starmaker, The 25
Steinem, Gloria 90, 104
Stevens, George 24, 84, 88
Stranger, The 24
Strasberg, Lee 8, 9, 10, 17, 18n5, 23, 32–39, 43, 47n24, 88, 96, 105, 113, 114, 115
Strassberg, Morris 111
Streetcar Named Desire, A: authoritarian masculinity 28; bohemianism 67–68; Broadway production 50–53; emergence of Method in 22; Hunter's view of Stella 50, 51, 52–53, 58, 66, 67, 68; Kazan's view of Stella 50–52, 66, 67, 68; managing men's trauma 29; "natural" acting 41; Oscars 5, 75; PTSD 29–30; new ending 73–74; queerness 7, 71–73; realistic portrayal of abuse 58–59, 61–64; sexual relationship of Kowalskis 68–71; Stella's defiance 63–66; Stella's protection of Blanche 60–61; veteran reintegration 53–58, 72; *Wanda* and 130, 131, 132
Strindberg, August 36
Stronger, The 36
Stroppel, Elizabeth 35, 134
Suicide Squad 46n14
Summer and Smoke 22, 34–35
Sunday in New York 107
Sundown Beach 23, 96
Sunset Boulevard 82
Swanson, Gloria 82, 103n22
Sweet Bird of Youth 3, 22, 98–102

Taubman, Howard 103n18
Taxi Driver 14, 110, 124
Taylor, Aaron 13
Taylor, Elizabeth 83, 84
Tender Comrade 53, 68, 77n13
Terminal Station 41
Tewksbury, Peter 107
They Shoot Horses, Don't They? 125
Three Faces of Eve, The 4–5
Three Sisters 9, 18n5, 35
Tilly, Meg 115
Tootsie 128
Trask, Michael 26
Truckline Cafe 76n12
Trumbo, Dalton 68, 77n13

Vadim, Roger 107, 109
Van Druten, John 91
Van Fleet, Jo 3, 5, 14, 17, 133
veteran reintegration 53–58, 77n17, 118, 120
Victoria Regina 84
Voight, Jon 120–123

Waiting for Godot 24
Walerstein, Rachel 93
Wallace, Irving 107
Wanda 128–133
Waters, Ethel 14, 102n1
Wayne, John 1, 45n4

Weber, Lois 11–12
Welles, Orson 26
Wexman, Virginia Wright 43
White, Patricia 92–93, 102n9
Who's Afraid of Virginia Woolf? 6, 133
Wild One, The 24
Wild River 3, 14, 129
Williams, Linda 121, 122, 125
Williams, Tennessee: as Method playwright 7, 9, 33; *Period of Adjustment* 116–120; *Streetcar* 49, 50, 53–58, 59, 64, 67, 68, 74; *Summer and Smoke* 34–35; *Sweet Bird of Youth* 98–101
Winchester '73 84

Winters, Shelley 5–6, 9, 18n5, 19n15, 42, 43, 83–90, 91, 102n1, 105, 107, 108, 129
Wise, Robert 96
Woman Under the Influence, A 134n3
Women's Media Center 104
Wood, Audrey 49, 55
Woodward, Joanne 4–5, 17, 123

Young Lions, The 28
Youth 105–106, 123, 125n3

Zinnemann, Fred 3, 9, 11, 14, 18n5, 27–28, 44, 45–46n10, 46n13, 76n12, 93–94, 120

For Product Safety Concerns and Information please contact our EU
representative GPSR@taylorandfrancis.com
Taylor & Francis Verlag GmbH, Kaufingerstraße 24, 80331 München, Germany

www.ingramcontent.com/pod-product-compliance
Lightning Source LLC
Chambersburg PA
CBHW052129300426
44116CB00010B/1829